EXPLOSION

IN

VILLA RICA

Elaine Bailey

Lillium Press

Explosion in Villa Rica

Copyright © 2010 by Elaine B. Bailey

All rights reserved. No part of this book may be reproduced or transmitted in any form or by any means without written permission of the author.

ISBN 978-0-9628023-6-2

Cover designed by John Kirby

Lillium Press

Dedicated to those twelve

who lost their lives and to

the loved-ones they left behind.

Explosion in Villa Rica

Table of Contents

Acknowledgments --- 1
Preface -- 3
Chapters
1. The Days Before the Tragedy ----------------------------------- 7
2. Early Morning, December 5, 1957 ------------------------------ 17
3. The Moments That Decided—Life or Death ---------------------- 29
4. The First Minutes After the Explosion ------------------------ 35
5. The Community Reacts to the Sudden, Violent Blast ----------- 51
6. The Search for Loved-Ones ----------------------------------- 59
7. Rescue Efforts: Civil Defense/Red Cross/National Guard ------ 69
8. Families Learn of the Disaster ------------------------------ 81
9. A Town, Crippled -- 89
10. At the Hospitals -- 95
11. Memories, Stories, and Affidavits -------------------------- 105
12. The Days After the Tragedy -------------------------------- 115
13. New Organizations -- 127
14. Lawsuits Against Southern Natural Gas Company ------------- 135
15. Lawsuits Against Dr. William L. "Bill" Berry -------------- 141
16. Lawsuits Against the City of Villa Rica ------------------- 151
17. 40th Anniversary and 50th Anniversary Memorial
    Remembrance Ceremony --------------------------------------- 171
In Memoriam --- 179
Credits --- 189
Bibliography -- 199
Index --- 201

Acknowledgments

Putting this book together was like finding a half-a-century-old jig-saw puzzle in a dusty attic, opening the box, finding odd pieces, and trying to fit them all together. Many of the parts went together beautifully. Of course there were missing parts. Some pieces didn't seem to go together at all, but I included them. What we have here is not a jig-saw puzzle but a story—one based on old newspaper articles, rich interviews from the people of Villa Rica, and on an unexpected find. When I visited the Federal Archives I found over one thousand pages of court documents from lawsuits that followed the Villa Rica explosion. These documents contain extensive testimonies of those involved in the central event. There are many things we will never know, but from the facts found in research, this book will come as close to telling the complete story as anything.

Thanks to all those who have helped me: This became somewhat of a family project which made it all the more rewarding in spending this interesting time with my loved-ones. John Bailey, my husband, shared personal memories of his involvement in this tragic story. Having lived in Villa Rica in the fifties, John was able to find some of the residents he remembered from the past. He also proved invaluable in helping me with the research as he spent many long hours into the night at the computer searching for facts from the past.

Thanks to other family members: to Kevin Smith, my son-in-law, who put the newsreel, *Explosion in Villa Rica,* on YouTube and developed a great website. Thanks to my daughter, Sueann Bailey Smith, for her skill in the critique of the book. Then my mother-in-law, Mary Bailey, shared her clear but sad memories of that fateful day.

My most important help came from Valerie Storey, of Dava Books, who gave me guidance in editing that helped bring this story alive to the reader. Next are: Jeff Robison, Ted Williamson, and John McPherson who contributed photographs they had collected, many of which are originals taken at the time of the tragedy.

Acknowledgments

Ann Bell shared with me twenty original black and white photos that her Uncle George Holloway had taken minutes after the explosion. She gladly brought these for me to scan. These were published in the Villa Rican, the local newspaper, at the time of the tragedy.

Charlotte Barber, Winnie Baxter, Valerie Berry Wilhelm, Charlotte Doyle, and my cousin, Patsy Bollen, literally made this book possible by loaning the newspapers they had collected and saved as guarded treasures. This book could not have been written without those original papers as the search for the same information at libraries on microfilm was tedious and almost always disappointing in what we did not find.

The technical support I needed came from Spencer Crawford at the *Villa Rican* who gave me instructions on placement of the photographs included among the text. Mayor J. Collins shared a most valuable document: a college, history research paper his mother, Brenda Collins wrote, dated August 5, 1993 titled, *Explosion in Villa Rica*.

Ethyleen Tyson, Irma Ree Carnes, and Paul Free, my guides and mentors, came to recognize my voice on the phone whenever I called and said, "I need your help again." Usually they could identify someone in the old photograph or tell me whom to ask. They always knew who I should contact for information.

A special thanks goes to the Berry family: Valerie Berry Wilhelm, Kippard "Kip," Randall "Ran," and Mark Berry who shared documents, pictures, original newspapers, and personal family papers for this project including an *Affidavit* by Annie Powell Berry.

Those who wrote and shared their very personal memories greatly enhanced this story: Leslie Powell Carter, Randy Wallace, Perry "Bill" Bailey, Faye White Williams, and Martha Faye Bailey Beedle. Bill "Perry" Bailey also gave me valuable leads, pictures, and a video, "Villa Rica Explosion 1957."

Appreciation goes to librarians at the Villa Rica Library and to the archivists at the Carroll County Courthouse and the Federal Records Center in Morrow, Georgia for helping me find very old documents.

My greatest appreciation goes to all those people I interviewed. They were willing to open up their minds and reach back to memories that have almost faded, and to open up their hearts to feel love and pain for those that were lost. There was so much fear and devastation that tragic day, but each person I interviewed seemed willing to be a part of this remembrance as they too knew it would be totally lost in another generation if not for this book.

Preface

The town of Villa Rica, known as City of Gold, was incorporated by the Georgia General Assembly in 1883 from the earlier villages of Hixtown and Chevestown. These early gold mining regions sprang up when the pioneer farmers in this northwestern Georgia area dug for the precious metal. In 1825 after Carroll County was formed, the state ruled that the mineral rights were state property. But this did not keep thousands of gold prospectors from rushing into this area to mine for gold. From 1827 to 1828, land value shot up one hundred times what it had been. At Pine Mountain, just north of Hixtown, the small mining town of Pine Town went into operated before 1830. The words *Gold Region* are stenciled on an 1830 map of west Georgia right on the northern edge of *Carroll County*. By 1832 three hundred men were working in the mines. From 1830 to 1840 prospectors mined 20,000 pennyweights of gold dust annually.

Little mining was done from 1844 to the end of the Civil War, then things picked up again when the gold miners of Villa Rica persuaded the Georgia Pacific Railroad (now the Southern Railroad) to lay the tracks through Villa Rica in 1862. This would give them access to the nearest gold market in Augusta, Georgia. Before the miners had much time to benefit from the use of the rail lines, the mine's gold wealth began to wane. Only a few mines remained in the last three decades of the 1800s. Gold mining diminished after 1900. All that remains today to remind us of Villa Rica's rich history in gold mining is the Pine Mountain Gold Museum located on Pine Mountain north of Villa Rica.

Historians as early as 1913 were saying the town of Villa Rica had "disappeared from the map." Then Villa Rica became famous for its cotton known to be even more beautiful than Egyptian cotton. This product which was in great demand and brought top price brought prosperity to the town once again.

Preface

Over the next fifty years, this small agricultural community became a thriving town because of its industry. In January 1957, a newspaper reported Villa Rica's new gold mine was its rich industrial boom that had enveloped the town. Villa Rica boasted at least twenty-two industries, producing caskets, hosiery, anklets, caps, lawn furniture, sports shirts, fertilizer, aluminum window frames, newspaper and job printing, feed stuff as well as several lumber mills and cotton gins.

In 1957, Villa Rica, Georgia, with a population of 3,600 was just a spot on a map on the main road, U.S. 78 Highway, that ran atop a ridge for a little over a hundred miles from points west of Atlanta to points east of Birmingham, Alabama. This ridge afforded spectacular views of vast green countrysides to the left and right for any traveler.

Anyone driving west would be impressed by the charm of this rural countryside. The vivid green landscape was broken by the red clay of the farmlands dotting the land around unpainted tenant houses. Within the expanse of grassy pastures, two-story white gabled farmhouses were inhabited by second—even third—generations of the same farm family. White steepled churches gave distinction to many corners of town, and country churches located down dirt roads and across low lying creeks stood out as beacons in the community. These country, dirt roads cut the terrain and sometimes plowed through any water that might accumulate in a creek-bed that crossed the road.

Villa Rica, located forty-five miles west of Atlanta, was for the most part unremarkable unless you value the fact that this was a friendly, Christian based community. This small town seemed to be made up of relatives and friends that would do anything for anybody, even strangers passing through that needed a helping hand.

Like most post war small towns in the South, the older citizens well-remembered "hard times." Those that survived World War II were around to tell stories, or maybe keep the stories to themselves. There were even a few granddaddies around that could tell stories of World War I. These veterans with lined faces and "old injuries" were thankful to be alive and took pride in the uniformed pictures of themselves on the mantle.

The women of the returning soldiers knew the difference between hard times and good. The old folks could tell stories of the Depression. There might have even been some ration stamps in the top bureau drawer to pull out and show the grandkids how sugar, coffee, and tea were rationed back in the 1940s.

In Villa Rica everybody knew everyone else and were even kin to many of their neighbors and fellow churchgoers. Families had between three and eight children. The women were mostly housewives and the men had jobs in town or Atlanta or Marietta but

Preface

still farmed a crop and raised all their own meat.

The older women in town wore cotton dresses, thick stockings in winter, long coats that swung from the back yoke, and headscarves when it rained or was windy. On Sundays they kept their hair in bobby pins until they got to church. There they took the pins out while still in the car and then combed through their hair right before going into church. That way their hair would hold the curl all during the service.

But people were seeing change in Villa Rica as they were in the rest of the world. Many second and third generation farm boys were leaving the country and heading to a job in Atlanta. The boll weevil and the army worm that had attacked the crops for the last ten years had taken the profit out of farming.

The Russians in the late 1950s were really giving the U.S. a licking in the "space race" after putting "Sputnik," the first unmanned satellite, into orbit. In December of 1957, the eyes of the nation were on Cape Canaveral on the coast of Florida, when our rocket, the Vanguard, was poised on the launch pad with plans on putting the first U.S. satellite into orbit. It launched a few feet and crashed.

But the real hope of the future was in the eyes of the teenagers. Their thoughts, ambitions, music, even their way of dress was different. The girls wore bobby-socks, saddle oxfords, poodle skirts, and the more crinolines, the better. The boys wore jeans, buttoned-up cotton shirts, and had the hopes of buying a leather jacket. These were the years of crew cuts, flat tops, and pony-tails.

The world was coming alive with anticipation. The young population of Villa Rica in 1957 would say this was a grand, carefree time. Buddy Holly and the Crickets had appeared for the first time on Sunday night on the Ed Sullivan Show. Every teen in town wanted a '57 Chevy convertible, but most teens drove the 1940 Ford or Chevrolet their dad bought for a couple of hundred dollars. Then they had to work in the afternoons after school to pay him back.

Villa Rica thrived in resources. There were reputable family doctors who were from second and third generation of practicing physicians in town. Solid businesses were run by families whose grandfathers or even great-grandfathers had started in the same building where they were still located. The new Villa Rica Hospital building had opened two years before, in 1955, two miles north of town on Dallas Road. The grammar and high school could take care of all ages—first grade through twelfth grade. There was a basketball, baseball, and football team, and there was a college in Carrollton, West Georgia College, in the next town south of Villa Rica.

Preface

This small Southern town and its people were taken completely unaware and unprepared when a horrific explosion rocked the business district on December 5, 1957. The town had for a long time been stagnant in its progress toward the future and thought of only how things were and how things had been in the past. The town was without sufficient funds as the citizens disapproved of higher tax rates. Much of the yearly property tax revenues came from taxing farmland. Higher taxes for the local industries was out of the question because so many of these factories had been plagued with fires—seven fires in five years. The newly elected City Council voted in a Civil Defense organization in August of that year, but tabled the discussion of buying equipment based on lack of funds. On December 5, the hospital, though only two year old, had only six available beds. This was due to an influx of people coming in because of a flu epidemic. Villa Rica had only a volunteer fire department and its chief qualified by being a well-liked store owner. The town was referred to in an editoral from the local Villa Rican newspaper as being "like growing boy who, upon reaching young manhood, continues to wear the trousers of an adolescent."

Then catastrophe came unexpectedly and the townspeople had to cope with the events of the day and meet the challenges in the coming days and years that lay ahead.

1

The Days Before the Tragedy

*Teens gathered at the pharmacy for a cherry coke
and played music of the fifties on the juke box.
John Bailey, teen and employee of Berry's pharmacy.*

In December of 1957, the main part of Villa Rica was a row of stores not much more than two blocks on either side of the Southern Railway tracks. This two block area of town was the hub of business for everyone. On the north side of the tracks was the train depot with a few industries claiming a half a block behind and beside City Hall. There were other stores sprinkled about the adjacent blocks as well as the small, white framed houses that edged the roadsides farther out.

Almost everybody in town lived within walking distance of the stores, school, and factories. Very few families had a car. Men who worked too far to walk to work or who happened to work in Marietta or Atlanta, rode to work together with as many as six riding in one car or station wagon. The housewife stayed home, rode with a neighbor, or walked wherever she needed to go during the day. The town's one school was half a mile west of the business district. Most of the school children in Villa Rica walked to school, and the kids who lived in the rural areas rode the school bus.

The main road U.S. 78 Highway was also called Montgomery Street as it went through downtown. The two blocks of stores that formed the business district was bordered on the west by Westview Drive; on the south by Wilson Street; on the east by Carroll Road; and on the north by Montgomery Street. Candler Street ran between the movie theater and Reeves Jewelry, crossed Montgomery Street (U.S. Highway 78) and went over the railroad

Explosion in Villa Rica

track. On the corner of Montgomery Street and Candler Street in a line all the way to the next corner—that of Montgomery Street and Carroll Road were stores where a person could find anything he or she needed.

On the corner of Candler Street and Montgomery Street was Reeves Jewelry. Cliff Reeves and his wife, Eunice, were a nice middle-aged couple who had run their business for several years but had only been in their current location for one year. In the back of the store, the Reeves' daughter, Charlotte, ran the Villa Rica Florist. Next door, to the left occupying the same building was the A & B Dress Shop which Camille Adams and Bernie Bell owned together. Next in the line was the historic Powell-Marchman building, built in 1895. This two-story red brick building was now occupied on the first floor by Berry's Pharmacy. Upstairs above the pharmacy was Dr. Burnham's dental office where he came on Wednesday and Thursdays to his new practice. Although Berry's Pharmacy was the tallest building in town, the movie theater on the corner was the largest structure in town.

To the right of the two-story building was the Empire 5 & 10 Cent Store. Then there was Jack William's Tri-County Clothing Store, Mullinax Groceries, and M.D. Henslee's Department Store. To the right of Henslee's Department Store was Hughie's 5 & 10 Cent Store, and at the end of the block were Hoyte Easterwood's Grocery Store, a barbershop, Joe Brock's Furniture, and a few other shops. On the end corner of this row of stores was Star Department Store

Dr. William L. "Bill" Berry owned and ran the pharmacy, employing two other pharmacists. Dr. Berry was the president of the Georgia Pharmaceutical Association and often directed the young people who worked in his store toward getting a higher education.

Bill Berry's wife, Margaret, ran the store with him. She kept a line of cosmetics and helped with the customers. A petite, dark-haired mother of three, Margaret was well thought of and was always working to make Villa Rica a better place and to help its citizens.

Also working at the pharmacy was Ray Tyson, manager of the soda fountain and sandwich bar where he had worked for eight years. Ray ordered all the supplies for the soda fountain and made pharmacy deliveries. Ray was energetic, small in stature, thirty-nine-years-old, married, and had five children. He was the president of the Villa Rica Saddle Club and had been a member since it was formed in 1951. Ray was dependable and known to be an honest man and a man of his word.

Ann Pope Smith, a petite pretty brunette, had worked for Berry's Pharmacy since she graduated from high school several years earlier. In school, she was voted the most athletic. She married her high school sweetheart, Billy Smith, right after high school. Ann

1. The Days Before the Tragedy

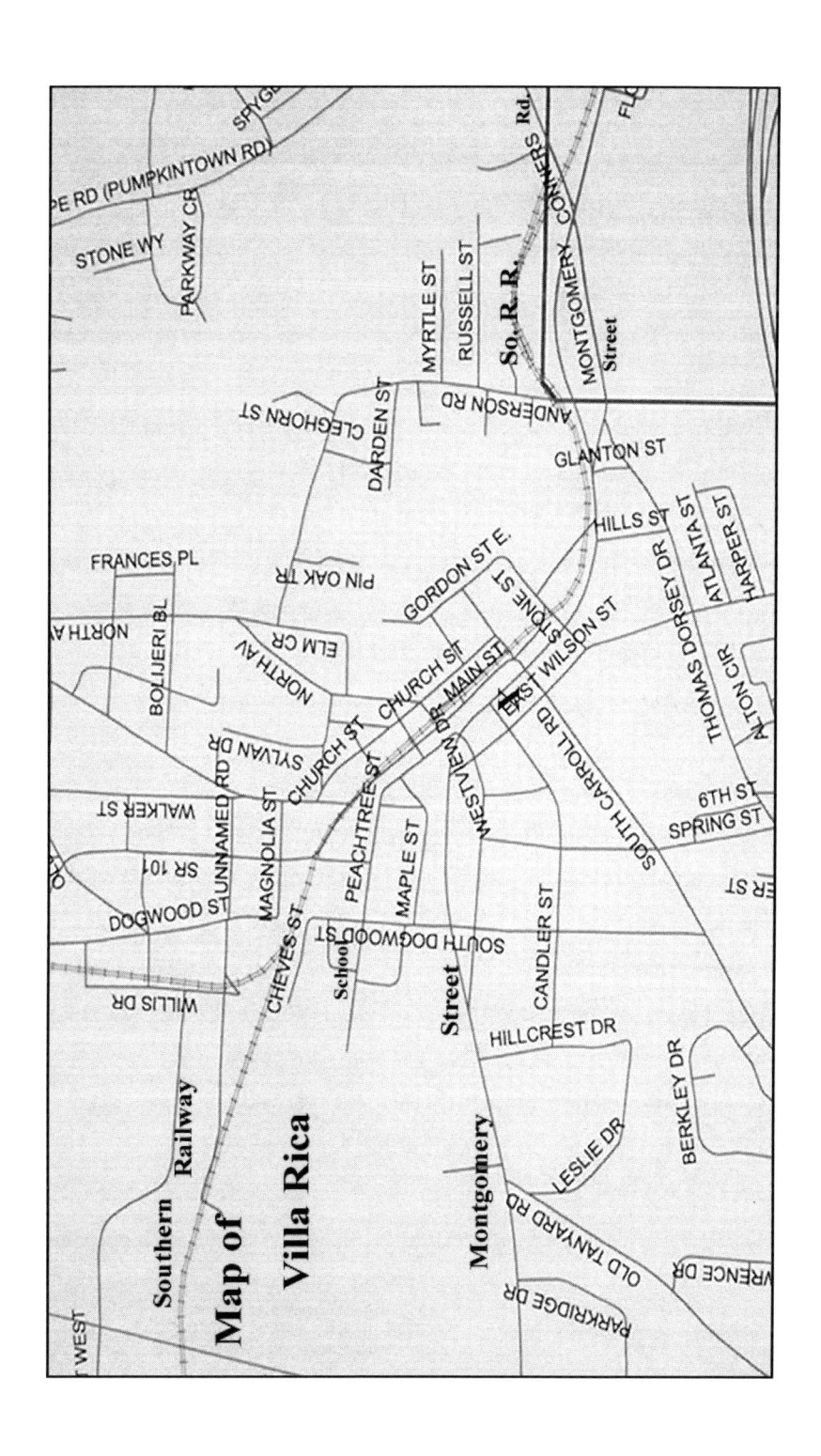

Explosion in Villa Rica

worked in Berry's Pharmacy in many capacities, but she mainly worked with billing and invoicing. She kept the books at Berry's with the assistance of Bill Berry's mother, Annie Powell Berry, who came in most every day to get her mail, see her family, and help with the paperwork.

Don Bohannan was one of the two pharmacists employed by Bill Berry. Don was a short, well-built man with dark hair who could not keep the mischievous look from showing in his eyes. He was ready for a prank or trick whenever the opportunity presented itself.

The other pharmacist was James Harrison. James was dependable and likable. The young people that worked part-time after school learned to admire James and to look up to him.

On Monday, December 2, Eunice Reeves called Tom Pope, an assistant to the superintendent at the City Municipal Gas Company of Villa Rica, to come by Reeves Jewelry on the corner of Candler and Montgomery Streets to check for a gas leak. Tom had worked for the city since the gas system was installed in 1954. His duties were to keep up the lines and read meters. When Tom Pope got to the store, Eunice told Tom there was some kind of odor in the store and that she thought she had smelled gas. Tom did not notice the smell of gas when he walked in but later smelled fumes from the radiant heater that sat midway of the store. Tom found it was out of adjustment. He readjusted the heater then checked the gas lines to determine if there was a gas smell, but smelled nothing unusual. He checked the Y-shaped connection and shut-off valve that ran off the two and one-fourth inch main gas line that ran at the back of the stores. One line of the Y ran into Reeves Jewelry. The other part ran next door to the A & B Dress Shop. He knew the natural gas that was piped into Villa Rica from the pumping station six and a half miles south of town was odorized, as he and Oscar Hixon, the Gas Superintendent, were the ones who put the odorizing agent, mercaptan, in twice a year. The odor of raw gas is very unpleasant and could be compared to "rotten eggs, or to the smell of a "pole cat" or "skunk." If leaking, it would be so unpleasant a person could not stay in the room. Tom left Eunice Reeves, reassuring her that things were fine.

Up at Berry's Pharmacy, Ann Pope Smith was waiting on a customer when her dad, Will Pope, came by to see her. He smelled the odor of gas. Later (in court testimony) he said, "I am familiar with the odor of natural gas because I usually light the gas stove or heater and before it lights there is an odor of gas. The odor I smelled in Berry's Pharmacy on Monday was the same odor as I smell when I light my natural gas fixtures."

That same day, Mrs. L. W. Leathers walked up the long flight of stairs from the

1. The Days Before the Tragedy

street to the dental office located on the second floor above Berry's Pharmacy. Later in Mrs. Leather's court testimony, she said, "When I walked up the stairs, I smelled an unusual odor; it smelled like gas to me. I have natural gas in my home furnished by the City of Villa Rica. When I turn on the stove at my house and when it does not catch immediately, I've smelled that same odor. When I got up the stairs it seemed as though my eyes began to burn; my nose smelled something real strong and it smelled like gas to me. The office was closed, so I returned down the stairs."

On Tuesday, December 3, Oscar Hixon, the Superintendent of the Villa Rica Gas Company, received another call from Reeves Jewelry. He went to the store and double-checked everything Tom had done the day before. Oscar found no gas leak. Oscar had worked for the City Gas Company for a couple of years and Tom was his only assistant. Villa Rica received the natural gas from Southern Natural Gas Company at Sandhill, which was about six and a half miles south Villa Rica and the neighboring town of Carrollton. It came in at one hundred pounds per square inch pressure.

Oscar had odorized it in June or July, putting three drums of mercaptan that arrived by Barnes Freight Lines. There were fifty gallons in each drum. The one hundred and fifty gallons would last at least six to eight months. The gas was sufficiently odorized so that it could be detected in case of a leak. The mercaptan went into a storage tank and then left the storage tank and went into the line. The odorizing station was ten to fifteen feet from the Southern Natural Gas meter station. There was no way the gas from Southern Natural Gas Company could <u>not</u> pass through Villa Rica's odorizing station. It was Oscar's job to check the regulator and odorizing station every day. Tom went in with him at least once a week. The gas went through the regulator and odorizing station and then flowed into town through Villa Rica's regulator station through a six-inch steel gas main. The more gas that was used by the City of Villa

Two story Berry's Pharmacy Photo courtesy Ted Williamson

Explosion in Villa Rica

Rica, the more odorant that would go into it and the faster the odorant would be used up.

The gas flowed through a steel pipe to the regulator station, and there the pressure was cut from one hundred pounds to fifteen pounds per square inch. After being reduced to fifteen pounds it was reduced again to about four ounces per square inch to be distributed to the 1,000 customers in the City of Villa Rica. Under this Rockwell system, if the pressure got too high, there was a pop-off valve. If it got too low, there was an alarm system which turned on a light and an alarm.

On Wednesday, December 4, about 9:00 o'clock that morning, Ray Tyson, who managed the soda fountain part of the pharmacy for Bill Berry, smelled an unusual odor." I got a whiff of something like fumes from a Greyhound bus," he later testified in court. "I went back and checked the radiant heater in the back of the store to see if it was turned on high. I then looked in the trash cans. I considered it might be decayed food—but found nothing. We had not had that odor in there before."

The Villa Rica Theater   Photo courtesy Ted Williamson

Wednesday was Bill Berry's day off, so Ray took it upon himself to ask M.D. Henslee, who ran the M.D. Henslee Department Store four stores up from Berry's, to come down and check things out. M.D. Henslee, known to everyone by his initials, also served as fire chief in the local Volunteer Fire Department. M.D. testified in court the happenings of that morning. "I left my store unattended and went down to Berry's. I stuck my head in the door and said, "Bring me a cup of coffee—I'm trying to watch my shop." Ray told him, "Come here, M.D. I want to see if you can smell anything in here. I have smelled odorized

1. The Days Before the Tragedy

natural gas in my home when I change the heater and I am familiar with that odor, but this is not the same." M.D. replied, " I haven't got anybody to watch the store."

Ray said, "I will stand in the door then and see if anybody goes in your store."

Bill and Margaret Berry   Photo courtesy Valerie Berry Wilhelm

M.D. went to the end of the soda fountain where Ray had poured a cup of coffee for him.

"You know what that is," he told Ray, "that's a downdraft."

"What's that?" Ray asked.

"That's just the wind blowing down the flue, " M.D. replied.

"Any danger in that?" Ray asked.

"No. That's gas that has already been burnt. There is no danger in that at all. The natural gas lines are not the problem. Also tell Bill to call a plumber to check for sewer gas leaks." M.D. took the coffee and told Ray he had to get back to his store.

After M.D. Henslee left, he walked back to his store thinking about the backdraft and the peculiar smell. In 1954, he had been part of a crew who had changed Bill Berry's system from butane to natural gas. The pipes at that time were in good shape. The gas pipe in Berry's store came into the rear of the building at the crawl space underneath the floor and came up through a hole into the pharmacy through another hole in the floor the same

Cliff and Eunice Reeves   Photo courtesy Charlotte Reeves Lee

size as the pipes. The A & B Dress Shop did not have a basement but a crawl space. Reeves Jewelry had a basement in the back part of the store.

The two gas meters behind Berry's Pharmacy had a cut-off valve where one could shut off the flow of gas into the building. This was true of the A & B Dress Shop and Reeves Jewelry. It was an easy matter to cut off the gas into the building. Oscar Hixon had tested the system after the 1954 installation and found no leaks at the time. M.D. Henslee put the thoughts of the backdraft aside.

Even though Wednesday was Bill Berry's day off, he came in about 9:30 that morning after M.D. Henslee had left. Ray was busy at the soda fountain and after the other employees came in, he made some deliveries. He was busy and did not think to tell Bill about M.D. Henslee saying there was a downdraft.

Ray continues the story. "But that day when I went home at noon to eat dinner, I checked the fuel oil heater. It was burning kerosene in it at the time, and it (the wind) was blowing down my flue and had spewed (spread) kerosene fumes all over my house. When it whiffs, the heater will make a popping noise. I told my wife, 'We are having the same trouble up at the pharmacy. Maybe the wind will change tomorrow.' When I got back to the work at 1:00 o'clock, an hour later, I did not smell the same odor again that I had that

1. The Days Before the Tragedy

morning. I thought no more about it that day. It passed my mind."

The reason Bill Berry had come in on his day off was to met with Joe Cutcliff, a Rexall Drug Company salesman who had been in the business for thirty-seven years. That morning, he and Bill went over the entire pharmaceutical stock of goods in the store. They finished about 2:00 or 2:30 that afternoon. Joe Cutcliff said later in a court testimony, "I was in the store about five and a half hours and do not remember smelling anything unusual in his store on that day. I do not remember any sensation of my eyes burning or anything unusual whatsoever. I heard no conversation concerning any reference to any smell or burning sensation of the eyes during that period." Joe Cutcliff and Bill went to Bill's house for dinner (lunch) and Bill came back to the pharmacy about 5:30 that evening.

Wednesday was the day to mop, and after Ray finished about three o'clock, it was his rotating day to be off for the afternoon. He left after John Bailey, the afternoon high school help, came in to work. John was a high school senior who worked at the pharmacy two afternoons a week, on Saturday, and every other Sunday.

John and two of the pharmacists, Don Bohannan and James Harrison, often had some sort of prank going on. That afternoon John was caught by one. If John happened to get a customer's order wrong when he fixed them a hot dog, he lay it aside and made them another one, as ordered. After they left, he would eat the one he had laid aside. James Harrison saw John lay a hot dog aside to eat later. Then James went over and without John seeing him, he filled the hot dog full of a bitter quinine. Everybody in the pharmacy was watching as John reached for the hot dog and took a big bite. When they all started laughing at him, he looked up and with a mouth full of hot dog said, "What?" He kept on eating, finishing the hot dog. He looked around having no idea what they were laughing about.

James Harrison said, "How did you like that hot dog?"

John said, "Fine. Tasted good."

James replied, "I don't see how, I filled it full of quinine."

Down at Reeves Jewelry that same day, Wednesday, Cliff Reeves noticed an odor that seemed to come in from the back of his shop. "The odor seemed to be different, and I did not know what it was," he later said in his court testimony. "It seemed to come in when the back door was open and drift through the building occasionally. It was not noticeable all the time. I called Oscar Hixon, the Superintendent of the City Gas Department about 6:00 o'clock in the afternoon and asked him to come by my place. He came immediately and checked my heater and gas line back to the meter. Oscar Hixon told me I did not have a gas leak. No odor was noticeable while he was in my store. Later that night, I called O.T.

Explosion in Villa Rica

Dyer, a plumber, who said he would come by on Thursday morning."

Back at the pharmacy, Bill Berry and Don Bohannan left for the day. James Harrison filled the last of the day's orders and helped the last few customers. The day had been busy with filling prescriptions as there was the Asiatic flu epidemic going around this season. There had been several hundred students absent from school in the previous weeks and the hospital nearby had been busy. Even the high school football game had been cancelled the Friday night before because half the players were sick with the flu.

After everyone left, John Bailey cleaned the soda fountain counter and dishes, straightened all the chairs and tables, and watched the clock waiting for nine o'clock to come. At 9:00 o'clock, he went to put his apron in the closet to the right of the sofa fountain counter. When he opened the door to the closet and hung his apron on a nail inside the closet, he got a strong whiff of gas. He looked toward the crawl space that was accessible from the closet and then closed the door. He turned to James, "Hey, I smell gas. Seems like it's coming from the crawl space."

"I'll call someone to come and check on that." James reached for the phone as John left and locked the door behind him. John walked to his 1940 Pontiac, parked at the curb, and headed home to Walker Street, about a half mile north across the railroad tracks. This chilly December night, John had no way of knowing that tomorrow would bring about catastrophic events that would be remembered for lifetimes and would affect so many lives.

2

Early Morning, December 5, 1957

*Workers from the factories planned on taking their lunch break
to do a little Christmas shopping in the stores that day.*
Elaine Bailey, author

Early Thursday morning, Donald Willis went to work at the cabinet shop located in a tin building right behind the theater. This cabinet shop stood diagonally from Reeves Jewelry.

Between seven thirty and eight o'clock that morning, a hundred or so workers came to their jobs at the Villa Rica Hosiery Mill which was located at the end of the block east of the business district and over the tracks from the intersection of Carroll Road and Montgomery Street. Many of the workers already planned on doing a little quick Christmas shopping after they ate lunch at the pharmacy like they did many days on their lunch break.

Adjacent to the hosiery mill sat the police station and City Hall. To the left of City Hall, was the Camp Cap Company that employed about a hundred workers who also planned on taking their lunch somewhere in the city of Villa Rica.

Sometime during the early morning activities in this small unaware town, Tom Pope left town and headed east down highway 78 toward Douglasville, the nearest neighboring town. He was driving a dump truck, going to the rock quarry eight miles away for a load of gravel. He never suspected as he left this quiet little orderly town that a major disaster would occur while he was gone and that things in the town would never be the same. He could never imagine that when he came back he would have the shock of his life.

At eight o'clock, Don Bohannan parked his 1954 blue Chevy in the usual place in

Explosion in Villa Rica

front of the pharmacy. The morning was cold; the weather forecasted a high of 50 degrees and a slight breeze. The street was quiet. It was too early in the day for Christmas shoppers, but Don knew they would be coming to this block of stores soon. The pharmacy should be busy again today because of so much flu going around—and he remembered, today was election day. That meant more people would be in town than usual. Right now, only a few cars moved up and down Montgomery Street—the main street—which ran parallel to the Southern Railroad track.

As Don went to unlock the double doors of the pharmacy, he realized they were already unlocked. Bill Berry had arrived before him. Don smelled an odor of some kind as he entered the building. "It wasn't strong enough to make me believe I was in danger, but was different than anything I had smelled in the store," Don said later in his court testimony. "I did not associate it with any drug or product that we sold in the store. It did not bother me. I either got used to it or it wasn't present all the time."

Ray Tyson came in right behind Don and said, "Well, he beat us here today." He referred to Bill Berry who was already in the back filling prescriptions.

When Bill Berry came in that morning, he had not noticed anything unusual at first. But after he had worked at the prescription counter for about fifteen minutes, his eyes began to burn. He had been working in the veterinary section of the pharmacy. He opened up the double doors in front of the store, the back door and the windows behind the pharmacy counter. The cold air came in, but he wanted to get this smell out of the pharmacy.

As Bill Berry was opening the doors and windows, Ray Tyson, the manager at the soda fountain, related to him that M.D. Henslee had been in the day before and had checked, briefly, the peculiar odor and said it could be a backdraft, or burned gas fumes. Ray Tyson told Bill Berry that M.D. Henslee also said that the natural gas lines were not the problem, but to call for a plumber to check for sewer gas leaks. As Ray was telling Bill he could still smell the strong fumes that burned his eyes like they did the day before. He compared the smell to a Greyhound bus exhaust only it was stronger this morning than before.

Bill admitted to Ray, "Yes, I smelled something when I came in here burning my eyes a little bit. I'll call the Dyers and see what they think about it."

Ray said later, "I told Bill that Henslee and I thought the trouble yesterday was because the wind was blowing, but the wind was not blowing that morning and I said that I didn't believe it was a downdraft blowing the fumes all over the store. Bill made a phone call but I did not stay to hear what he said."

Ray continued: "I went to the back of the store and lit the radiant heater with a

2. Early Morning, December 5, 1957

match. Then Don Bohannan asked me to go light the heater upstairs for Dr. Burnham, so the rooms would be warm when he came in later. So I went upstairs. I did not smell any odor up there nor did my eyes burn. I lit the heater in his office and one in the reception room. A little after 9:00 o'clock, I left the building and went on a delivery. When I came back, I did not notice the odor any more that day. I had a little burning of my eyes but did not smell an odor."

A few blocks away on Walker Street, John Bailey loaded his two sisters and two brothers in his '40 Pontiac. As they left to go to school, their dad, John Bailey, Sr, a fireman at Lockheed Aircraft Corporation in Marietta thirty-five miles away, came in from work. John Bailey, Sr planned on a late breakfast and on going to bed as he had worked the night shift. John Jr carried his brothers and sisters to school as they all went to the Villa Rica Grammar and High School. Then he went to his twelfth grade class to take a test.

Villa Rica High School and Grammar School

Also at school about that time, thirteen-year-old Bobby Roberts went into the office to tell the school secretary he had a dental appointment that morning at 10:30. He had broken a crown off his front tooth during football practice the previous evening. Bobby's mother, Marie Couch was in Birmingham visiting her sister who was sick. Bobby and his younger brother, Ron, were staying with their Grandmother Mae Hambrick until his mother's return. Carolyn Davis, a co-worker of Bobby's mother at Marie's Beauty Shop, was to accompany Bobby to the dental office that morning. Bobby had been picked to play on an All Star team at Georgia Tech Grant Field later in the year and knew there would be a picture taken. He didn't want to have a broken tooth showing, so Carolyn Davis had agreed to meet him at the dental office about 10:30.

Explosion in Villa Rica

Across town, Olin Thomas Dyer planned to pick up his son, Johnny, who worked for him as a plumber at the Dyer Plumbing and Heating business he owned. They were to go to Atlanta to pick up blueprints for a job they had recently contracted. Winnie, Johnny's wife, usually rode in to work with them to do the books and payroll but today she took the morning to stay home with Marion Ann, their two-and-a-half-year-old daughter. She thought Olin Dyer, who was know to everybody as O.T. Dyer, and Johnny would be gone all morning to Atlanta, so she told them she would come in later in the day.

Right before O.T. left home to pick up Johnny, he had received a call to go by lawyer Jeff Cole's office located across the tracks from Montgomery Street to check for a gas leak because he had smelled gas in the office. O.T. already had a call the night before to go over to Reeves Jewelry to check things out as they had smelled gas. They usually did not do repair—they mainly installed plumbing at hospitals and schools. But O.T. thought it good to help the people in his hometown when they needed him.

After Ray Tyson told Bill Berry that M.D. Henslee had said they might have a sewer problem in the Berry's, Bill immediately called, O.T. Dyer's home. O.T.'s wife told Bill that he had gone to lawyer Jeff Cole's office and was then going by Reeves Jewelry and she thought he might be there by now.

Bill walked out of the pharmacy and down to Reeves Jewelry. When he went in, he talked to Cliff Reeves relating the problem to him that they seemed to keep having—one of a peculiar odor. Cliff Reeves said O.T. Dyer had just gotten there and was checking to see if he could find the problem. Bill then walked back to where O.T. Dyer was and asked him to come over to the drugstore when he finished there.

Bill later remembers when he testified in court, "When I returned to the store, I did not smell anything unusual at first then my eyes began to burn again, then after a few minutes, I noticed a peculiar odor again. The odor I began to smell was not that of odorized natural gas. I told Ray Tyson, I was going to City Hall to find Oscar Hixon because I was going there to vote anyway.

"I then went into City Hall, and told Ralph Smith, the assistant clerk, that I had a peculiar odor in the store that had been smelled for a day or two. 'I'm getting dubious about it,' I said to Ralph Smith. 'I'm going up the street and ask the rest of the store owners if they smell this peculiar odor or if anyone had complained of their eyes burning.'

"As I returned to the store, I saw M.D. Henslee on the street. I asked M.D. to check the building to see if any of the gas heaters were out of adjustment."

When M.D. Henslee came into the drugstore, he told Bill Berry, "The odor smells

2. Early Morning, December 5, 1957

like a vent is stopped up, and is something like a downdraft smell."

While Bill was gone to City Hall, about 9:30 Ray Tyson carried some gratefruit juice to the ladies at the A & B Dress Shop. "I smelled this same odor and my eyes burned while I was in there, Ray testified later. "It was stronger in there than I had smelled it in the drugstore when I came in that morning," Ray told Camille Adams and Bernie Bell and they talked about the odor for a few minutes. "You all have got more of a downdraft in here or gas fumes than we do in the pharmacy."

One of the ladies mentioned, "And we don't even have a flue. We just decorated a Christmas tree—I wonder if the odor is coming from the tree?"

"After returning to the pharmacy," Ray said later, "I went into the closet to the right of the soda fountain. This closet fit into the underside of the stairway that went from the street outside to the second floor. In this closet, I opened up the trap door and went down into the crawl space (under the Berry's building) with a flash light as there was no light or light socket down there. I didn't smell anything under the floor, nor did my eyes burn. I didn't go all underneath the floor of the store; I just walked around under there where the floor went down for a short space. I had on white clothes and there were spider webs and everything under there. I didn't go far back enough to see any pipes that came in from the back. The opening or trap door was about 20 to 30 feet from the front of the store. There were cob webs and stuff down there. As I went farther back, the floor got lower so I could stand up. I didn't want to get back there and get dirty. The radiant heater was about forty or fifty feet from the front of the store. The gas pipes came from under the floor and go up to the ceiling."

When Ray came out of the crawl space and into the closet and back out into the pharmacy, he saw Bill talking to M.D. Henslee. Then M.D. came over to the soda fountain where Ray was and reached to the glass jar of straws sitting on the counter, took out one straw and his lighter, and lit the straw. He went around the store with the open flame trying to find the source of the smell. He spent quite a while that morning going along the natural gas pipes and heating appliances in the pharmacy using lit straws to see if there were any leaks along the lines and trying to find the source of the smell.

Dr. Burnham came into the store and said that his eyes were burning. He asked M.D. Henslee to come upstairs and check his dental office and waiting room. Henslee then went upstairs to Dr. Burnham's office and lit a straw to check the pipes and heating appliances there.

Bill remembers what happened next. "Later, M.D. Henslee came down from upstairs and told me he had checked there and everything was all right in the waiting room, but he found a small gas leak around the valve in one of Dr. Burnham's heaters in the dental office. He told me that he cut off the heater and that I ought to sent someone up there and have it fixed.

"M.D. said I had a downdraft and stated that heaters which were not properly regulated would give off that odor. M.D. Henslee had helped install my system when I converted from butane gas from a tank to natural gas, so I thought I could trust him. Henslee was around both the pharmacy and Dr. Burnham's dental office checking for a leak all morning.

Ray Tyson remembers, "When I returned from a delivery, I saw M.D. Hensley on the other side of the water heater which was midway on the right side of Berry's. He was back there going up the pipes with a lighted soda straw."

Bill went back into the prescription department and worked for awhile. "I thought about the matter of plumbing facilities. We had no problem or trouble with gas odors coming into the store from the plumbing facilities. There were two toilets downstairs on the lower level close to the snack bar—where the juke box and tables were—toward the back and down a couple of steps. We had one restroom on the main floor-level. We had previously had trouble with this toilet, but I did not remember how long ago. These were flush toilets, and I had a sink in the soda fountain area. I telephoned the City Hall and asked Ralph Smith again if Oscar Hixon had come in and that I needed him here at the store."

It was, by this time, mid-morning, and outside five-year-old, Ricky Hammond held his mother's hand as they walked passed the pharmacy and down Montgomery Street. Ricky

L-R: Warren Powell, Gene Holloman, Lamar Furr, and James Harrison, pharmacists. Photo 1958 Villa Rica High yearbook.

2. Early Morning, December 5, 1957

thought about how cold it seemed as his mom, Cleo Hammond, had shopped the stores up and down the street all morning. They were waiting for his dad, Ray Hammond, who worked for a wholesale grocery and was up the street at Mullinax Grocery Store taking an order. When Ricky and his mom got cold and tired of shopping, they went back to wait for his dad in the family car parked in the alley directly behind Berry's Pharmacy. Ricky played on the driver's side turning the steering wheel of the '56 Brown, two-toned Buick left and right in a rocking motion like small kids do.

Eunice Reeves left the jewelry store and walked across the railroad tracks to a beauty shop to get her hair fixed. She left her husband and daughter, Charlotte, to run the store. She

Inside Berry's pharmacy. Ray Tyson standing behind the counter in the center of the photo (shortest) in a white cap. Photo courtesy Ted Williamson

planned to be back within an hour—before they got busy.

About 10:30 Shirley Whitworth took a break from the Hughie's 5 & 10 and went to Berry's for a morning break. There she ordered hot chocolate and a snack from Ann Smith, who worked behind the soda fountain this morning in the place of Ray Tyson. Shirley got her order and went down a couple of steps at the end of a hallway to where the tables were in the snack area and sat down. Ralph Fuller, a barber who worked at the end of the block, came in and ordered coffee and a sandwich from Ann. He got his order and also sat at one of the tables in the snack area.

23

Explosion in Villa Rica

Martha Wynn, age seventeen, was staying with her grandmother, Mattie Wynn, up on Dogwood Street two blocks west of the main strip of town. About 10:30 that morning, Martha walked three blocks from her grandmother's house on Westview Drive to Berry's Pharmacy to pick up a prescription for her grandmother. Before Martha left, Mrs. Wynn told Martha, "Now I want you to be back here to have my lunch ready at 12:00, noon. I don't want to wait. I want it served to me at 12:00."

When Martha entered the pharmacy, she smelled a heavy noxious odor that reminded her of rotten eggs. As she stood in line at the drug counter to pick up the prescription, her eyes and nose began to water from the strong smell. She quickly picked up the prescription from Don Bohannan.

Martha walked toward the front door to leave. She saw Margaret Berry to her right standing behind the cosmetic counter. For a brief instant, Martha glanced around at the cosmetics and felt tempted to look longer, but she remembered that her grandmother wanted her lunch served exactly at 12:00, so Martha left the store. "I felt glad to be out in the fresh cold air," she said later. Martha turned left, walked past the movie theater and made another left, and went down Westview Drive the way she had come. She walked up the hill toward the Jones Funeral Home which was located in a large white house that sat up on the hill.

About 10:30 Bobby Roberts checked out of school and began walking toward town to go to the dental office. Carolyn Davis, who was to meet him there, left Marie's Beauty Shop and walked toward Berry's Pharmacy. She met Bobby outside and they both went up the long flight of enclosed stairs to Dr. Burnham's office.

Mrs. Gladys Bishop had gone in Dr. Burnham's office that morning to have a tooth pulled. As Gladys walked through the reception area to leave, she saw Carolyn Davis and Bobby Roberts in the waiting room. As she closed the door behind her and went down the stairs, she too smelled the strong odor of natural gas.

Right after 10:30, Bill Berry told Ray Tyson, "M.D. Henslee didn't find anything when he was back there checking."

Bill felt impatient and worried about the peculiar odor. He told Ray, "I have been trying to get the Dyers up here to see about this odor, but they haven't come to check. I called over to Ralph Smith at City Hall and he told me where Oscar Hixon was working. I want you to go out there at Marvin Suddeth's on Dallas Highway where he is working and get him to come up here to see if he can tell what the odor is and where it is coming from. Get in the truck and find Oscar Hixon, and ask him to come to the store."

Ray Tyson drove to where Ralph Smith said Oscar Hixon was working with city

2. Early Morning, December 5, 1957

laborers. Ray drove one mile north to where city workmen were making a gas and water tap on Paulding Road to hook a gas line from the main to the Suddeth's house. Harold Evans, Horace Chism, and James Bailey later testified that they had worked there all morning with Oscar Hixon directing them. When they cut into the main gas line, about 9:15 that morning, gas came out of the pipe and they each smelled the familiar odorant in the gas. James Bailey remarked when the gas came out, "I never smelled anything that smelled as bad as that." As they made the tap and connected a line to run to the Suddeth's house, they also checked and found that the required 15 pounds of pressure was in the line.

As Ray pulled over in his pick-up truck he hollered, "Where's Oscar?"

"He left about fifteen minutes ago. He's gone to the Villa Rica Hosiery Mill," was the reply.

"I drove toward the hosiery mill," Ray said later. "I saw Oscar coming out of a cafe where he had stopped to get a cola. I told him that we had an odor at the drugstore and that we couldn't tell what it was and that we wanted him to come and see if he could help."

Oscar Hixon replied, "I'll go there right now and see what I can find." Ray Tyson followed him in his pick-up truck back to the store.

About 10:50 the pharmacist, James Harrison, who had worked the night before was dropped off out front of Berry's Pharmacy after accompanying a doctor on a house call. He walked toward the pharmacy intending to go in and have a soft drink and relax before going to work at 1:00 that afternoon. As he walked inside, he remembered it was election day, so he decided to go vote. James came right out, got into his car parked near the pharmacy, and drove north on Candler Street across the tracks, passed the railroad depot and to City Hall to vote.

Robby Robison, the editor of the Villa Rican newspaper, left the pharmacy and walked around town selling ads.

The postman was running late that morning. Mrs. Gladys Brown, Mrs. R. L. Williams, and Mrs. Rosa Lee Williams were due at the dental office, but waited patiently for the postman to come first.

Preston Lancaster, from Bremen, parked his gas tanker truck on Wilson Street behind Berry's. He went inside to have a cup of coffee and collect payment from Ray Tyson for fuel oil he had delivered to Ray's home and for what he had put in Ray's mother's fuel oil tank earlier that morning.

Homer Vaughn, a former truck driver and part-time farmer, came into the pharmacy at the same time with Preston Lancaster. Homer Vaughn was there to ask Ray Tyson to bring

Explosion in Villa Rica

a penicillin shot out to his farm for a sick horse after he got off work. Homer ordered a Coca-cola and stood at the counter talking to Preston Lancaster. Both men were waiting to talk to Ray Tyson. Ann Smith told them Ray was on an errand and would be back shortly.

Earnest Lee "Buck" Jackson, one of the gas workmen employed by Dyer Plumbing and Heating, has vivid memories that fit in detail but as the series of events unfolded, it causes you to wonder how *all* of it could have possibly happened. Buck Jackson pulled into O.T. Dyer's driveway on Wilson Street in the black, panelled plumber's truck that he drove for Dyer when at work. O.T. was coming out of the house and hollered, "We've got to go to Berry's and check for a gas leak."

Buck followed O.T. as he drove his white Studebaker the block and half to Berry's. Buck parked the truck right behind the pharmacy. When Buck went into the basement, O.T. was already talking to Johnny who was somewhere out of sight—probably in the crawl space trying to find the source of the gas leak. Buck tells this, "We could hear Johnny, but could not see him. O.T. had been called when City Hall could not get in touch with Oscar Hixon."

Buck remembers, "You could sure smell the gas in that basement."

O.T. Dyer looked at me and said, "Go get the pipe-dope out of the truck."

"We're out. We used all we had yesterday," I told him.

"'Go on to the hardware store and buy some,'" O.T. replied.

"I went up the steps to the pharmacy, walked through the store, saw Homer Vaughn and Preston Lancaster standing at the soda fountain and hit each on the shoulder as I walked by. I went out the front double doors that were wide open and crossed the road and headed toward B. Powell's Hardware Store that was directly in line with the pharmacy, but past the depot and down Candler Street on the north side."

As Buck was walking through the pharmacy and out the front door, Ray Tyson had followed Oscar Hixon to Berry's and each parked his pick-up truck out front at Berry's. Ray remembered later in court testimony, "When we arrived, the Dyers were getting out of their truck in front of the drugstore (which means they must have moved their truck to the front of the pharmacy.) Johnny Dyer got a couple of wrenches out of the truck and both of them went into the store. Oscar Hixon entered about twenty feet behind them, and I was behind Oscar."

At 10:50, M.D. Henslee had to leave Berry's when one of his customers from his department store came in and asked him to come back to his store and write up an order for him. As M.D. Henslee left Berry's he saw O.T. and Johnny Dyer come in. Each was carry-

2. Early Morning, December 5, 1957

ing a wrench in his hand. "As I left, I saw Oscar Hixon coming in right behind them. I told Oscar, 'As soon as I'm through with my customer, I will come back and help.'"

Ray Tyson tells what happened next. "When I entered the store, the Dyers had stopped just beyond the water heater which was about half-way of the store on the right side. There was a pipe that came from underneath the store through the floor next to the gas heater which was to the right. The water heater was to the left of the gas heater. The water heater had a pilot light that burned all the time. Both the gas heater and water heater were vented into an old chimney on the right wall of the pharmacy.

It was about ten minutes until eleven. At that time, I didn't notice any odor or burning of my eyes. Hixon stopped about half way between me and the Dyers and turned around and said: 'This is not gas that I smell.' Hixon said that it wasn't gas fumes or gas either that he smelled. Hixon turned and went down where the Dyers had stopped.

"I walked behind the soda fountain and began talking to Preston Lancaster and Homer Vaughn, who both stood at the counter. Ann Smith walked from where I was to the other side of the Dyers. While there, I heard Ann Smith, say to the Dyers, 'Now, you all are not going to do anything that will blow this place up or anything, are you?'"

O.T. Dyer said something to her which I could not understand. Johnny Dyer was tightening up something; I saw his arm go up and down about twice. I know he was working on the pipe that came from underneath the floor. Johnny Dyer was closest to me; O.T. Dyer was on the other side; and Oscar Hixon was standing behind them looking. I then heard a sound in the back that went: 'Shoosh.' Black smoke came high, over their heads. Whether it come [sic] through the wall or whether it come from around there somewhere I don't know. But it was just a second, and then everything flashed over with a kind of red—blue flame and then I heard a loud noise."

3

The Moments That Decided—Life or Death

*There was no foreboding of tragedy, no preparation for disaster.
It came in the twinkling of an eye.*
The Atlanta Constitution, Friday December 6, 1957

That morning business at the pharmacy had seemed unusually busy. There were Christmas shoppers coming to look through the new holiday displays; there were people coming in to buy medicine and get prescriptions filled because a member of their family had the flu; and since it was election day, some of the voters stopped in for a few minutes before or after going to City Hall to vote.

About 10:40, Don Bohannan stood behind the drug counter, which was located on a step-up area that ran across the back of the store, talking to Bill Berry who had come back from the gas company. Mrs. Berry had just gotten back from the bank a few minutes earlier. She called to her husband, "Bill, the gas men are here."

Don Bohannan remembers in his testimony later, "I glanced up and saw O.T. Dyer and his son, Johnny Dyer, come in the door. The Dyers each were carrying a wrench. Oscar Hixon who walked right in behind them, said in a loud voice, 'This is not gas that I smell.'

"The next time I glanced up," Don related, "I saw that all three of them had disappeared from my line of view. There was a wall that blocked a hallway beyond the overhead heater. On the left of the hallway was a small utility closet where a sink and the water heater was located. The gas heater was on the right hanging from the ceiling then at the end of the hallway, there were three steps that went down to the snack area. Customers went down the hallway, and down the steps to the snack area in the back right corner of the pharmacy.

"Margaret Berry stood behind the same counter that I did about six feet behind Bill

Villa Rica Railway Depot   Photo courtesy Ted Williamson

and me and to the right. Ann Smith stood about six feet in front of us at the cash register. We had one customer, Rob Broom, who stood waiting to pick up a prescription that Bill was filling for him.

"Carl Vitner, a pharmaceutical salesman, who came in only about once a month, sat at a small table waiting to talk to Bill.

"Ralph Fuller and Shirley Whitworth were the only people in the snack area. Ralph got up and put a nickle in the juke box and made his selection.

"Ray Tyson talked to two customers, Preston Lancaster and Homer Vaughn at the counter. Preston was there to collect for gas he had delivered to Ray's home. Homer was standing there at the counter drinking a Coca-cola."

Don Bohannan continues, "My first knowledge of the explosion was just a sharp cracking noise and then a kind of bright flame all around me and a lot of pressure. I was either going up or down, and there wasn't any time to think about it.

"The building exploded upward. For just a split hundredth of a second, I glimpsed blue sky. As the building went up, it exploded outward. I landed about where I had been standing, but the large shelving with the cubbies that held the medications landed on top of me. When I got free of the shelving, I crawled and dug my way toward Bill who lay on his back under the same shelving that also trapped him. I knew he was alive as I cleared debris from his face. He had a long bad vertical gash going back from his forehead. 'I'll get you

3. The Moments That Decided-Life or Death

to where you can breathe. I'm going to get help.' I looked up and saw the sky through a hole in the collapsed roof. I started climbing over debris, upward. When I got to the roof, I saw two men getting a beam off a man, but I could only see his two legs coming out of the debris. I didn't stay long enough to see who it was or if he were alive. I still don't know who he was.

"When someone helped me off the roof, I saw that the fire had picked up and came from the center of the drugstore about where the end of the soda fountain had been. The whirling smoke rising up somehow sounded to me like rain."

Buck Jackson, the plumber from Dyer Heating and Plumbing, was on his way to the hardware store to buy pipe dope for the leaking pipe. He had just put one foot over the railroad tracks, when it hit. Buck Jackson remembers, "I jerked around and stood there in shock watching the smoke boiling upward. I could not move and in about thirty seconds, another explosion hit. This time there were more flames. I could hear crumbling going on inside the building. I took off running, thinking there might be another explosion around me. I really just ran instead of doing any thinking. When I went inside the hardware store, I saw that the door had been blown off and was laying on the floor. The store clerk said, 'Where are you going?' I said, "I don't know, and ran out the back door. He said, 'I'm going too' and ran out behind me.

"By that time, we ran back to the front of the building and watched. People were running to the fire and some were still running from the fire. I knew I had to go back. There were piles and piles of bricks no one could climb over. The cars in front of the stores were crushed. I pulled out someone and helped him until he could stand. Someone helped me pull out another guy and we laid him down on the sidewalk. I don't know who it was, but he was unconscious. Then we began to dig. We could do nothing more, so we went up the street and down Carroll Road to Wilson Street then to the back of the explosion site."

When the explosion hit, it rocked City Hall on the other side of the railroad tracks. Herman Holloway was inside at the voting booth. Herman Holloway, a part time postal employee, had just left his dad, Herman Sr, who worked at Richard's Motor Company located a block east of town on the 78 Highway. Herman Jr had walked down Highway 78, and had been planning on going into Berry's for a sandwich and cola before going to work but decided to go vote first. When Herman went into City Hall, there were several people standing in line to vote. Bill Black, a deputy, was on duty.

Herman Holloway tells this, "When the loud percussion shook the building, everybody in the building ran to the front door. Deputy Bill Black grabbed the door knob to jerk

Explosion in Villa Rica

the door open to see what had happened, but then realized the explosion had hit so hard that it had warped the door frame and the door was stuck. Bill, who weighed over two-hundred-and fifty-pounds, got a running start and rammed his shoulder and body-force into the door and managed to pry it open."

Herman Holloway was outside in an instant and could see only thick dust everywhere. He looked up and saw debris and papers raining downward. "It looked like hundreds of old prescriptions papers floating through the air. When the secondary percussion came we had just come outside City Hall to see what had happened.

"I ran immediately across the railroad tracks and down to the stores to help," Herman Holloway tells. "There was too much fire in front of the building to get in and rescue anyone, so I went down Carroll Road to Wilson Street to the back of the buildings to see if it were possible to get in and help. There, city personnel were looking for the cut-off valve for the gas line but no one could find it. I think it might have been buried under the debris. I knew Villa Rica needed help. As I realized some of the phone lines were down I drove by way of Stockmar Road and through Dark Corners, near Winston to the next town east—to Douglasville to get help."

James Harrison, the pharmacists who had driven over the tracks to City Hall and parked to go inside had just walked up the steps of City Hall when the explosion took place. James was lucky enough to find a working phone and quickly call his wife to let her know he was all right. He knew she would have heard the explosion and would be wondering what had happened. Then Harrison went back to the scene. James later told the newspaper reporter, "I was at City Hall ready to vote when all hell broke loose. I ran back toward the store but saw there was nothing I could do. It was total chaos as one might imagine."

M.D. Henslee had been back at his department store for only a few minutes. In later court testimony he told what happened. "I returned to my store and wrote out an order for a customer. I started to the door to go back to Berry's when the explosion occurred. I heard either two explosions or a 'down concussion' of the brick falling back as the second noise. I do not know which. After the first explosion, I ran to the door of my shop and saw stuff falling everywhere. I told the people in my shop to run and I started out again and stepped outside and the second concussion or explosion knocked me back through a plate glass window. I would estimate that the time between the two explosions was one-half minute to one minute. There was a little interval between the first explosion and the time of the second one. If the second was due to material falling, the material would have had to go pretty high in order to take that much time to come back down."

3. The Moments That Decided-Life or Death

A few seconds earlier, at the Empire 5 & 10 Cent Store, eighteen-year-old Melinda Doris Hembree had started to go to lunch when she heard the radio disc jockey play the song "Why, Oh, Why?" She paused, wanting to hear the song. "We had not had many customers that morning, and I paused a minute to listen," she told the reporter later.

"Why, Oh, Why?" could have been a prelude to what happened next. "I was standing there when all of a sudden a big noise came and I didn't remember anything for a few minutes.

"When everything quit falling down around me," Melinda Hembree said, "I heard Rozelle Johnson, the manager of the dime store, who was working three feet away from me. She was crying, 'Oh, my legs! Can't you help me?' I tried to reach her, but I couldn't move the counter that hemmed her in."

Rozelle was frantic; Melinda felt desperate and helpless. She did not know what to do. She hoped help would come soon.

4

The First Minutes After the Explosion

*When the explosion sent shock waves over the small town
of Villa Rica, the neighborhood literally shook.*
Elaine Bailey, author

Frank Carnes, the local depot agent, stepped out of his office at the train depot and hooked a mail bag to a "switch arm" on a tall steel pole beside the railroad tracks. The "switch arm" held the mail bag out for a person on a passing train to reach out with a hook and grab the bag as the train passed. At the very moment the passenger train sped by, he saw the explosion happen in front of him. He described the scene to a reporter as being like a house of cards falling, so rapidly did the stores disintegrate and catch on fire. The air was filled with clothing, papers, wood, bricks and other falling debris that came toward him and landed on the roof of the depot and all about him on the ground. Frank Carnes ran back inside to depot to avoid getting hit by the falling objects.

Several minutes before the explosion in Reeves Jewelry and Flower Shop, Cliff Reeves had been waiting on a customer. Charlotte, his daughter, had seen the Atlanta Linen Service route man, Kenneth Hendrix, get out of his red paneled delivery truck parked across the street and come in to pick up the soiled linen and deliver the fresh ones as he usually did once a week.

After taking the fresh linens from Kenneth, Charlotte had walked to the back of the store and Kenneth had just enough time to get to the sidewalk, when she felt the percussion and force of the explosion. She stood horrified as she watched the outside wall of the store fall out onto the cars that were parked along the street. She stood there until her dad started yelling, "Run and get away from the store, he yelled. "It might blow again."

"I looked down and realized my shoes were gone, and I knew they had literally been blown off my feet. A hideous smell filled my nostrils and a sickening feeling flooded my body as a dark, thick smoke boiled upward and hot flames were coming from all directions. There was burning destruction that only seconds before had been the pharmacy. I got out, but could not do anything because the flames were so hot."

Donald Willis, at the cabinet shop behind the movie theater, felt the shock of the explosion like a loud earthquake. "It shook the entire building and dust flew everywhere.

Approximately six minutes after the explosion.

Photo by John McPherson

I thought a train had run off the tracks. I ran toward the front door of the cabinet shop and as I got to the outside, I looked up and saw debris falling—a lot of debris. I realized there had been an explosion that had rocked the entire area. I could see several buildings had just blown up. I didn't see them go up. I got there as they came down. People were on their knees, everywhere, as I guess those who were walking on the streets had been blown down. Everybody ducked and tried to get away from the falling debris. Papers were flying in the air."

4. The First Minutes After the Explosion

Donald Willis ran toward the demolished buildings wanting to help. "I looked up again and saw no fire but dark smoke billowed hundreds of feet into the air. I looked toward Reeves Jewelry. The entire building had collapsed but not all the way to the ground. The heavy tin roof was in one piece like it had been draped over the collapsed building. The right wall of the jewelry store had been blown into Candler Street as piles of bricks and rubble filled the entire street. The highway in the center of town was blocked by debris. The front wall of the pharmacy, a two-story brick structure, fell into the street, crushing several cars. I saw that Berry's Pharmacy had been the hardest hit and the whole back had been blown out.

"Several buildings beyond the pharmacy had exploded but the heavy smoke made

Approximately eight minutes after the explosion.
Photo by George Holloway

it impossible to see all that were involved. As I neared the Reeves' building, I could not avoid stepping on the fallen power lines that lay everywhere. The bottom half of a utility pole in the front of the Reeves' building had been blown away and the upper half swung loose, dangling from wires."

Cliff Reeves, Charlotte, and a customer—an elderly man—had come out the back of the building. The elderly customer had slipped on glass and had fallen. Reeves helped him up and the three of them came out of the collapsed building.

Once outside Cliff Reeves was joined by Donald Willis. Both of the men heard screaming coming from next door, at the A & B Dress Shop. Both followed the sounds and Bernie Bell came out crying, "Save Mrs. Adams. She's trapped." Cliff Reeves and Donald were joined by N.J. Defore, who also worked at the cabinet shop.

Donald Willis continues his story: "As the three of us went in the back door of the A & B Dress Shop, we saw the roof had collapsed, but we made our way inside, climbing over broken counters and continuing to follow the sound of the screams. Near the back of the shop, we could see someone's hands waving over a partition. It was Camille Adams. She was pinned down by some lattice work and a big fan."

Camille Adams' statement to the newspaper takes up the story here: "At first they were afraid to move me, afraid they would hurt me, but I yelled, "Pull, pull, pull. Dr. Ernest

Approximately fifteen minutes after the explosion.

Photo by George Holloway

Powell came in about that time. They pulled me over the partition."

"After we pulled her free," Donald Willis said, "the four of us with Camille Adams climbed over the rubble and had just made it to the stoop, outside the back door, when a secondary explosion came with a 'whoof' sound and force. It knocked us all down and burned my hands and face. Cliff Reeves was burned on his face also."

While Donald Willis helped Camille Adams out, Bill Berry was helped out of the building by a stranger who had gone in, saw a way out, and literally shoved him through an opening.

4. The First Minutes After the Explosion

As Donald Willis reached the outside, he remembers, "I looked up and saw Bill Berry standing out behind the demolished pharmacy. What had been the pharmacy looked like a pile of smoking rubble. I could hear moaning, crying, and hollering coming from inside. Bill looked dazed and soot covered him from head to toe."

Right then, Dr. Powell ran to Bill Berry, who gasped for air. Dr. Powell helped support him. Bill coughed and was choking from coming through the thick smoke which boiled upward inside the torn-up pharmacy. Bill managed to say, "Margaret's still in there. Can you get her out?"

At some point, Bill Berry was put in the back of a pickup truck and carried to the Villa Rica Hospital, about two miles north.

Dr. Powell, took a step into the burning building, tried to peer into the boiling grey

The back of Reeves Jewelry. At left, the roof of the depot and the "switch arm" are visible. Photo by Robby Robison

smoke and could make out two stories of fallen and burning timbers piled between the demolished walls. He knew they needed rescue equipment to get the trapped victims out. He could hear screaming and knew Margaret Berry was still in the smoke filled building.

Margaret Berry who had been behind the cosmetic counter moments before the explosion had walked to the back and had stood beside the pharmacist's counter. She now lay trapped in the rubble, pinned down by a timber that had fallen on her leg. She was screaming, calling, "Someone get this off my leg."

Seconds before the explosion, Shirley Whitworth sat at the snack bar table finishing her snack and Ralph Fuller had sat back down after putting a nickle in the juke box when the explosion occurred. "I saw what looked like a red flash," Fuller later said to a newspaper reporter. "At first I thought the juke box had blown up, but I was blown out of my seat and slammed up against the wall (eastward) opposite from the A & B Dress Shop. As everything came crashing down around me, I realized the whole building had blown up. Stuff kept falling on me," he said. "I felt like there wasn't any air. I was covered in debris. Shirley Whitworth and I were trapped in the wreckage as the blast had buried both of us and we were under the rubble. I thought I was going to suffocate. Then I saw a light, so I knew I wouldn't smother. I stuck my leg up through the opening. I could hear people talking above me, saying, 'There's somebody in there, let's get him out.'

"The rescue workers found us and pulled us out. Both Shirley and I were burned

The Candler Street side of Reeves Jewelry. Note the flower vases still standing. Photo by George Holloway

badly. I got burned on my arms and face. After we were out, it was a few minutes until we were taken to the Villa Rica Hospital."

Shirley Whitworth's only memory is that she regained consciousness several times as she rode in the ambulance to the hospital. She knew she was hurt badly.

Preston Lancaster, the gas man from Bremen later testified in court that he saw a wall of fire coming from his left, from the back of the store. There was a loud roar and he went up in the air and fell back down. The floor had blown out underneath him before he was blown twenty to twenty-five feet into the air. He fell through the floor into the crawl

4. The First Minutes After the Explosion

space.

"The flame was yellow," he remembered as he testified. "It moved toward me and reached me. I came down in the same position I was in when I was blown up [sic]. I ended up with second and third degree burns on my face, neck, arms, hands, and legs. The explosion burned my hair off and my eyebrows and took all the hair off my body. When I went into the pharmacy that morning, both front doors (double doors) were wide open. It was about five minutes until eleven. I did not notice any odor when I went in the pharmacy that morning, but I had impairment of my sense of smell because I worked near diesel fuel and kerosene and at various times I had fuel oil on my clothes."

Homer Vaughn who had stood in front of the soda fountain beside Preston Lancaster, was also blown into the air, before falling through the floor. He later testified, "As the explosion happened, I saw a flash.... I had not noticed any smell of gas and had not heard anyone talking about leaking gas. I would say that within four minutes of going into the store, why *SHEBANG*! Everything went up and we went up. ... It sounded like dynamite went off. I went up and as I came back down through the floor I was left hanging upside down. I weighed two-hundred-and-twenty pounds. It was just as dark as 'midnight under a washpot.'

"I didn't know where I was," Homer Vaughn continued in his court testimony. "There was hollering and a lot of noise. I called on the Lord for help and no more than I did, some wires caught afire [sic]. When the wires caught fire, I could see and was able to grab a large post that was close by and some wires. I pulled myself up and got loose. When I did, I fell into the crawl space. I heard Lancaster in the dark saying 'come this way!' We kept crawling and found our way through the dark and out the back and were rescued."

Homer Vaughn and Preston Lancaster were probably rescued before the secondary explosion and fire that came seconds later. Homer had a nail with a board attached to it sticking into his leg. He was burned badly.

Ray Tyson had his wallet in one hand and his money in the other hand paying Preston Lancaster for his fuel oil. "I first heard a hissing sound," Ray remembered as he talked to a newspaper reporter. "Then I heard something go 'swoosh' and a puff of black smoke rose about head-high going up in back of the pharmacy to the ceiling.

"A split second later I heard the explosion and I felt a lot of heat rushing at me. I was blown up into the second story. I thought a bomb had hit the place. But I knew it was gas. We had been smelling that peculiar smell for a day or two. I felt a hot flash, and then burning all over. I got a little burn on my shoulder, but not on my face. My back and sides were hurt. The billfold containing three-hundred-sixty-five dollars was blown out of my hand.

"I could hear people screaming and hollering and begging for help. A water pipe broke behind the counter and the hose on the fountain miraculously sprayed water all over me, keeping me from getting burned. Some timber hit me on the head and back. I struggled to get free. I moved a lot of timber and got out. I crawled through a hole. I don't exactly remember coming out."

Men with water hoses on the rooftops on the right. Photo by Robby Robison.

Ray continues, "When I came to, I heard screaming in the dime store next door. I crawled toward the scream, got out through an opening at the front of the pharmacy. I moved stuff. You feel like you can move a ton when you see fire. I made my way into the dime store. It was Rozelle Johnson screaming and Melinda Hembree was trying to move a counter. I took Melinda out, then I got dizzy and don't know what happened."

Ray Tyson passed out. He was taken out by Gene Doyle.

Despite a severe blow on the head and some burns and scratches, Ray Tyson was later reported in fair condition by the attendants at the Villa Rica Hospital.

Melinda Hembree who had paused a few minutes to listen to the radio play, "Why, Oh, Why?" first went to the Villa Rica Hospital then she was transported to Tanner Memorial in Carrollton.

4. The First Minutes After the Explosion

Two blocks away from the pharmacy, Martha Wynn, the seventeen-year-old who had picked up her grandmother's prescription, felt the huge explosion. She had been going up the hill in front of Jones Funeral Home when she felt the earth shake like an earthquake. She thought that a train had run off the tracks and into the stores in the business district. She never looked back but ran the rest of the way to her grandmother's house.

A few minutes after she got there, her mother, Mrs. Metta Wynn arrived. She had just learned of the explosion and came quickly from the elementary school where she was a third grade teacher. Metta ran inside, frantic, until she saw that Margaret had made it back home. She knew her daughter had planned on getting the prescription for the grandmother that morning. If Martha had not minded her grandmother in getting back home promptly to fix lunch, she could have been in the explosion. If she had stopped at the cosmetic counter for five minutes as she wanted, she could have been killed.

Owners of the adjacent stores were among the first to participate in the rescue efforts: J. P. Spinks, who operated the dry cleaners a block from the demolished stores, heard a deafening roar and ran into the street to see debris flying and smoke and flames gushing hundreds of feet into the air. Spinks, a volunteer fireman, was able to help pull several people from the wreckage. Joe Brock who ran the furniture store went into the Empire 5 & 10 Cent Store and brought out Mrs. Willie Mae Tackett. Joe almost got blown out of the store himself when the second percussion occurred.

On the streets outside the pharmacy, Don Bohannan stood in a daze. He later told what happened. "As I climbed upward over the debris and got to the ground, I realized how badly I had been burned. Every bit of my exposed skin had been burned and was black with soot. My shirt had been burned off, but some of my tie remained. My nylon socks were burned out of my shoes, even inside my shoes the socks were gone. My hair, that I was letting grow out from a crew cut, had burned to the roots. I had lost my glasses, so I could not see well. I knew my hands were burnt badly.

"I walked around in the back of the pharmacy for a few minutes. People were running all around me. There was shouting and a lot of noise. Anyone who noticed me, passed me by knowing I was alive, but they were intent on going in to rescue anyone else they could find. After I stood there a few minutes in terrible pain and trying to get my breath, I heard someone say, 'Can I take you to the hospital?' I looked around and saw it was John Bailey, the high school kid who worked at the pharmacy several afternoon a week." John helped Don Bohannan into his 1940 four door Pontiac and headed for the hospital.

John Bailey had been taking a test in school when the explosion shook the school.

Explosion in Villa Rica

He had run to the window. The teacher told him to sit down and finish his test. In a matter of minutes, someone came and said John was needed at the explosion site. Because John worked at Berry's and knew everyone, he could help identify those who were hurt since all the burn victims were covered with black soot. He had driven there to see how he could help.

When the secondary explosion occurred M.D. Henslee had been knocked back into his glass store window. He got up and immediately ran for the firetruck which was housed across the street in a building across from to City Hall where he saw people running out of

The first ambulance arrives.   Photo by John McPherson

that building. "Someone had already activated the siren on the utility pole in front of City Hall. This blasted an emergency signal that could be heard for miles." M.D. Henslee said later. "I never looked back until I got on the firetruck. I knew it would be bad and I knew we had to have the truck if we were going to be of any help. Men came running to the truck and we shot across the road. We got there within two minutes of the explosion, but by then the block looked like an inferno. I couldn't tell if my store was burning or not. All I could think about was trying to help. I don't know who all was helping, but I could hear screams and when we got the hoses hooked up, we started pouring water to the flames as hard as we could. It wasn't doing much good, but somebody took the hose and we started digging through the flames and rubble."

Someone hollered, 'Shut off the gas! Nobody had cut off the gas! Where is the cut-

4. The First Minutes After the Explosion

off? Get that tanker truck out of here! Move it!' They located Preston Lancaster who had driven the gas truck from Bremen. Preston was burned badly and the rescuers were trying to persuade him to go the Villa Rica Hospital. Preston gave them the key to the tanker truck then he flagged down a passing motorist and asked them to take him to Bremen to the hospital. Lancaster wanted to be in a hospital close to where he lived.

Hoyt Easterwood and his wife, Dora, heard the explosion from the grocery store they owned at the opposite end of the same block. They stepped out onto the street to see what had happened. They saw debris falling on the railroad depot roof across the railroad track. Then they heard a woman screaming. Hoyte Easterwood hollered to his wife, "Call an ambulance! Call an ambulance!" Dora Easterwood went back inside and called Jones Funeral Home.

"We then ran out into the street and across the tracks and looked back to see black smoke boiling up and the buildings that had been flattened," Hoyte Easterwood later told a newspaper reporter. We looked down at the smoldering, torn-up, and tossed pile of bricks, wood, and roofing that had been the four stores. It looked terrible. We turned around and saw the town's only firetruck, a 1942 Chevrolet firetruck, already crossing the tracks at Carroll Street and turning right onto Montgomery Street."

"As they were stretching out a hose," Dora Easterwood said, "my husband asked the firemen if they had called any other fire departments. They said they had not. He went back into his store and called for help from the neighboring towns—Douglasville, Carrollton, and Dallas."

People began to look around and find that buildings several hundred yards away were damaged. Four cars were completely smashed. Fortunately, rescuers found them to be empty.

Inside the hosiery mill, some four hundred yards away from the blast, the workers went into near panic with fright. "It sounded like an airplane hit the roof," Thelma Knowles, a worker there, said later. "I thought we had been hit. So did everyone else. We all ran for the door." The workers in the Camp Cap Company, located near City Hall, also knew something really bad had happened.

When the explosion hit, Gene Mullinax who owned a grocery store two door up from the devastated area saw his groceries knocked of the shelf. He later told a newspaper reporter, "A colored fellow and I were the only ones in the store. I didn't know what had happened, but I knew it was bad and I hollered for him to run." Gene looked toward the huge piles of charred wreckage blown out onto Montgomery Street. There were piles of Christmas

Explosion in Villa Rica

decorations, wrapping paper, and ribbons laying in the rubble. He could see tricycles and toys among the debris. Gene ran to the nearest phone and started calling for help from the surrounding counties. He told them to send firetrucks.

Kenneth Hendrix the twenty-two-year-old delivery man who had taken linens into Reeves Jewelry was on his way toward Berry's to deliver linen, aprons, and towels used for the soda fountain, when the explosion occurred. He had been walking past the buildings and was hit with the flying debris and bricks. He was killed instantly. His body was the first recovered. The first ambulance on the scene took him to Jones Funeral Home in Villa

L-R Tri-County Clothing, the demolished Empire 5 & 10 Store. John Bailey, Sr—hands on hips looking left. Photo by George Holloway.

Rica.

Later, Jack Williams at the Tri-County Clothing store recalled: "My wife, Ruth, and I were the only ones in my store when the explosion hit. She was sitting in a chair and I was standing up. The explosions knocked me down onto a counter. I saw the plate-glass window of the store shatter. I looked up and the wall by the dime store seemed to be rocking. I heard my wife scream and ran to her. She was still in the chair. She seemed to be frozen there. She finally jumped up, and we ran out the back door. I heard screams coming from the Empire 5 & 10 Cent Store next door. It was Rozelle Johnson. She was screaming for someone to get her out. It seemed like a long time that I just stood there. I didn't know what I could do. She was crying and screaming, 'Help me, help me, I'm burning up . . .' Rozelle Johnson was buried under loads of debris in the building. I tell you it's awful when somebody is begging you to get them out and you can't reach them."

When the explosion sent shock waves over the small town of Villa Rica, the neigh-

4. The First Minutes After the Explosion

borhood literally shook. Down on Walker Street, John Bailey, Sr, the off-duty fireman, had just gone to bed but was not asleep. When the explosion went off, he knew something terrible had happened. He jumped up and quickly pulled on his clothes. As he and his wife, Mary, ran to the front porch, he exclaimed, "What was that?" He looked toward town and saw a column of black smoke rising at least two hundred feet above town. Many of his neighbors were outside in the streets. Someone called out, "It's downtown! There's has been an explosion!"

John Bailey, Sr drove his car to the scene of the devastated area in about three

L-R Tri-County Clothing, Empire 5 & 10 Store after some clearing. Note -two holes in wall - midway. Photo by George Holloway.

minutes. He joined Jack Williams from the Tri-County Clothing Store—that adjoined the demolished buildings. Jack was trying to knock a large hole into a wall between his store and the dime store next door where Rozelle Johnson still lay behind the counter, trapped behind a wall of bricks. John Bailey, Sr and Jack Williams had a sledge hammer and took turns using it until they discovered a beam where they were trying to knock a hole. They had to start another hole adjacent to the first one. As they hammered, Rozelle Johnson's screams intensified. They felt panic-stricken and helpless, but kept trying to knock a hole in the wall to get to her. At one point they got a chainsaw to try and cut through the bricks, the two by fours, and the wallboard. When they could not get the chainsaw started, they continued with the sledge hammer.

Ed Elsberry, who was twenty-years-old and was planning on going into the Navy soon, came on the scene and was able to help. He had been driving down Wilson Street with his dad behind the row of buildings that suddenly exploded before his eyes. Smoke and fire

Explosion in Villa Rica

blew out the back of the stores as he parked his car and then ran down Candler Street. When he heard hammering, he was drawn to help. He grabbed one of the fire hoses that had just been connected to the fire hydrant on Carroll Road and tried to crawl through the hole to Rozelle Johnson, but the hole was too small for him to fit. Instead, he sprayed water as best as he could while John Bailey, Sr and Jack Williams continued to take turns with the sledge hammer, working as hard and as quickly as possible.

Finally, Ed Elsberry, who was a trim, muscular one-hundred-and-fifty pounds, went into the hole with the water hose. It was dark under the debris where the roof had collapsed and he could not see a thing as he crawled toward Rozelle Johnson who now only moaned. The fire that surrounded her, had gone out, so he set the hose aside. He then followed the sound of her moans until he could reach out and touch her. He felt her hair and body in the dark and was able to get behind her putting his arms under her shoulders. He managed to pull her near the hole in the wall. Miss Johnson was a large woman and difficult to move in the debris. Ed struggled to get her shoulders near the hole. Then John Bailey, Sr went through the hole to help Ed. With Jack William's help the three of them managed to bring her out.

Williams related: "We knocked two holes in the wall, but the fire got to her before we could reach her. When we brought her out through the second hole in the brick wall, she was still breathing, but she had been burned, horribly," Rozelle Johnson was taken by ambulance to the Villa Rica Hospital."

Earlier at the very second of the explosion, an out-of-town businessman, Elbert Moseley of Greenville, South Carolina had been walking across the railroad tracks directly toward the now destroyed buildings. He watched with horror as the four stores collapsed. He ran toward the scene of disaster and was among the first outsiders to reach the victims. He saw smoke and heard the screams of persons trapped inside the row of wrecked stores. He and a group of other passersby began feverishly to make their way through the obstacles of the wreckage in an effort to reach those trapped inside. Elbert Moseley said they found three persons burned to death. It was impossible to reach the others whose screams and calls for help came from somewhere in the rear of the store. Unable to do anything else, Elbert Moseley turned his attention to putting in telephone calls to Atlanta for help.

When the explosion occurred, Robby Robison, the editor of the Villa Rican Newspaper, ran back to his newspaper office, grabbed his camera, and started taking pictures documenting the occurrence of events.

George Holloway who worked at the car dealership at the east end of town, heard the

4. The First Five Minutes After the Explosion

explosion, grabbed his camera, and ran to the scene. Some photos were taken approximately six minutes after the explosion and show smoke boiling from beneath the pharmacy roof.

John McPherson, a twenty-two-year-old plumber's assistant, worked for Horace Bagwell but had taken the day off to take his wife, Nancy, Christmas shopping. John was outside on his mother's farm on Van Wert Road, three miles west of Villa Rica when he heard the explosion and saw the column of smoke rising on the horizon. John called a friend, Durwood Herrell, who ran the Shell Service Station on the corner of Montgomery and Westview Streets and asked what had happened.

Durwood exclaimed, "The whole damn town just blew up."

John McPherson grabbed his 35 millimeter camera that happened to have color slide film in it. He and his wife, Nancy, were in Villa Rica in less than six minutes. As he entered town, he began to take photographs of the unbelievable scenes before him. He took twelve color photos that documented many of the events of the day.

John and Nancy McPherson stayed in Villa Rica for several hours photographing the demolished areas — the first ambulances to arrive, and the first rescues made. At one point John went to the roof of the theater building and took a photo of the crowd that had gathered across the tracks. He made several photos of the hundreds of people who had collected to watch the rescue effort.

Then John and Nancy went home to think about all that they had seen and heard; They were numb with shock from the experience.

Ricky Hammond, the five-year-old who sat in the car parked behind Berry's, remembers very clearly what happened. As an adult now, Ricky recalls, "When the explosion went off, the force of it lifted the car Mom and I were in up a few feet and then set it back down exactly where it had been. We saw glass explode out of every window of every store. Mother grabbed me, screaming. She said how lucky we were that we were in the car and not still on the street. I heard an alarm signal go off seconds later.

A short time later, my Dad ran up to our car, got in, and grabbed us both. He had been looking up and down the street for us. He thought we could have been in the exploded, burning buildings, but thought to come to the car first before he went looking for us in the demolished, burning areas. He said as he ran toward the car he had to step on many wires that covered the ground. There had been no way to get to us except to step on these wires. My dad was in shock and held onto both my mom and me for a few minutes.

"After Dad was in the car with Mom and me for only a few minutes, emergency

Explosion in Villa Rica

vehicles pulled into the alley and parked behind our car. We could not leave. Our car was blocked in by the firetrucks and ambulances that had begun to line the street. I saw people coming out of the burning buildings and each person was covered in black soot or had been burned black. After a long time, we were able to leave. We had been as close as we could possibly have been to not actually have been in the fire. Even though I was only five at the time, these images have stuck with me for a lifetime."

5

The Community Reacts to the Sudden, Violent Blast

The Villa Rica Tragedy was listed as being among Georgia's Most Memorable Disasters.
The Atlanta Journal-Constitution February 22, 1959

Some members of Frances Hughie's family came within a "Gnat's Hill" of being in the explosion. Frances tells this story: "I was working in Hughie's 5 & 10 Store that my husband and I owned near the corner of Montgomery Street and Carroll Road. My husband, C.T. "Cula" Hughie had gone to Lee's Chapel to work on cleaning off his mother and daddy's grave. The young lady that worked for me, Shirley Whitworth, had left to go to Berry's Pharmacy for an early lunch break. Only Florene McWhorter, better known as just "Grandma" and I were in the store. When the explosion hit, it sounded like a bomb went off. When the windows to the store blew out, Grandma hit the floor behind the counter and started beating on the floor, screaming, 'It's a bomb. We're being bombed.'

"No, Grandma. I don't think it's a bomb." I replied nervously and stepped out from behind the counter and went to the sidewalk to look west down the street. "I saw the black smoke boiling up from the rooftops at the end of the block. Then I ran back inside and out the back door to my mother's house. My mother, Ellen Tant, lived in a house directly behind our store. There was only an alley between the Hughie's 5 & 10 Cent Store and my mother's house which faced Wilson Street. Gladys Henderson who took care of my mother and my two-year-old daughter, Ann, should be there. I wanted to be sure they were safe. I

Explosion in Villa Rica

ran into the house and saw the look of shock on everyone's faces. I looked at my mother and little Ann and saw that they were okay.

"Then Gladys Henderson, our caregiver, began to wring her hands and tell her story. She and little Ann had been walking to Berry's Pharmacy to get a prescription filled, when little Ann said she had to use the bathroom. Gladys Henderson and Ann turned around and went back to the house. As they stepped up on the first step of the porch, the explosion went off. The force of it knocked a flower pot off a shelf and it would have fallen right on Ann's head had Gladys not caught it. 'We came within a Gnat's Hill of being in that explosion,' she related excitedly to everyone. I gathered them all up and drove them to my sister's house across the tracks. Then I walked to the school to get my other daughter, Kay.

"At the school, I found that the classes of children were lined up on the field and playground area. Some of the classes were in lines, some were huddled together in groups. But all were with their teacher. When I found Kay's class on the playground, her teacher said they were not to let the students be picked up as they were not sure that the gas could pass down the line and cause more explosions. But after I waited for a while, the teachers were finally authorized to let parents pick up their children.

"My husband, C. T. "Cula" Hughie, was driving back from the cemetery when he heard about the explosion on his car radio. He could see the black smoke in the sky over Villa Rica. It scared him as to what he would find when he got back to his store. As he neared town, road blocks were already set up. He parked his car on Dogwood Street near the school and ran the three blocks to his store. 'Where's my wife?' he asked. A Civil Defense worker already on the street told him, 'She's safe.'

"The State Patrolmen who had just arrived quickly blocked off the demolished area to keep bystanders from interfering with the first rescue efforts. They also began to set up road blocks east and west of town. Rescue units began to pour into town after a few minutes."

Families and individuals began to gather in town to search for their loved-ones. One woman looked broken-heartedly at the rubble that had been a pharmacy and dental office. "Rob Broom was in Berry's to pick up a prescription for his daughter, Mildred, who was at his home recuperating from an operation," she said to a workman. "I know he was in there. His smashed car is parked in front of the pharmacy. His brother, Joe, said he had gone to pick up a prescription for her. But they haven't found him yet!"

In the meantime, another store owner joined in the rescue efforts. James Conner who ran J & J Auto west of town and another garage, by the same name, east of town

5. The Community Reacts

felt the shattering explosion that rocked the car his employee had just finished repairing. James jumped into this car and started driving to the scene but was stopped at the Carroll Road—Montgomery Street road block that had just been set up. He parked the car and ran the length of the block to the site of the explosion. When he saw that the entire second floor of the Berry building had collapsed into the first floor and the first floor had fallen into the crawl space, he knew he had to help.

"I went to the back of the building immediately," James remembers. "A black man and myself could get eight feet inside the building, but the heat, thick whirling smoke, and flames shooting out the back of the building made it impossible to go any further.

James Conner knew they had to clear the heavy timbers in order to get the others out. He could hear screaming at the back of the building He knew what he had to do and then ran all the way back to his garage.

At his garage, James Conner quickly took two of his wreckers and two employees for each vehicle. They were back to the scene in no time. Their main focus was to hook the wrecker cables to the larger timbers in the debris and start pulling them out. Other people moved the cars out of their way so they could go in as far into the area as possible. Piles of bricks made a front entrance to the Berry building almost impossible. First they began to move these so Conner and his team could get to the burning beams inside. "As my crew gradually began to clear from the front to back, the volunteer rescuers began to pull people out. For many it was too late."

As rescuers worked and as timbers were moved, M.D. Henslee got as close to Margaret Berry as he could through the debris when he heard her calling out. She called to anyone that could hear her, "Tell my family to take care of my children." Margaret could not be rescued in time to prevent her death. She died of smoke inhalation. Rescuers took her body out of the debris; an ambulance took her to a funeral home, but none of her family were notified that she had been found.

James Conner joined several men who were clearing brick and debris by hand. They took out Rob Broom who had perished in the explosion. An ambulance had just arrived and a stretcher was bought out. Rob Broom was taken to a funeral home in Villa Rica.

For those involved in the rescue effort, James Conner tells, "It was noisy. Everywhere people were hollering and there was screaming coming from inside several of the buildings. There were motors running and large pieces of tin were being dragged on the street away from the demolished buildings.

Explosion in Villa Rica

All main roads coming into Villa Rica were blocked off by the State Patrol who took over and freed the police for other badly needed duties. With the force of the State Patrol all side roads coming into the main road—U.S. 78 highway were blocked within a several mile radius.

A road block was set up one mile east of town at the intersection of Conners Road and U.S. 78, (Bankhead Highway). No one was allowed to drive west to the town but those who lived in Villa Rica. They were allowed to detour through the back streets by way of Sunset Drive. A road block was set up on the ridge above town on Carroll Road that went south to Carrollton. Another road block had been set up at the corner of Montgomery Street and Carroll Road, half a block from the scene of the devastation. Those who lived in Villa Rica who got through by the back streets, had to park their car and walk to their homes.

The local newly formed Civil Defense and the State Patrol were the first to respond. W. C. Cole, of the Civil Defense, Trooper Tom Bentley, and Trooper Frank Durham

Volunteers try to bring the blaze under control.

Photo by John McPherson.

were on duty from the time the latter road block was set up throughout the entire afternoon. They kept in contact with Captain Fain of the Atlanta Fire Department by police radio throughout the day as they rerouted traffic to Sunset Drive and back onto the main 78 highway at Conners Road.

All roads west of town that came into U.S. 78 from Birmingham to Villa Rica were closed, so there was very little traffic coming into town from the west—only emergency

5. The Community Reacts

vehicles and those who lived in Villa Rica. At the edge of town, another roadblock was set up one block below the devastation at the corner of Westview and Montgomery Street. Any vehicles making it this far into town were routed over the railroad crossing and to Highway 61 that went north of town.

Rescue efforts first came from those survivors on the scene. Then owners of the nearby stores and their customers ran to pull victims out of the burning building and from the debris. There were people passing through who joined in the effort. The response was immediate and overwhelming. Actually there were more willing hands to help than there were places to use them.

The townspeople uninjured in the blast performed heroic service to their neighbors. The thickness of the smoke was intense, making it almost impossible for workers to stay in the building for any length of time. Yet they stayed and persisted in order to rescue those who could be reached.

One high school student, Bud Streetman, who had left his second period agricultural-shop class to go to the post office for his teacher, J. A. Ariail, jerked around when he heard the explosion. He stood shocked and stunned before he ran to the accident scene. As he ran, he saw many others also running toward the smoke and fire. He went to the back of the pharmacy building. The black smoke almost overcame Bud as he tried to enter the building. Bud remembers throwing up after he inhaled the thick, black smoke. He had to come out to breathe. Later when he went back into the building, he was overcome by the smoke and passed out. He was given oxygen from one of the ambulances that had arrived. Bud Streetman continued to help remove debris until the rescue units arrived.

Several persons working in the smoke and fire collapsed.

Jerry "Moe" McClung, the high school football coach, went to the scene with several of his football players. They worked frantically to save those trapped inside until the fire departments could to arrive.

In the meantime, Herman Holloway, Jr who had been at City Hall voting when the explosion occurred arrived in the neighboring town of Douglasville asking for help. "I went to City Hall and the police station there in Douglasville and called on "Monk" Redding, the sheriff of Douglas County to send the fire fighters." The Douglasville Fire department was among the first on the scene.

Firemen from other counties began to arrive and hook up the hoses to the fire hydrants which were located around the demolished stores. One hydrant was at the front of the theater adjacent to the flaming area, a second hydrant was at the corner of Wilson and

Explosion in Villa Rica

Candler Streets behind Reeves.' Another hydrant was on the corner of Wilson Street and Carroll Road, and a fourth hydrant sat across the tracks to the right of the City Hall. There was also a fire hydrant down past the railroad depot. The fire hose attached here ran across the tracks to the explosion site. Firemen soon lined the roofs of the Reeves' collapsed building, their hoses stretched across the smoldering buildings.

At the Villa Rica Elementary and High School, the students had heard the explosion. Ron Roberts, Bobby Robert's younger brother, had no idea his brother had gone to the dentist. Ron remembered that the windows of the school rattled. After an hour, school let out and Ron walked to where his grandparents owned C. W. Hambrick Grocery located across the tracks from Berry's. He saw the demolished area burning and all the activity of the firemen. Then Kathleen Candler, owner of Candler Drugs, saw Ron in the huge crowd that had begun to gather in the area. She called him aside and took him to his grandmother so he would not see the note left at Marie's Beauty shop stating that Carolyn had taken Bobby to the dentist. They sent Ron home so he would not know his brother was missing while they tried to find out if Bobby had left the dental office or if he had been in the explosion.

In Villa Rica two miles away from the explosion site, Ethyleen Tyson had heard a percussion and saw a column of smoke fill the sky. To her it sounded like a loud boom. "We thought it sounded like a bad thunderstorm…the noise vibrated the whole house and shook the windows. It was a beautiful day so we wondered what it could have been.

"We heard the news shortly afterward on WSB-TV when the announcer interrupted to say, 'there has been a bad explosion in Villa Rica—people are being asked not to come to town simply out of curiosity, only emergency vehicles are being allowed into the city.' People were busy helping to search for bodies. We were kept up to date on what was happening by watching the television. The people got on top of it and lots of bulletins updating the situation were given out."

In the town of New Georgia, seven miles north of Villa Rica, Alton Morris stayed home with his young daughter, Ann, who had the mumps. When they heard a far away boom and felt a tremble, Alton looked puzzled and said to Ann, "Somebody must be using dynamite." A little while later, Stella Morris, Alton Morris' wife, came home from her job at Cannon Casket Company where they had let all the employees go home because they didn't know what would happen next. They were afraid something else would blow up.

In Carrollton, eighteen miles south of Villa Rica, on Alabama Street, Herman T. Broom was at work and looked up and saw smoke billowing upward in a pencil-like column far away on the horizon.

5. The Community Reacts

Horace Luther, Superintendent of the Water and Sewer Authority and Louis Harris, one of the city workers who assisted him, were coming into town from a job, when the explosion happened. They immediately went to the scene. Horace realized the gas lines behind the buildings were ruptured and were feeding the fire that had just broken out. He went to City Hall and located the Valve Book that showed the location of the turn-off valves at the back of the three stores. Horace Luther could not get to these valves as they were under the debris and fire.

About 11:20 that morning, Tom Pope, the assistant to the gas superintendent who had driven the city dump truck into Douglasville, eight miles east of Villa Rica, earlier that morning, finished getting the load of gravel and left the rock quarry. He turned left heading

The back of Berry's Pharmacy. This is thought to be Louis Harris in the center with the light hat and dark jacket. Photo by Robby Robison.

west down U.S. Highway 78. When the winding road straightened and he came to a slight elevation, he could see far on the horizon the dark appearance of something that billowed upward. As he neared Villa Rica, he gradually began to understand the implications. As he neared his destination, he drove faster and was gripped by fear. When he got to the road block at U.S. 78 and Conner Road, he was told what had happened and was allowed to go right on into town a mile away.

Tom Pope made his way to the back of the burning buildings intending to cut the

Explosion in Villa Rica

gas off at the valves, knowing exactly where they were. The Y-shaped connection and shut-off valve ran off the two and one-fourth inch main gas line that ran at the back of the two stores—there was Berry's, and there was the A & B's on the same line with Reeves'. In later court testimony, Tom told that when he neared the scene, he saw the devastation and knew he could not get to the valves. The ruptured gas lines were spewing gas out and were feeding the fire. The cut-off valves were under the burning debris behind the two stores. Horace Luther was there with the Valve Book not knowing what to do.

After Tom Pope arrived on the scene, there was quite a frantic discussion as to what to do. Could they go into the burning debris to find the cut-off valves? How long would that take? How could they get close to the valves if gas was shooting out? They knew it was too dangerous to try, but they knew the gas flow had to be stopped quickly. The only alternative was to cut off the gas to the city of Villa Rica at the power and odorization station at Sandhill. But that was more than six miles away. They had no choice. That was the only option. Both Tom Pope and Horace Luther jumped into a pick-up truck and took Louis Harris who worked with Horace Luther. The three of them sped to the regulator and odorization station, six and a half miles south of Villa Rica at Sandhill. As they drove they realized they did not have the key to the station or to the equipment that powered the gas, piping it into the city. The only key was with Oscar Hixon and he was missing, presumedly lost in the explosion.

Once there, Louis Harris took a pick ax, sharp on the front and blunt on the back and broke the lock to the station. Once inside, the three of them saw the large wheel attached to the cut-off valve and the pipes bringing gas into the station. They knew they had to close the valve by stopping the pump. They could only cut off the power with a key which they did not have. Horace Luther and Tom Pope directed Louis Harris, the city worker, to stop the pump. Louis managed to jam the pick between the turning gears, temporarily stopping the pump. Then they closed the valve. This shut off the gas to the city of Villa Rica.

As the three of them drove quickly back to Villa Rica they thought about the gas that still filled the lines and wondered if there would be any chance of this gas escaping or coming into the burning buildings.

From all later estimations, by the time the three men got to Sandhill and stopped the gas flow into Villa Rica, it was about 11:45, forty-five minutes after the explosion occurred. The wreckage burned for an hour after the explosion at 11:00 o'clock before the blaze was controlled. Firemen beat back the flames as rescue workers watched and waited.

6

The Search for Loved-Ones

*"Villa Rica was having elections that day and
folks were also out doing their Christmas shopping.
It's only the Lord's mercy there weren't more killed or hurt."*
Ethyleen Tyson, Villa Rica resident.

A few minutes after 11:00, Winnie Dyer got a call from Sarah Camp. They were friends who saw each other almost daily since Sarah lived close to Winnie's husband's business on Wilson Street in Villa Rica and Winnie lived two miles out of town. Sarah Camp told Winnie, " I think a train ran off the tracks and hit Berry's Pharmacy." Winnie grabbed her daughter Marion Ann and got into her car, but before she could back out of the driveway, it filled up with cars. Concerned friends, neighbors, and relatives had come to bring her the shocking news.

"The pharmacy blew up, someone told her. "I think your husband and O.T. were in there. O.T.'s car is parked out front of the pharmacy." Winnie thought both her husband and father-in-law were in Atlanta by now, but when she heard O.T.'s car was out front she began to fear. Friends took her to the site of the devastation. There she saw the crushed car.

Winnie later remembered: "We were not allowed to get close to the burning buildings, so we joined the crowd that had begun to gather across from Montgomery Street, around the train tracks and the train depot.

"I began asking everyone I knew if they had seen Johnny. No one was able to tell me anything about him. I walked through the crowd of people solemnly milling around and joined them as we watched workers go through the debris." Crying, I kept asking everyone,

Explosion in Villa Rica

'Where's Johnny? Where's Johnny? Have you seen him?'

"Then we were told his body had been found and had been taken to Jones Funeral home on Westview Drive two blocks behind the exploded business district. But someone went there and came back and told me that it wasn't true. I wanted to have hope, but in the afternoon my brother-in-law, Gid Robinson, found that both Johnny and his Dad, O.T., had been taken to Almon Funeral Home in Carrollton, some twenty miles away. I had told my brother-in-law before he left for Carrollton what Johnny had been wearing. He came back and told me he found Johnny and had confirmed that it was Johnny as he had on a leather jacket and khaki pants. We were told that both Dyer men died of suffocation. They were not burned, but were covered with black soot from the initial burst of the explosion. My brother-in-law had gotten Johnny's ring and gave it to me.

"I just sat there stunned. How could this be true? I remembered back in 1954 when a meeting was held to discuss putting the gas lines in under the streets running to each building, the councilmen were skeptical. O.T. Dyer, my father-law, had stood at the meeting and cautioned, 'You need to get an experienced gas man to do the installation of the gas lines. This gas can be dangerous.' Now his worse thoughts had come true and he had become a fatal victim."

The town's business section had been crowded with shoppers, and no one seemed sure who was missing or if everyone had been accounted for. There was always a chance that a person from out of town might be covered in the piles of debris and their relatives might not know that he or she had been in the area. Even when a body was found but not

Aerial view

Photo courtesy Jeff Robison

6. The Search for Loved-Ones

identified, those loved-ones waiting would not know where the body had been taken. Was their loved-one at the Villa Rica Hospital? If he or she had died, was he or she at the Jones Funeral Home less than a block away from the devastated area or had they been taken to the Almon Funeral Home in Carrollton, about twenty miles away? There was mass confusion, grief, and fear enough to feel it tangibly as it spread from family to family.

It was a day of anxiety and tears and horror. Dazed residents of the area were still searching for missing relatives long after the scorching flames had become embers. One salesman said he saw several women rushing around asking distractedly, "Have you seen

View from the front of the theater at street level.
Photo from the Atlanta Journal, December 1957..

my daughter?" or "Have you seen my husband?" then rush off to repeat the question to other groups of spectators.

"Where is Ann?" one woman pleaded to a rescue worker. "Have they found her?"

The rescue worker turned and said grimly: "I don't know—I'm not sure. They did take out the body of a girl wearing a purple blouse. It might have been her."

Ann Pope Smith, the young lady who worked at Berry's Pharmacy and had stood at the end of the pharmacy counter at the time of the explosion was missing. Her brother-in-law was Herman Holloway, Sr who had gone to Douglasville for the fire department. While he had access to a phone, he had also made calls to get to in touch with Ann Smith's two sisters and mother. He had called his sister-in-law, Catherine Pope, who worked at Grady Hospital in Atlanta. He asked her to go to Rich's Department Store in downtown Atlanta and

Explosion in Villa Rica

find his wife, Mary Nell Pope Holloway and her mother, Gladys Pope, who were Christmas shopping. He said to tell them to come home—Ann was missing. "Ann was in an explosion and nobody can find her."

After Herman talked to Catherine at Grady Hospital, she told the officials there at the hospital about the disaster. This resulted in a team of doctors and nurses being sent from Grady Hospital to the Villa Rica Hospital to help out with the burn victims. After Catherine Pope found her mother, Gladys and her sister, Mary Nell, at Rich's Department Store, she brought them back to Villa Rica to join the vigil in front of the depot and to wait for any

Friends console one another as they wait for news about loved-ones.
Photo by John McPherson

news of Ann. After Catherine Pope left her mother and sister, she then went on to the Villa Rica Hospital to join the team of doctors and nurses who had come from Grady Hospital to help.

People began to pour into town anyway they could get there. Since the main roads were blocked, those who drove just parked their cars on the roadside and began to walk in small groups toward town. The side roads were soon lined with parked cars. Housewives who were home during the day and who did not have a car either walked to town or got a ride with a neighbor. As they walked the detour they began to gather on the ridge above

6. The Search for Loved-Ones

the devastated area—across the railroad tracks and in front of the railroad depot. The immediate area was roped off to keep spectators back from the scene as the fire was brought under control.

As many as six ambulances were lined up down Montgomery Street in front of the demolished block of stores to take the recovered victims either to the three hospitals in the area or to the funeral homes in the surrounding communities. When a body was brought out and put into an ambulance, there was no one person or agency in charge of keeping up with where each person had been taken. If the ambulance was from Carrollton, the body went to Carrollton. If the ambulance came from Bremen and recovered a body, then the person was taken to Bremen. Most of the fatalities were burned and covered in black soot and oil and each one's hair had been burned to the scalp. This made it impossible to identify them.

Though there were three women in the fire, each small in stature, when one of the women was recovered and taken to a funeral home, no one knew who had been found or where they had been taken. The Berry family knew Margaret's body had been recovered, but had to search the hospitals and funeral homes until she was found at the funeral home in Bremen, twenty miles away. Later Dr. Irving De Garrett made the final identification.

Victim being carried to a waiting ambulance.
Photo by John McPherson.

After the fire was under control, the rescue efforts started at the front, the back, and the top of the burned-out buildings. From the wreckage near the roof, Dr. Burnham's body was found and brought out. Then Bobby Robert's body was found. He was still in the dental chair.

Explosion in Villa Rica

Newspaper accounts were heart wrenching as they told of families searching for missing loved-ones:

News traveled quickly to Bremen's many manufacturing plants, twenty miles west of Villa Rica, where Carolyn Davis' mother, Evie Davis, worked. Mrs. Davis immediately came to Villa Rica to join her husband, Carl Davis, who had reported as usual that morning to his job in Villa Rica. They were joined at the scene of the devastation by Mrs. Davis' sister, Mrs. Evelyn Clower and Carolyn's best friend, Imogene Williams, who worked just down the street from the center of the demolished site.

"We knew Carolyn had gone to the dental office to take little Bobby Roberts," Mrs. Clower said to the small cluster of friends who gathered across in front of the train depot.

"She must be dead—she's in there too!" cried Eva Davis when news of the death of Dr. Burnham and Bobby reached her. But they still held out hope.

Carolyn's parents, Carl and Eva Davis, were led to a parked car to continue their wait. Mrs. Clower walked anxiously through the crowd of people that lined the street along the depot opposite the destroyed stores and looked fearfully into an ambulance where a volunteer rescue workers had just put someone on a stretcher.

"It's not Carolyn," the ambulance driver told her. "It's a man." She glanced back to the piles of burned bricks and debris across the street, hoping she might see Carolyn in the crowd wearing the bright corduroy suit she had bought the day before in Atlanta.

Back in the car a few minutes later, Mrs. Davis told a newspaper reporter on the scene, "I didn't want her to go to the beauty shop to work today, she had such a cold. She asked me yesterday if I had her Christmas present yet, and I told her I wasn't going to get her one. Of course, I was teasing—the cedar chest she wants so much is at her grandmother's. Oh, I wish I'd told her about it!"

Word came that several bodies had been taken to the Jones Funeral Home. "I've got to go see if one of them is Carolyn," Mrs. Davis said.

At the funeral home, Mrs. Clower offered to view the unidentified victims.

Mrs. Etta Shierling and Mrs. Clyde Jones, of the funeral home, tried to prepare her for what she would find. "There's only this watch to go by," Mrs. Shierling said, carefully exhibiting a charred ladies' watch.

"Carolyn bought a new watch last week," Mrs. Davis said. "That looks like it. Her's is white gold."

Someone produced a kitchen knife and scratched the back surface of the watch. "This one is yellow gold," he announced. The victim matched Carolyn's height and weight,

6. The Search for Loved-Ones

but there was no way to be sure it was her.

"Her teeth!" Mrs. Davis cried suddenly. "Can't you tell by that?" Then came more minutes of anxious waiting.

"This is not the girl," Clyde Jones, funeral director, announced after an examination.

Meanwhile, relatives of Ann Pope Smith came to the funeral home hoping not to find Ann. "I don't think that's her watch," tearfully declared Martha Golden, sister-in-law of the missing girl.

Mrs. Davis' nephew, Howard Daniel of Douglasville joined the group and announced, "Another girl has been taken to Almon's Funeral Home in Carrollton. It could be Carolyn."

The group then journeyed to Carrollton. They were silent in their trip hoping against hope that Carolyn had not been killed and that they would not find her body there either.

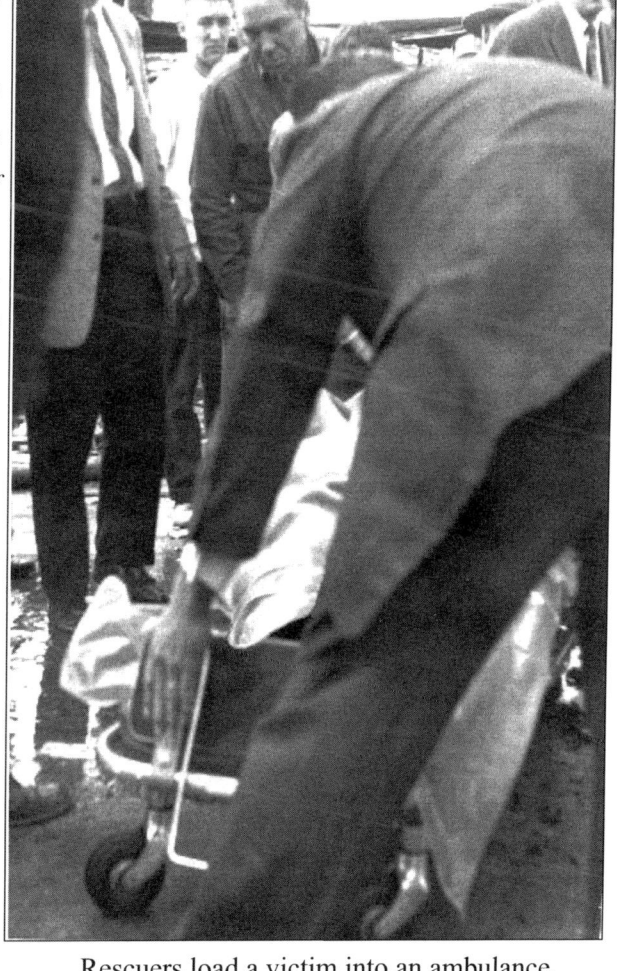

Rescuers load a victim into an ambulance.
Photo by George Holloway.

Dr. Ernest Powell, Jr of Villa Rica, a friend of the Davis family, and W. D. Scott of the funeral home, met the group at the door. "It's Carolyn," Dr. Powell said quietly. Evelyn and Howard accompanied the doctor to make the identification official.

"But are you sure? Couldn't I see her myself?" pleaded the mother, who could cry no more tears.

"Three of us who have known Carolyn all her life couldn't be wrong," Howard said.

"But her clothes—what is this girl wearing?"

Mrs. Davis insisted that what material remained be brought to her. Evelyn returned

Explosion in Villa Rica

in a few minutes, bringing three scraps of bright corduroy the size of silver coins. "Yes," Mrs. Davis whispered, fingering the material. "This is it." She clutched the bits of cloth a few seconds, then carefully put them in her purse.

Mr. Davis, who had been silent practically throughout the long ordeal, turned his back. His shoulders were shaking convulsively as he let flow the heartrending tears that only a father can weep. "I guess we can go, now," he said finally. "We've done all we can for her."

Hundreds gather across the tracks in front of the depot.

Photo by John McPherson.

Back in Villa Rica, John Bailey, Sr, the off duty fireman from Walker Street, had been at the explosion site for over an hour helping in rescue efforts. His wife waited at home for news from the downtown area. She knew something bad had happened when she and her husband had heard the initial explosion. Together they had gone out onto the porch and into the yard as many of their neighbors had done. Now, an hour later, Mary Bailey decided to walk to town to see what had happened for herself. A neighbor, Louvie Bone, went with her. As they walked down the streets, they followed droves of people walking toward downtown. As she neared town, she was amazed to see hundreds of people gathering at the depot. The siren on the utility pole at City Hall still blasted an emergency signal that she could hear stronger and stronger as they got closer into the center of town. The main street, Montgomery Street was blocked off at Candler Street.

6. The Search for Loved-Ones

Mary told later, "The whole town went crazy. Hundreds of people were there—gathered at the railroad depot There was chaos everywhere. I waited across the tracks from the smoldering buildings, safe, out of the way. I waited for several hours for my husband. The day was cold and I pulled my coat tight around me. The sun was warm toward the afternoon. I waited a long time and finally my husband came out of the shattered buildings. When he found me in the crowd, he had a look of stricken grief that I had never seen on anyone's face. His arm had been burned badly in trying to rescue Rozelle Johnson. The rescuers wanted him to go to the hospital with his burned arm, but he went later to the Powell, Berry, Powell Clinic on Carroll Road instead. He never talked about the woman that he had helped bring out. I knew she was severely burned; he took it very hard that she could not be rescued sooner."

Mary Bailey continues, "These stunned townspeople stared at the string of stores lying in ruin. They talked about what had happened—where they were when they had heard the explosion, and many had stories of how they had just left one of the stores which was now a pile of blackened rubble. But most people just stood and stared, not believing what they were seeing." The explosion had leveled an entire half block of the tiny two-block town.

Lewis Wayne, one of the people in the crowd who was standing in front of a building about 200 feet west of the scene of the wreckage, said, "I saw it blow up. Wreckage must have gone several hundred feet in the air. When the pharmacy disappeared, the other stores collapsed. It didn't take but five minutes before at least one person was carried off in an ambulance. Wreckage from buildings rained on a brick grocery store some 75 feet from the rear, smashing windows and damaging the roof."

The terminal station area was littered with debris. Even the roof of the station had been showered with debris. Trash could be seen several blocks away. The tracks were covered with standing droves of people who came to see what had happened and to console each other.

C. M. Griffin, Villa Rica's mayor, told a reporter later that he heard the explosion from his store across the railroad. "I not only heard it—it knocked all my windows out."

Herman Keaton, from the C & S dry cleaners, joined the crowd gathering in front of the demolished area. He later told his family when he got home, "I was going to Berry's Pharmacy to give a dry cleaning bill to Ann Smith, but I couldn't find a parking space out front of the pharmacy, so I decided to head toward home. I turned right at the end of the block and then took another right onto Wilson Street that runs parallel to Montgomery Street.

Explosion in Villa Rica

When I got directly behind the stores, they blew up. The force lifted my truck off the ground and sat it right back down where it had been. If I had gone in the pharmacy, I might have been killed. I feel like someone or something was looking out after me."

Martha Wynn, the seventeen-year-old who had gone for her grandmother's prescription minutes before the blast went to Villa Rica with her family later that day. She now crossed the railroad tracks to stand on the hill above the devastated area to see all of the destruction.

Everyone talked about the timing of the explosion. Someone said, "If it had happened at 11:30 that is when the mill workers from the Villa Rica Hosiery Mill, the Camp Cap Company, and the Bryant Hosiery Mill would have turned out their people for lunch. Many of them usually ate in the pharmacy and many were planning on doing a little quick Christmas shopping at the other businesses scattered around this main part of town."

Members of a family rejoiced as they found each other. Others still desperately searched the crowd and remaining stores for their loved-ones trying to make sure they were accounted for and not in the explosion.

The scene was made even more heart-wrenching when family members found each other amidst others still desperately hunting in the crowds, wanting assurance that the one they knew was not in the disastrous explosion.

7

Rescue Efforts:
Civil Defense/ Red Cross/National Guard

Orders were sent to the Southern Railroad to hold all trains going into Villa Rica for an indefinite time.
The Atlanta Journal, Friday December 6, 1957

When the first calls went out from Villa Rica for help, it set into motion a massive disaster-relief coordination of the State Civil Defense Department. The Atlanta police received the first calls and notified J. L. "Jack" Grantham, Sr, Communications Officer for the State Civil Defense, at 11:18 Thursday morning. "A hell of an explosion has hit Villa Rica. Could Atlanta send fire equipment?"

The report was quickly verified when Jack Grantham contacted the City Clerk of Villa Rica, Ray Dodson. Jack Grantham had access to the combined radio networks of Civil Defense, the intercity police hookup, amateur ham operators, the state highway patrol, and the state highway department maintenance. The Civil Defense communicator radioed fire departments in Bremen and Carrollton for help. He called the State Highway Patrol and ordered all roads to Villa Rica barred to all but emergency vehicles. For several hours after that, no one got into the town without police escort. The Villa Rica Police Department were on duty doing all that they could: Roy Yearty the Police Chief; the night Police Chief, Henry Martin; and deputies, Bill Black and Otis Newman cooperated with the officials coming into Villa Rica throughout the rescue efforts.

Explosion in Villa Rica

Jack Grantham dispatched two Atlanta fire-fighting units and called for a rescue truck. Next he contacted the five adjacent counties around Villa Rica calling for ambulances. They came from Austell, Marietta, Smyrna, Rome, Cedartown, and as far away as Jonesboro, about forty-five miles southeast of Villa Rica. He sent a communications officer from Atlanta headquarters to coordinate all calls into and out of Villa Rica.

Grantham arranged for front end loaders—road clearing machines—to be sent from Calhoun and DeKalb County which were several counties away. He also arranged for maintenance trucks to be sent from the Highway Department and ordered ten dump trucks from Atlanta National Guard headquarters to pick up bricks to clear Villa Rica's streets. He made arrangements for medical aid from the State Health Department.

Representatives from several different agencies soon arrived to the scene from surrounding communities including The Salvation Army, and the Red Cross.
The Civil Defense and National Guard were called.

Another victim is carried off the roof.
Photo by John McPherson.

Colonel Donald Mees, executive officer to the State Department of Defense, sent ten National Guardsmen from Atlanta, Douglasville, Rome, and Calhoun to help in traffic control and to guard supplies and materials left unprotected by the blast. Searchlights and additional equipment arrived toward the late evening.

The Third Army Headquarters and the Federal Civil Defense Administration officials were notified to go to Villa Rica to determine whether the area would qualify for

7. Rescue Efforts

relief funds.

CW4, (Chief Warrant Officer) Alfred B. Smith the unit administrator of Company D, 122nd Infantry Regiment, 48th division in Douglasville remembers, "Most of our troops heard about the disaster on the radio and television and came to the armory headquarters in fatigue uniforms without being called. We had our trucks lined up ready to go when mobilization orders came. We took several two and a half ton trucks filled with armed troops. Each troop had a field pack and we drove another truck with minimal equipment, rations, and kitchen equipment to maintain the troops for three days.

"Our troops were on the ground in Villa Rica within thirty minutes of the call to deploy. Around ninety troops descended on Villa Rica and reported to the Police Chief, Roy Yearty. Our mission was to guard the streets and shops that had been damaged and to take over the road blocks that had been set up east and west of town.

"Another immediate duty was to recover the lost merchandise of the jewelry store. There were cartons of merchandise and loose jewelry scattered around the area. I dispatched troops to recover these items. Loose jewelry was picked up and put into envelopes and sealed. Then these envelopes and the damaged cartons, found on the site, were put into boxes. We sealed the boxes and stored them temporarily in an empty railroad boxcar sitting on a sidetrack adjacent to the site. When we were satisfied that all had been recovered we put a guard on the boxcar until the merchandise could be carried to Douglasville and stored in a vault at the armory until the store owner could come and claim the goods."

In the afternoon the National Guard engineering unit of the 878 battalion sent dump trucks and front end loaders to aid in clearing the debris.

Hundreds of rescue workers from the surrounding communities poured into the disaster area during the afternoon to help dig through the rubble and debris for bodies. John Bailey, Sr contacted Lockheed Aircraft Corporation and they sent two firetrucks. "This was a day of heroism as grim faced, sweating workmen worked frantically beneath standing, fire weakened walls searching for and pulling out victims of the fire and explosion," stated the Atlanta Journal in the next day's newspaper.

When the water hoses were strung across the railroad tracks from the hydrants adjacent to City Hall and from the intersection behind the train depot, the trains had to be stopped or delayed. Two passenger trains and a freight train were backed up on the tracks for several hours until a crane, which was brought into Villa Rica in the late afternoon, could lift a firehose above the tracks so the locomotives could pass underneath.

The other water hose was lifted—hoisted by a large fork-lift or a wrecker to the

Explosion in Villa Rica

"switch arm" on the tall steel pole beside the railroad tracks. This "switch arm" was usually used to hold a mail bag out for a person on a passing train to reach out with a hook and grab the bag as the train passed. When the two hoses were lifted above the tracks, this allowed the three trains to pass underneath and be on their way.

Robert and Horace Stewart who owned the City Supply Company on Lucille Avenue in Carrollton ordered the entire supply of elbow-length, heavy duty gloves to be rushed to Villa Rica for the volunteers to wear as they removed the smoldering bricks, cement blocks, and debris in an assembly line fashion. Someone on the rescue team called out instructions to the volunteers using a megaphone (bullhorn). Volunteers came from nearly every town in west Georgia. Rescue workers lined up in a long row and passed the debris by hand to try to get to the people who might be buried, looking and hoping to find someone alive in the jumbled mass of bricks and timbers.

Donald Willis, who worked at the cabinet shop across from the Reeves building, remembers that the prisoners came from the State Camp in Carroll County. Prisoners from three prison camps worked in frantic haste until late on Thursday night to save lives and salvage whatever property could be saved.

Pat Allen, a salesman from Forest Park in Atlanta, who drove into town about half an hour after the explosion related, "When I was about ten or twelve miles away, I knew

Rescuer recover another victim.
Photo by George Holloway.

something was wrong in town. I saw a column of black smoke towering several hundred feet in the air. It looked like a big bomb had been dropped on the town. When I got here, I saw men—some dressed in business suits—were digging into the debris for victims. They had to chop holes in the roof of a store to get inside. As they made holes, air got inside and the fire flamed. The rescuers had to back off and let firemen pour water on the fire.

"I saw a blue-jean clad boy about seventeen-years-old climb up onto the roofs of the wrecked stores after helping pass down four bodies. He was almost in a state of shock and

7. Rescue Efforts

was wringing wet, either from sweat or water from the firemen's hoses. He was trembling and pale. He was revived with oxygen from an ambulance." As the workers removed the debris piece by piece, it was piled up and giant loaders picked it up and placed it on trucks to move it to a different location—out of the way.

The heavy traffic on U.S. Highway 78 from Atlanta to Birmingham was routed around the stricken town. The local Boy Scout Troop #108 of Villa Rica and the city Schoolboy Safety Patrol helped direct traffic. Sixteen Boy Scouts and the seventeen School Boy Patrolmen from Villa Rica Public School aided the Georgia Highway Patrol to reroute heavy traffic through the outskirts of Villa Rica. Traffic to and from Atlanta was rerouted by way of Dallas, the neighboring town to the north of Villa Rica.

The boys were mobilized around 12:50 by the Boy Scout District Executive, Harry L. Wheeler, from the Atlanta Area Council, who lived in Carrollton. Some of the boys missed their lunch and went with the patrol. The School Patrol Director who was also the grammar school principal, E. A. Holloman, and Scoutmaster J. A. Ariail, Jr, a teacher, directed the boys in their traffic duties.

Several factors interrupted the flow of traffic, locally, and congested the area. Abnormally heavy traffic was created by parents who picked up their children from school, and by curiosity seekers. The two passenger and one freight train that were stopped from going through town had traffic backed up at the railroad crossings.

Within the hour after the catastrophe several ambulances with doors open begin to line the street in front of the pharmacy waiting to rush victims to the hospital. The out-of-town ambulances and emergency vehicles had arrived from Atlanta and five other surrounding counties. One worker stood close by the rescuers holding a stretcher ready for the next recovery, a grim reminder of the havoc wrought by this nightmare.

Hundreds of people flocked in to watch the search. National guardsman patrolled the area and kept the crowd back from the damaged area. The section around the shattered ruins was roped off to protect on-lookers from getting close to the smoldering debris and the rescue efforts.

The Salvation Army dispatched three Atlanta officers about 12:30 that afternoon with a truckload of clothing, food, and other supplies. A Columbus unit moved three workers with a mobile canteen into the area. Three others brought supplies from Rome.

At 2:30 Captain Fain of the Atlanta Fire Department reported that twelve bodies had been recovered from the debris. He gave this summary of the findings: The first victim to be recovered was Kenneth Hendrix. Rozelle Johnson, who had been taken to Villa Rica

Explosion in Villa Rica

Hospital and then to Tanner Hospital, died there. That morning, Rob Broom's body had been recovered and taken to a funeral home in Villa Rica. Margaret Berry's body had been taken to the Bremen Funeral Home. As workers cleared the debris from the top of the pile, they found the bodies of Dr. Burnham, Bobby Roberts, and Carolyn Davis.

At 12:40, Oscar Hixon's body was found beside a heater on the first floor of the pharmacy. Then Ann Pope Smith, Carl Vitner, and O.T. and Johnny Dyer were found. When rescuers were able to move the collapsed debris that had been the upstairs of the pharmacy building, they could search what had been the first floor, now collapsed into what had been the crawl space at the bottom of the debris.

Thursday afternoon, about 2:30, bulldozers were brought in and that speeded the work of clearing the area. Roy Richards of Richard's Construction Company of Carrollton sent a boon to lift debris and aid in the recovery and cleanup.

Late in the afternoon a huge crane arrived from Atlanta on a large truck and after half and hour, began the task of picking up the roof of the collapsed jewelry-florist shop—piece by piece and loading it into scores of trucks which hauled the debris away. Workers edged under the huge collapsed roof as it was lifted piece by piece looking for bodies and possible survivors. Although the explosion ripped the roof and crumbled most of the wall of the combination jewelry and flower shop, it did not damage several beautifully arranged floral decorations. Some flower pots and empty floral boxes

Volunteers clear piles of debris onto waiting dump trucks
Photo courtesy of Ted Williamson

7. Rescue Efforts

were undisturbed by the blast. This seemed ironic to anyone who noticed the arrangements of fresh roses that only a few feet away on the other side of the wall, people had died—burned to death.

"We won't stop turning over these stones," Sergeant T. E. Bentley, of the Georgia Highway Patrol said, "until we're sure no one is buried there." Police estimated at least fifty people had been in the buildings at the time of the explosion and fire. There was no way to be sure everyone had been found at this point.

The Police Chief of Villa Rica, Roy Yearty, said a check of townspeople had not been completed but he felt "sure" there must be other people buried in the debris.

As the volunteers and prisoners worked into the late evening, one of the guards was asked if he were afraid that some of the prisoners might escape. "I've never even thought about it and I don't guess they have," he replied. "The job now is to see if we can get any-

View from the roof of the theater.

Photo by John McPherson

body else out of there." The prisoners continued to move freely up and down the block as they worked into the night.

Fireman were still pouring water on smoldering ruins late in the afternoon. The debris was loaded onto dump trucks that lined Montgomery Street close to the destroyed area. At first the debris was taken to the city dump, but then workers realized the massive amount would soon take up the space needed for household garbage. So an alternative place

Explosion in Villa Rica

was chosen. The solid rubble, the bricks, and burned timbers were dumped west of town on the corner of Dogwood Street and Highway 78 beside a creek. After this area had been filled, loads of debris were taken from the site of the destruction to an empty field one mile east of town and piled on the right side of Highway 78, back a couple of hundred yards.

Red Cross Canteen in background; prisoners taking a break in the foreground. Photo by Robby Robison.

As the rescue efforts continued into the night, a bonfire was built that blocked both Carroll Road and Montgomery Street—78 Highway. This fire served as warmth for the workers to take a break on this cold December night. It was forty or forty-five degrees now and these water soaked rescue workers were chilled. They were drawn to the fire to try and get dry and to rest before going back to their grim job. This bonfire also served to block traffic from both streets. It was later noted that this fire, which burned most of the night, actually did damage to the pavement at the intersection.

Late in the afternoon, rescue workers were being fed by women of the community who brought food from the Villa Rica school lunchroom. Pastry was donated by a bakery a few doors from the disaster zone.

7. Rescue Efforts

A Volunteer Red Cross unit from Villa Rica notified the Southeastern headquarters shortly after the explosion occurred. Hudson Bacon, deputy director of disaster services for the Southeast, reported that within an hour of the explosion one field representative had been recalled from Gadsden, Alabama and a district representative and two nurses from the Atlanta office had been assigned to the area. Their first duties were to take a survey to determine what services were needed and to see that the people were adequately taken care of in the hospitals. Bacon said medical service was the primary need since "homes were not destroyed." Chairman of the Carroll County Chapter of Red Cross, J. W. Warren came to the scene as well.

The work continued into the night. Photo by Robby Robison.

Jennie Ramsey, northwest Georgia field director helped set up emergency headquarters and medical supplies were furnished by the Atlanta chapter.

By Thursday afternoon a Red Cross disaster team moved in to offer aid any way they could to residents affected by the gas explosion. Part of the Red Cross team were volunteers who furnished sandwiches and coffee to the men working into the night.

A local resident who had been a Red Cross Aide came to Villa Rica to help. Mrs. June Albertson, who lived in Winston with her husband, Bill, learned about the explosion from her mother who heard the news announcement on the WSB Atlanta radio station and then called her. June's mother told her, "The whole town of Villa Rica has blown up." June

Explosion in Villa Rica

had a small son and was six months pregnant. She had been a Red Cross aide both at Grady Hospital and at the Veteran's Hospital in Atlanta while her husband, Bill, was in Japan during the Korean War. She had quit a few years back to have a family.

When she heard the news, June quickly dressed in her Red Cross uniform, and took her son to her mother's house. Then she drove toward Villa Rica where she had no trouble getting into town when the police at the road blocks saw her in uniform.

In Villa Rica, there was chaos everywhere. A Red Cross Unit worker saw her and

Floodlights allow a full crew to continue into the night.
Photo by Robby Robison.

quickly called her over. One Red Cross worker there was so glad to see June that she hugged her. June was put to work immediately in the canteen area to furnish food for the rescue workers. Tables and coffee makers were set up right in front of the demolished buildings. There was a paneled truck with sides that raised where the food was stored. June began making sandwiches as fast as she could, stacking them up on trays. Soft drinks were also furnished. She remembers another worker fussing about only having cheese sandwiches. After a while the supply was replenished with sandwich meat and bread brought in by the community. When this supply was depleted, a volunteer went to the store as the day wore

7. Rescue Efforts

on and brought back what was needed.

"Everyone that day was good to each other. We were like a family. We all loved those people who died. We were each trying to do our part. We tried to stay out of the way of the main rescue effort but do just what we could to help."

When the rescue workers came by to take a break and eat, several gave June a pat on the back and thanked her. She kept busy, but could hear the hollering going on among the workers. She saw the men who came by her table had tired, dirty faces lined with pain. She

Note workers on utility poles in the background. Photo by Robby Robison

saw that their clothes were covered in soot and were wet from the water they had sprayed on the fire and torn from crawling through the debris. She remembers being so sad. Berry's Pharmacy was her pharmacy. She knew all the people there. The search went into the night for some ten hours after the blast. The hot drinks and food provided by the Red Cross on this cold night with its blistering wind was welcomed by the citizens who still searched.

June Albertson stayed until 11:00 o'clock that night. "The men who came to eat and to get warm at the fire up at the intersection looked sad, tired, and hollow eyed," she remembers.

Explosion in Villa Rica

At midnight, the rescue workers were still going strong, their work lit by emergency lights from gasoline generators. But workmen suspended operations when a brick wall on an adjoining building threatened to fall. Both the side and front walls of the Empire 5 & 10 Cent Store were so weakened by the blast that they were about to collapse.

The National Guardsmen on site patrolled the block throughout the night even though the windows of each shop had been boarded up by the owners during that day. A great deal of merchandise had been recovered from stores surrounding the devastated area and this merchandise was placed in surrounding buildings and kept under guard until the owners could reclaim what was theirs. These guards on the street protected the vulnerable town against the temptation of any looters with a shift of two hours on and four hour off. The troops also maintained the road blocks during the night with the same shift of two hours on and four hours off as they continued rerouting traffic around Villa Rica.

For the next two days, the National Guard troops not on duty were housed and slept in a large empty building adjacent to the jail, close to City Hall. The kitchen equipment and three field ranges were set up in another, empty building in order to feed and maintain these ninety troops that stayed in and around Villa Rica.

In the wee hours of this cold December morning, the only movements in town were that of the National Guardsmen and the occasional whips of smoke that escaped upward from the charred timbers. The heavy equipment, the half-filled dump trucks, and the crane posed over the collapsed roof sat motionless until daybreak when the clean-up effort would continue.

8

Families Learn of the Disaster

*"...the explosion is not a pleasant part of the city's history, but it is an important chapter.
So many of the key players, of our parents' generation, are no longer here.
We are the ones left to tell their stories..."*
Leslie Powell Carter, daughter of Dr. Ernest Powell, Jr

At the Villa Rica Elementary and High School a half mile west of the downtown area, Mark Berry was at lunch down toward the old football field. He didn't hear the explosion like the other kids did up in the classrooms. "I was seven-years-old and in the second grade and I remember seeing the white smoke boiling up on the horizon as all the kids were evacuated from the school. I saw Jack Williams come to school and get his son, Steve. Many other parents started picking up their kids. There were people afraid that the gas coming into our school might explode, so all the kids were moved out in front of the school on the old practice field.

"As all of us students marched in line to the field. I saw my cousin, Valerie Berry, sitting in a car talking to someone. She was distraught as she had just learned her mother, Margaret Berry, was in the explosion and presumedly had died. I learned later that Valerie was taken to our other cousin's house.

"I also learned later that my mother, Sara Berry, had intended on going to see Margaret Berry at the pharmacy to pick up a pair of cowboy chaps Aunt Margaret had gotten for me or my brother. But before Mother left the house, she got a call that something had

Explosion in Villa Rica

happened. Clarence Brown, who owned the Hosiery Mill, had called his wife, then she called my mother and asked what she could do. Mother asked her to pick up Margaret's two boys, Kip, age ten, and Ran (Randall), age eight, and to also get me and my brother, Bob, age eleven, from school.

"Mrs. Brown soon picked up the four of us and took us home with her to her house on the 78 Highway where we stayed outside. Kip, Ran, Bob and I—we were just a couple of kids hanging out, confused, not knowing what had happened. We were out in the pasture walking around. Every now and then, we looked toward town watching the white smoke still boiling up. Then we were amazed to see a couple of small airplanes —piper cubs that started circling Villa Rica.

"I also later learned that my Dad, Dr. Robert L. Berry had been driving to the pharmacy to have his usual morning coffee with Bill Berry, his brother. When he was down on Dallas Highway, he met an ambulance driven by Clyde Jones. Clyde waved him down and told him about the explosion and that he was on his way to the hospital with the first burn victim. Dad then turned his car around and followed the ambulance to the hospital.

"Later that afternoon, the four of us were taken to my house where some relatives and my grandmother Annie Powell Berry told Kip and Ran that their mother did not survive the explosion and fire. Both the boys were very upset as you can imagine. After they cried for a long time, my grandmother asked me to take Ran for a walk. The death of his mother was just about too much for two small boys to process. I remember saying, 'We will get through this together.' When we went back into the house, Grandmother Berry was laying down and had a small space heater turned on close by her. She told the boys, 'Margaret is singing with the rest of the angels in heaven now.'"

After the tragedy, Grandmother Berry, Annie Powell Berry, mother of Bill Berry and mother-in-law to Margaret Berry wrote this affidavit.

"Every day, I was in the pharmacy at least once—often two or three times. My children were there, my mail came there, and I did some work there.

"On Monday morning, December 2, 1957, I went in for my mail and to find whether Ann Smith was ready to begin work on the monthly statements with which I helped her. It was decided that we would begin Tuesday morning. I was in the store helping Ann all day Tuesday, December 3rd. There were no unusual odors of any kind either on Monday or Tuesday. On Wednesday morning, December 4th, . . . I returned to work in the pharmacy about 10:00 o'clock and stayed until about 3:00 in the afternoon. Ann got off at noon. There was no odor in the store that day—no one mentioned smelling anything out of the ordinary.

8. Families Learn of the Disaster

I was in the store again about 6:00 that night—no odors of any kind.

"On Thursday morning, December 5, 1957, I took my sister to the dentist. We reached his office around 9:00 or 9:30. In the waiting room we noticed an odor—not a strong odor but plainly noticeable. A lady sitting there said Dr. Burnham had gone downstairs to find out what it was. An open free radiant gas heater was going in the waiting room. I remarked that I didn't know what it was but it was certainly not a gas odor. A little later when we were called in to Dr. Burnham's office, he said something was making his eyes and nose burn. I said, "I smell something—it is not a gas odor—probably it is from the chimney. (I was recalling that we used to get an odor from those chimneys when the wind was from a certain direction.)

"Dr. Burnham stepped into an adjoining room for something and cold air came in from the open door. I jokingly said, 'If they didn't furnish heat I wouldn't pay rent.' He said, 'Don't blame Bill and Margaret—they are doing all they can to find out what it is.' He went on to say how much he thought of Bill and Margaret and that they were the most wonderful people he ever worked with. Two heaters were sitting in the office—I am under the impression that an electric heater was going.

"After giving the patient (my sister) a medication of some kind, Dr. Burnham asked us to sit in the waiting room for a few minutes until the dose took effect. I ran downstairs to see about my mail, and noticed the odor there. The odor was nothing to be anxious about. I didn't see Margaret or Bill. I went back upstairs. Dr. Burnham soon called us to his office, and he went right to work with the patient (my sister). He answered the telephone a couple of times and told the callers when to come on in. He didn't again mention that his eyes and nose burned and didn't mention an odor, and I didn't notice or think of the odor any more. When he had finished with my sister, he asked me to take her by the doctor's office for a shot which he would call about. We left his office sometime between 10 and 10:30. Downstairs after getting my sister in the car, I stepped back into the store to see about a package. The odor was gone. I did not see Margaret. Bill was talking on the telephone. When we were parking in front of my sister's home, Bobby Roberts passed us going toward town."

When the explosion occurred, Mrs. Annie Powell Berry drove back to the site. If she had not been held back forcibly by others, she would have gone into the smoke and burning timbers to search for her loved-ones.

Leslie Powell (Carter) tells her memories from the perspective of a twelve-year-old girl. "December 5, 1957 remains one of the most shocking days of my life. It was the day when I saw how something unimaginable and life-altering could strike with no warning at all. It was the first time I experienced the loss of people I knew well. And, most shocking of all, it was the first time in my life that I ever saw my father cry.

"Berry's Pharmacy, 'Ground Zero,' for the explosion, was owned and operated by my dad's cousin, Bill Berry. A block away was Powell-Berry-Powell Clinic, where my dad and grandfather (Doctors. J. E. Powell, Sr & Jr), Dr. R. L. Berry (Bill's brother) and Dr. J. I. Vansant based their medical practice. These four men made up the entire slate of physicians in Villa Rica at the time.

"Our family's life was closely intertwined with that of the Berrys. Not only was there the family connection and professional connection, but both Berry brothers had built homes on the same street where we lived. My brother and I were enjoying growing up close to our cousins. Hardly a day went by when we weren't with them, slamming screen doors at each other's houses.

"Bill and Margaret Berry had a wonderful capacity for finding interesting ways to entertain their children, and we benefited from this enormously. When they took up horseback riding, we got horses, too. When they bought a boat and learned to water ski, we soon followed. Dad was not going to be outdone. He seemed to feel an almost sibling-like rivalry toward Bill, but it was a friendly rivalry. Bill Berry was as close as Dad came to having a brother—his cousin, neighbor, and best friend. And, if time permitted between his hospital rounds and the start of patient appointments, his day often began with a stop at Berry's Pharmacy for a cup of coffee and a chat with Bill.

"The explosion occurred on a beautiful, clear December day. I had convinced Mom that, like my little brother, I was much too sick to go to school. The two of us were lounging in front of the television when we felt, rather than heard, the explosion. It shook the whole house, rattling the windows and shutting off the electricity. If it had been April, and a thunderstorm had been approaching, it wouldn't have seemed unusual, but this didn't make sense. I went to the kitchen and saw my mother looking out the back door at a tall column of smoke rising from the direction of downtown, a mile and a half away. After unsuccessful attempts to reach Dad by phone, she did something so out of character for her: she told my brother and me to get in the car and she started to drive TOWARD the danger, that ominous-looking tower of smoke.

"As we turned onto Westview Drive, we met my aunt coming in the opposite direction. She stopped her car in the middle of the street and got out crying, telling us to turn around and go back home. There had been an explosion at the drugstore, she said, and several people had been killed. It took a few seconds for that to sink in. The drugstore? Where the

8. Families Learn of the Disaster

Berrys definitely would have been and Dad might easily have been, too? THAT drugstore? There was nothing to do but go back home and wait. Disasters can turn ordinary mortals into superheroes. From all around, people converged on the scene of the explosion, ready to do whatever they could to help. My dad was one of them (running late that morning, he had gone straight to the clinic, bypassing his usual drugstore stop). He got there on foot just as rescuers were bringing an injured Bill Berry out. When Bill saw Dad, he told him, 'Find Margaret.' So Dad turned and walked inside what remained of Berry's Pharmacy.

"Afterward, he never wanted to talk about that experience, but I was a relentless interrogator. Gradually, I pulled bits of information out of him. He talked about the futility of what he'd been asked to do. The rear of the two-story building had collapsed, and there was little the first rescuers could do with no equipment to lift the debris. Thick smoke billowed from the rubble. He knew that if anyone in that part of the store had miraculously survived the blast, they would have quickly succumbed to smoke inhalation. His search would continue, but later, in other places. He never said so, but I heard from other sources that he helped with several rescues in surrounding stores before finally leaving the scene and heading for the hospital, which by then was being overwhelmed with the injured. And here he finally called to tell my mother he was safe.

"He also called hospitals in the surrounding area, asking to be notified if a small woman was brought in. He left the same message at nearby funeral homes. Late that afternoon, Dad came home. He pulled my mother aside and unfolded a piece of waxed paper he held in his hand. I heard him ask her if she could identify Margaret's watch. She looked and shook her head. She couldn't tell. I don't think that was what triggered what happened next. More likely, it was just the cumulative effect of all the horror he had witnesses that day, the terrible injuries and bodies burned beyond recognition. But, for whatever reason, my father did the most unbelievable thing. He walked to his bedroom, sat down and put his face in his hands and sobbed like a heartbroken child. It was the most frightening sound I'd ever heard.

"The days that followed were filled with more shock and sadness. One of the casualties was a boy I saw at school every day. Bobby Roberts, with his big smile and blond "flat top," had been a player on the Midget football team. He and the other victims were all identified, and funerals were planned. People followed the familiar rituals of caring for bereaved families, but had to repeat them over and over again. There were so many families affected. My mother tried to shield me from as much of this as possible, but I remember insisting on going to see my cousin, Valerie. Then I felt nervous because I didn't know what to say to her. As it turned out, the subject of her mother's death was too much for either of us. We spent my visit talking about clothes and tapioca pudding!

"Then life went on, as it always does… and should. The downtown area began to be rebuilt and eventually looked normal again. The explosion stopped being the only topic of conversation on everyone's lips. And a couple of years later, Bill Berry married a young widow from Carrollton who had three daughters, and they created their own version of the Brady Bunch. Their house was filled with kids and fun again.

"In some ways, Villa Rica today still looks like the town I grew up in. I'm glad to see my family "landmarks" intact. . . in fact, vastly improved! But the changes here are obvious, too. When I look at the new medical complex, for instance, I can't help but think how amazed my dad and grandfather would be! Progress is wonderful, but history is too. How fortunate that there is a group of Villa Rica citizens so determined to see it preserved. Even though the explosion is not a pleasant part of the city's history, it is an important chapter. So many of the key players, our parents' generation, are no longer here. We are the ones left to tell their stories and to think, as we do so often these days, "I can't believe it's been that long ago…"

The Associated Press picked up the story and by 12:00 noon, one a hour after the explosion, people around the country heard the report on the national noonday news. After the explosion and fire was announced, the news hit the afternoon and evening newspapers. Calls expressing sympathy "for the poor people of Villa Rica" and inquiries flooded the switchboard at The Atlanta Constitution-Journal shortly thereafter.

Fear and misinformation circulated when one caller asked about an hour following the tragedy, "Is it true that the whole town has been evacuated?" Another caller said, "I understand that West End (in Atlanta) has been devastated by fire."

A radio station in Hollywood, California called around 12:30 asking for details on the explosion. A newsroom employee said he had been obviously connected to a microphone in the radio station as he related what information was available at the early hour. "I definitely heard a click shortly after I started talking," the newspaperman recounted.

Numerous callers wanted to know to whom they could send aid for the stricken residents of the community. Many wanted information on the best route to take from Atlanta to Villa Rica.

Switchboard operators estimated over one thousand calls had jammed the boards at the newspapers by 3:15 that afternoon and were still running heavy.

Callers were told that highways to the town were blocked off to keep out non-emer-

8. Families Learn of the Disaster

gency personnel. Relatives and people who lived in Villa Rica were upset when they could not get to their loved-ones to find out if they were all right.

Melvin Ayers later told the newspaper reported how he found out about the explosion. Melvin lived in Villa Rica and worked in Atlanta at the Potter and Rayfield Company. Melvin always kept the radio on as he worked. "After I heard the announcement on the radio about the explosion in Villa Rica, I went to the office and told the boss. He called everyone from Villa Rica who was working there in that plant— about eighteen workers— to come into his office. He then told them about the explosion and dismissed them for the day to get on back home to Villa Rica.

We all rode together in two vans every day. So, Gerald Helton, the driver of one of the vehicles, drove us back to Villa Rica to see what had happened. We were trying to make as fast a time as possible. We got behind a firetruck coming from Atlanta when we got into Mableton. We jumped in behind it and with its sirens going we followed it right behind all the way to town.

"We found quite a destruction. It was quite a mess. They wouldn't let anyone close up to the scene but folks got out and began to help any way they could.

"We lived on Westview Drive, about a block and a half from the blast location. My wife had heard the explosion. My little girl and boy were in school at the time and they were not hurt in any way."

John and Nancy McPherson who had been in Villa Rica all day making photographs of the explosion went home in the afternoon stunned and shocked about all that they had seen and heard. In Philadelphia, John McPherson's in-laws heard the report on the noonday news and tried to get him by phone for several hours but could not get through because of the phone lines being down.

After John and Nancy McPherson were home a short while, the State Patrol came to their house. When John opened the door, the patrolman told him that his in-laws in Pennsylvania, Ralph and Florence Minetti, were very concerned as they did not know the gravity or extent of the explosion. They were especially worried since they knew he worked for a plumber. The patrolman told him, "Your in-law are concerned. They asked if anyone in your family was in the explosion. They don't know whether you and your wife are living or dead."

The State Patrol then gave them a police escort around the blocked off streets of Villa Rica to Douglasville, where they used the phone at the Rexall Drug Store. They were able to call Nancy's parents to let them know they were not harmed, just in shock and thankful

Explosion in Villa Rica

to be alive.

John's mother, Marjorie Eloise McPherson, was a greylady, at the Villa Rica Hospital. When she heard the hospital was filling up and that they needed all the volunteers to report, she went in to assist. Because of the help she gave that day and the good she did, Eloise decided later to become a licensed practical nurse. Eloise McPherson worked at the Villa Rica Hospital for many years until she retired.

After the Associated Press picked up the story of the Villa Rica gas explosion, newspapers around the nation carried the news. This is how Ruth Waller heard the story: "I had moved to Chicago but was from Villa Rica. My sister, Pauline, and brother-in-law, T. A. "Bert" Hall, still lived there. I worked from 7:00 in the morning until 3:00 in the afternoon at Western Electric in Chicago. At 3:00 o'clock, I came out of the plant and heard a *Chicago Sun Times* newsboy who held a newspaper high over his head calling out a shocking report, 'Gas Explosion in Villa Rica Georgia, ten killed, twenty injured.'

"Chills ran through my body. I fought back tears as I rode the bus home. When I got home, I called Villa Rica. After several tries, I reached my brother-in-law, Bert Hall, who told me he and my sister were fine. He had left Berry's that morning a few minutes before the explosion, after picking up a prescription for asthma. It hit as he walked back toward Fullerville, about a miles north of town. He had almost reached home, when he heard the thundering explosion."

At the time the *Chicago Sun Times* went to press there had only been ten found of the twelve who were killed. More than twenty had been hurt including rescue workers who were injured at the site.

The Associated Press aired the news of the Villa Rica tragedy abroad. Leonard Tyson, who was stationed in Puerto Rica, was watching television when a news broadcast interrupted the program he was watching and reported that there had been a gas explosion in America in Villa Rica, Georgia. He could not believe what he was hearing. He was born and raised in Villa Rica and had only been stationed in Puerto Rica for a few months. When a newsreel of the devastated area flashed on television, he recognized the surrounding buildings as those of his hometown. He became concerned for his family. Berry's Pharmacy was where his dad, Reverend E. C. Tyson, got his prescriptions filled. It took several days before Leonard could contact relatives to make sure all of his family were safe. When he heard the names of those who were killed, he was stricken with sadness because he knew most of them.

9

A Town, Crippled

"Our hearts were broken for the friends and family that we lost that day. Thursday, December 5, ended like no other day in the history of Villa Rica."
Robyn Doyle, The Villa Rican, November 22, 2007

Prior to the explosion, neighbors in Villa Rica mostly kept in touch by party lines and the occasional long distance calls. Telegrams were used for really long distance messages. Now with lines down and some utility poles broken in half, communication was about to become a huge problem for the rescue efforts. With the broken poles, the lines to all other poles on the block were disabled. To make matters worse, the radio at the Georgia State Patrol station was off the air, its power blown by the explosion.

In the sections of Villa Rica that still had phone service, the switchboards were jammed with more than five times as many long-distance phone calls as usual. Villa Ricans found it impossible to call out of the city as a result of so many calls coming into the city. Southern Bell Telephone Company put an "emergency only" restriction on callers coming in and urged telephone users to limit their conversations to three minutes. Newsmen and emergency workers depended mostly on ham radio operators to get messages out of the town.

Late Thursday long distance calls were being delayed more than four hours. A telephone company official said the backlog of incoming calls continued to be almost overwhelming. During this time linemen arrived late in the afternoon to work on restoring phone service to this area.

Explosion in Villa Rica

At 11:30 Thursday morning, Juanita Farr, who operated a ham radio station W4YEK, an alternate control station in the State Civil Defense setup, accepted an urgent call from Jack Grantham, State Communications Coordinator for the Civil Defense. "There's been a helluva explosion in Villa Rica," he told the licensed amateur radio operator, who worked out of her basement in Hapeville, Georgia, thirty-five miles east of Atlanta. Grantham ordered Juanita to take charge of establishing and maintaining radio contact with the wounded little town.

Fifteen minutes later, Juanita Farr dispatched William Kennedy to Villa Rica as a "mobile" as he had a unit in his car. With Civil Defense clearance, William Kennedy sped through the State Patrol blocks on U.S. 78. At 12:35, when the mobile arrived, William Kennedy established Villa Rica's first radio contact with the outside world. With her orders from Civil Defense headquarters, Juanita Farr instructed him to report the list of injured and dead and to give her a complete picture of what was needed in Villa Rica.

His report set up a chain of communications between the ham operators in Atlanta and Jack Grantham at the Civil Defense Headquarters. Each time Juanita got a report on the radio, she took off her headset and called it into Grantham.

For some reason, the Alabama Highway Patrol could not establish direct radio contact with the Georgia patrol to offer its assistance. Once again Juanita became the liaison to the Alabama patrol, giving instructions on routing eastbound traffic through Heflin, Bowdon, and Carrollton to Atlanta.

A call came through from a ham operator in Birmingham, Alabama early in the afternoon, "Can you get any information on Bobby Roberts? The boy's mother, Marie Couch, is here and plenty worried. He was due to be in the dental office about the time the explosion went off."

By the time the body of Bobby Roberts had been found and reported and the information passed on to the ham operator in Alabama, Bobby mother had left for Villa Rica to discover her loss for herself.

Juanita Farr stayed on the radio to William Kennedy and on the phone with Jack Grantham for eleven hours until they closed things down at 10:30 that night.

The gas to Villa Rica was supplied by the Southern Natural Gas Company and the distribution system was municipally owned and operated. Forty-five minutes after the explosion gas service was cut for entire town as everyone believed the accident had been caused by faulty gas heating. Tom Pope, the Assistant Gas Superintendent, cut the supply at

9. A Town, Crippled

the power station at Sandhill, on the corner of Highway 61 and Highway 163 (Highway 61 and Williams Road). This left approximately one-thousand people in town and in the surrounding area without gas service. That meant the houses were without heat and the people had to go elsewhere to get warm or wait it out, outside in their yards. People were warned not to turn on gas appliances and to not even go back into their houses.

E. B. Wilder, manager of the company's Carrollton office, fourteen miles from Villa Rica, was the first to receive a call for help and was the first employee on the scene. He was soon followed by a service crew from Carrollton under Superintendent Dick Tolbert. Joe LaBoon was immediately dispatched from Atlanta as the official company representative and he supervised the restoration of gas service, working through the Villa Rica officials.

Gas workers from Carrollton and Rome arrived to aid Villa Rica gas men about two hours after the explosion. The Carrollton crew, working under manager E. B. Wilder, planned to stay in Villa Rica through Friday.

A gas company spokesman said the explosion did not affect the city's gas mains and that chances of a single blast setting off a chain of explosions were small. To restore heating service gas crews must go to each home in Villa Rica and turn the gas back on.

Villa Rica's gas firm was owned and operated by the city and was not directly affiliated with the Atlanta Gas Light Company, but a twenty-five man crew from the Atlanta Gas Light Company soon arrived and worked until the pre-dawn hours of Friday to restore the town's natural gas service.

Although all employees involved responded to the call willingly, several employees were accidentally swept into the rescue effort. Lamar Maret of the Atlanta Measurement Department was returning from Rome when he was passed by several company trucks that turned off the Atlanta-Rockmart Road to the south. Guessing that there must be trouble, he followed them into Villa Rica, where he worked for twenty-four hours. James C. Logan, from Newnan, was off that day but went to Villa Rica with a friend who worked for the newspaper. James Logan wound up working with the service crews. B. H. Butler, from Buckhead, who left after work on Thursday to see about some relatives in Villa Rica, pitched in to help. Employees who assisted in the operation came from Carrollton, Rome, Marietta, and Cedartown.

After the gas supply had been turned off, the next action was to cut off all meters. By late afternoon the system had been checked and by early evening, gas was back on in some houses.

Mrs. Emily Roberson who lived about two blocks west of the explosion site, on

Explosion in Villa Rica

Westview Drive, tells about going without heat all day: "I heard the terrific noise and wondered what in the world had happened. After a short time, I received a call from a worker at City Hall telling me to get out of the house and not go back in until my gas lines and heaters could be inspected. They told me there had been a bad accident and that no one knew what would happen next. All feared fire could spread through lines and cause other explosions."

Emily went out into her yard and looked toward town. There she could see the massive amount of black smoke rising up and could hear the sirens in the distance. She saw more cars than usual and people were everywhere, walking in every direction, but mainly toward town.

Emily put on a coat and got jackets for her twins, Ray and Fay, age four. Then she spread a blanket under the huge oak tree in her narrow front yard and put her twins on the blanket and told them to sit there and not leave the blanket. A friend, James Ward, came by and helped her watch the twins.

Emily Roberson's driveway was directly in line with the driveway of The Jones Funeral Home set on a hill across the street. Each time the ambulance turned into the driveway of the funeral home, it came close to where she and the twins sat on a blanket. Emily felt tense and nervous. She knew that each time the ambulance turned into the drive, it probably held someone who had been killed in the explosion: someone she probably knew. Villa Rica was such a small, close-knit town, where everyone knew everyone else. The ambulance left and was back again in a short time.

A few minutes later her other children walked into the yard from school. They told her how the school had been evacuated. Judy, age 10, had gone to the lower field and Diane, age 7, was sent to the upper field. They had not been allowed to find each other as the teachers said each of the classes had to stay together. When the students were allowed to go home, the older sister, Barbara, a high school senior, had collected the two younger sisters, so they could walk the two blocks home together.

Emily dared to go back into the house to get lunch for her children, and they all ate outside sitting on the blanket. The children remembered the day as an adventure since school had let out early and they were having a picnic outside on the lawn even though it was wintertime and cold.

Emily's father-in-law, Guy Roberson stopped by and told them all of downtown had been destroyed. He usually walked to town from North Avenue each morning as part of his daily routine. He said he had just left the pharmacy and had made his way to the railroad

9. A Town, Crippled

tracks when the buildings blew up. If it had happened a few minutes earlier, he said he would have been killed. They were all serious at this point, and thankful.

They learned later in the day that Emily's seventeen-year-old son, Gene, had left school alone and had gone to town to see all of the activity for himself. Gene had climbed to the roof of the theater, the tallest building in town except for Berry's Pharmacy that now lay in smoldering, burning ruin below him. He stayed late in the day watching the firemen fight the blaze, and then the rescuers searching for survivors before he made his way home to tell all that he had seen.

About 5:00 o'clock in the evening, Roy Roberson came home to his family from his job in Atlanta at the Link Belt Company. At the barricade east of town, he had told the police he had to get into Villa Rica to his wife and children. When they let him through, he found a way to go down the back streets to his house.

Just after Roy came home, someone from the gas company arrived and inspected the house for any possible gas leaks. After checking the gas floor heaters throughout the house, he told the family it was safe to go back inside and to turn on the heaters. By this time, the weather had turned quite chilly and the whole Roberson family felt relieved to be inside again.

The work of turning on meters and lighting appliances that began during the evening, continued until about 3:30 the next morning, Friday, December 6.

Bobby Fendley, a Villa Rica resident, recalls, "I had worked at the explosion site clearing debris and rubble from about an hour after it happened for the whole day and into the night. I arrived back home at 2:00 o'clock in the morning. There was a knock at the door. It was men from the gas company who had come to check my gas lines and turn on the gas."

10

At the Hospitals

*As the Villa Rica hospital filled up, stretchers and mattresses soon lined the hallways.
For the most critical, a nurse took them to isolation and stayed with them.
Isolation was anywhere a place could be found.
Richard Smallwood, Villa Rica resident, 2009*

The number of dead and injured had overwhelmed the limited medical and mortuary capacities of the Villa Rica Hospital and the local funeral homes: Jones Funeral Home and Robert Miller Funeral Home. Even though Villa Rica had opened a new hospital two years before with a twenty-five bed capacity and with one private room, this hospital was not large enough to handle the incoming patients. This new hospital had twenty-three on their staff, but they were soon overwhelmed. The injured who could not be cared for at this facility were transported to the Tanner Memorial Hospital in Carrollton. When Villa Rica's Funeral Homes had reached capacity, the number of dead were carried to the funeral homes in Carrollton and Bremen.

Distress calls, meanwhile, had gone out over the radio at the State Patrol station and over the telephones spontaneously by citizens. Within twenty to thirty minutes, ambulances, doctors, and nurses began to arrive at the hospital.

Hospitals in Douglasville and Carrollton sent doctors and nurses to the Villa Rica Hospital. A team came from Grady Hospital in Atlanta. Doctors and nurses from as far away as Gainesville (fifty miles north of Atlanta) poured into Villa Rica as quickly as possible to assist Villa Rica's tiny hospital staff. The Bremen hospital sent medical supplies.

Many helping in the recovery efforts at the explosion site where injured or burned from moving hot bricks, concrete blocks, and burned timbers. These rescuers went to the clinic in Villa Rica know as the Powell, Berry, Powell Clinic on Carroll Road where Dr.

Explosion in Villa Rica

Earnest Powell Jr treated them. Their injuries were minor compared to those who were burned so badly during the gas explosion.

When Donald Willis was injured in rescuing Camille Adams, he went to the Powell, Berry, Powell Clinic where Dr. Powell bandaged his face and hands then told him there would be no charge. Dr. Powell asked Donald about Bill Berry as he had been busy with burn patients and could not go to find out how badly he had been hurt. Later Dr. Powell was able to go to the Villa Rica Hospital and check on Bill Berry. He was severely injured and burned.

Among the staff at the Villa Rica Hospital was Marie Harrison, the Director of Nurses. Marie Harrison had been rushing around the hospital because of the Asiatic Influenza Epidemic. From one-hundred-fifty to two hundred students had been out of school because of this flu the previous two weeks. Even a football game had been cancelled as fifteen members of the Wildcat Football team had been too sick to attend school that same week. Many Villa Ricans had been given the vaccine, yet some had been hospitalized recently.

Marie was busy attending to the patients when the lights flickered off then back on. She rushed to the operating room where her sister, Elizabeth Tackett, was assisting in surgery. After assuring herself that all was well she went back to the desk where a call came in with the news that they were about to be very busy because there had been an explosion in town. Shortly afterward, someone came by the hospital and told the staff, "The whole town of Villa Rica has just blown up." Marie immediately began to prepare for what lay ahead. She hoped her staff would be ready when the first casualties of the explosion arrived. The Red Cross was contacted to send extra blood as it would probably be needed.

Richard Smallwood, who worked in x-ray and lab, heard the news as word went around the hospital to be prepared. He felt an overwhelming concern for his wife, Shirley, and their six-week-old baby, Phillip. The Smallwood house was located at the corner of Candler and Wilson Streets, directly in line with and behind Berry's Pharmacy. Richard tried phoning Shirley, but the telephone lines in town were dead.

In a very short time the four ambulances from Jones Funeral Home and the Robert Miller Funeral Home in town started bringing in the burned and injured. Two of the town's three doctors, Dr. Robert L. Berry, and Dr. J. I. Vansant were at the hospital ready for the patients. The third doctor Dr. John E. Powell, Sr was out of town. He flew in that afternoon.

One of the first ambulances to arrive brought in Rozelle Johnson who had been severely burned. She was transported immediately to the Carrollton hospital—Tanner—where she died.

10. At the Hospitals

Most of the patients arriving were burned and covered in black soot. Many of them had their hair burnt down to their scalps. A triage was set up. The receiving nurses put a tag on each person's right wrist with a band. The patient's name was added as soon as they could be identified. Then each was checked by a doctor who wrote the seriousness of the person's condition. Only the most seriously injured were taken in. The rest were given first aid and sent on to other hospitals.

As the Villa Rica hospital filled up, stretchers and mattresses soon lined the hallways. The most critical were taken by a nurse to isolation where she stayed with them. "Isolation" was anywhere a place could be found. One person was taken to the operating room—not to be operated on, but to get away from the others so as to keep down bacteria and prevent infection. One by one, the small recovery rooms were soon filled with those needing to be isolated.

Richard Smallwood remembers, "After the doctors checked the patient and made an order for what kinds of x-ray should be made, I took those patient to be x-rayed. I was one of the technologists who did the lab work that was ordered by the physician which included cross-matching all who needed blood. The nurses then gave the transfusions that were ordered."

Over the following hours, twenty injured and burned victims were brought into the hospital. A knot of anxious Villa Ricans gathered outside the hospital shortly after the blast to hear news of loved-ones injured by the flames and by the initial concussion of the blast. When a loved-one could not be found in the debris, the family waited at the hospital for the arriving ambulances. The ladies huddled in groups in front of the hospital, their winter coats pulled close around them and their headscarves were tied tight as the day was brisk. They whispered in groups and shook their heads in sorrow when told bad news. People they knew were suddenly gone.

Inside the hospital, Marie Harrison, the Director of Nurses, and the other nurses and aides worked frantically with burn victims before the hospital administrator, Ruth Robertson, and Marie's husband, Lewis Harrison, approached her and took her away from her patients. Lewis, told her that two of the people in the explosion were her father and her brother, O.T. and Johnny Dyer. He said they had been working on a plumbing problem in the pharmacy and had been killed in the powerful blast. Marie stood stunned outside the emergency room of the hospital. Then she became faint with shock.

While others expressed words of sympathy to Marie, her sister, Elizabeth, continued her work unaware that death had come to their family and had taken their brother Johnny and their Dad, O.T. Marie bowed her head and fingered a handkerchief as her husband and the hospital administrator, Ruth Robertson, tried to console and comfort her. After a few minutes, a doctor walked up and asked, "Is there anything we can do?"

"You've done everything you could," Marie replied. "All we can do now is try to take care of the ones they're bringing in." Even as she spoke, rescue workers brought two more injured on stretchers into the emergency room. At one point, Lewis Harrison suggested to Marie that she go home and rest. She replied, "You all go on home; I've got work to do here."

As new victims arrived through the emergency room doors, Marie Harrison wiped her tears and went back to work.

Several of the doctors were also related to the injured: Dr. John E. Powell, Sr was an uncle to the injured Dr. Bill Berry, and Dr. J. Ernest Powell, Jr was his cousin. Dr. Robert L. Berry was his brother. Though related to the injured and to those killed, the staff, kept working until all the victims were cared for.

The Powell, Berry, Powell Clinic on Carroll Road.

The x-ray technician, Richard Smallwood did not leave the hospital for five hours. When he could get free for a short time, he drove quickly to Villa Rica. As the town was blocked off, he parked several blocks from his house. While he walked and ran the two blocks toward home, he looked around, amazed at the destroyed area. Near his house, he could see debris on the roof and saw that the windows were broken. When he went inside, he found his wife, Shirley, and his baby, Phillip, had escaped injury.

Shirley told Richard what she had seen. "When the shock of the blast boomed," she said, "it knocked out some of the windows in the house. I ran to look out the broken picture window at the front of the house. Boards came flying through the air toward me and crashed onto the roof. It looked like the whole block was on fire." Since the Smallwood's house was directly behind Berry's, Shirley had seen the dark mushroom cloud billowing

10. At the Hospitals

upward in front of her and saw the wall of the Reeves' building fall out into the street and the roof crash down.

When she turned to grab her baby to her, she heard a second explosion. Sirens began going off and emergency vehicles arrived. Shirley saw people, whose skin was black, began coming out of the stores. She said, "It was like having a front row seat to this horror." She tried to call the Villa Rica Hospital to let her husband know she and the baby were okay, but all lines were down. About an hour later the house grew cold. Since Richard had their

Dr. Powell and his nurse left the clinic to go to the site.
Photo by George Holloway.

only car, she was stranded at home trying to keep the baby warm.

After listening to what Shirley told and after comforting her, Richard then took her and the baby to her sister's house. The sister's house was far enough out of town that the heating was not affected by the gas being shut off in Villa Rica.

Richard then went back to the Villa Rica Hospital and stayed all night as well as for the next two days and nights getting little or no sleep. "I remember seeing the four to five boxes of blood that came in." The American Red Cross rushed forty-nine pints of blood to hospitals in Villa Rica and nearby Bremen and Carrollton. Twenty pints of blood went to the Villa Rica hospital from the Atlanta Regional Blood Center. This stack of boxes had to be kept iced down. Later in the day they dispatched a mobile canteen with five workers.

"We had to be very careful with the burn patients, in moving them, touching them, and treating them so as not to injure them further. Those who were still in pain were given

Explosion in Villa Rica

pain medication."

Right after the explosion, John Bailey, the high-school senior who worked at the pharmacy after school, took Don Bohannan, the injured and burned pharmacist, to the hospital. As the nurses worked with Don, John was taken to the emergency room entrance area to help. There, five or six stretchers were lined up from the most severely burned to those with lesser burns. "The nurses instructed the volunteers to scrub the burned patients," John remembers. "The nurse told me she needed me to scrub the skin of a woman who had been burned. I took the brush and very cautiously began to rub the patient's arm so as not to hurt her any further. The nurse came over and showed me how to scrub like one would scrub on a wash board. Then she demonstrated. She said I had to scrub vigorously to remove the burned skin and get the black soot off the skin. I did as she told me.

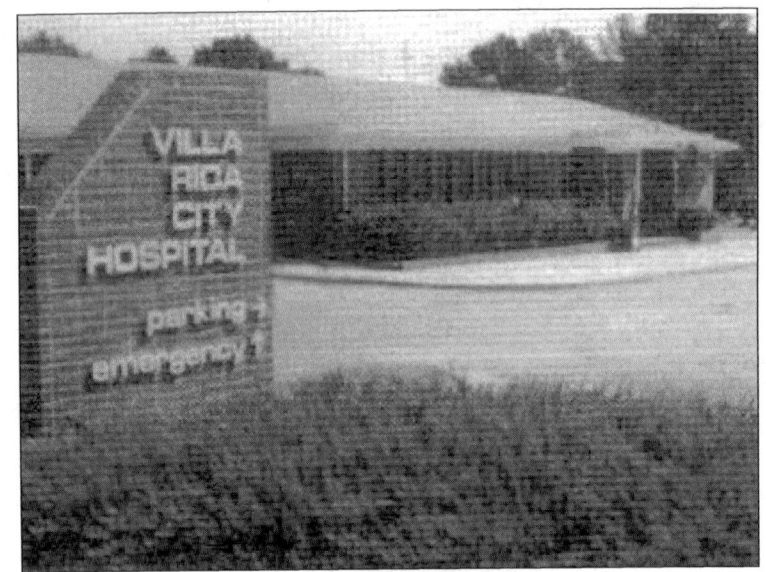

Villa Rica City Hospital
Photo courtesy of Perry "Bill" Bailey

"I looked over at Don who had been brought into this same area where I was scrubbing the burned patient. I looked at his hands which looked like he had on rubber gloves, but then I realized it was his skin hanging off his hands. One of the nurses took scissors and cut the hanging skin from Don's hands. She then handed me a brush and instructed me to scrub Don's burned arms and hands. It was a traumatic experience, but I knew the nurses needed my help so I did as I was instructed."

Don relates his experience. "The doctor told me I had shrapnel in my arm and the area above my ankle had been burned to the bone. My arms and hands were then soaked in a big pan of orange solution."

Arrangements were made with Don's father-in-law who happened to be a burn expert at Fort Oglethorpe Hospital in Chickamauga, Georgia. Don was given three shots of morphine and taken there by ambulance to be treated. "At the Fort Oglethorpe Hospital Burn Center, I was soaked in antiseptic solution to keep the infection down and pounds of

10. At the Hospitals

cold cream were applied to my skin. The weight and greasiness took away the layers of burned skin. As these layers came off I had no scars underneath. I stayed for three weeks in Chickamauga."

The small Villa Rica Hospital was filled with burned and injured patients. Donald Willis and Clyde Reeves were treated for burns they had incurred when they rescued Camille Adams. Ralph Fuller, the twenty-seven-year-old barber who was in the snack bar area, suffered severe burns about his arms, face, and head. When Ralph was first admitted to the hospital, his family came to visit him there and his own sister did not recognize him because of the burns on his face.

In the bed next to Fuller was Ray Tyson, the pharmacy employee who worked behind the soda fountain. Ray had surgery on his back for injuries sustained in the explosion. Both Ray Tyson and Ralph Fuller were later reported in fair condition.

Bill Berry was badly burned and had a serious injury on his forehead. He was listed in critical condition. It was two days until he was able to schedule his wife's funeral and be able to attend. Shirley Whitworth and Homer Vaughan were both admitted and later reported in serious condition.

Shirley Whitworth lay in serious condition with burns on her legs, arms, face and neck. Her long blond hair had been burned and doctors now cut it to an inch long stubble so they could see if her scalp had been burned. When Shirley's family got to the hospital later that day, they were given her watch and jewelry to help identify her. When they recognized the items, a nurse directed them down the hall to find her. Shirley's mother and daddy passed right by the stretcher she lay on, not even recognizing her.

Shirley's fifteen-year-old sister, Janie struggled to keep from crying as she waited in the hospital reception room talking to her other sister, Cora Mae, who was the hospital's record clerk.

"Shirley was looking forward to Christmas so much," Janie told her sister. "The rest of the family had done a little shopping but Shirley had all her presents bought and had them wrapped."

Cora stood in the reception area and answered questions of the victims' anxious relatives. When someone asked her about her sister, Shirley, she told them, "Shirley is one of the most seriously injured brought in here today."

Many of the most seriously burned were started on a new treatment. First, each burn victim had to be scrubbed. Then the affected skin was sprayed daily to do two things. One—this aided in the removal of old dead, damaged tissue, and two, it improved the

Explosion in Villa Rica

healing of the remaining skin. Once the burn victim got to a certain point in this process they were put into hot baths. This entire treatment worked so effectively that many times it prevented the patient from scarring.

Nine of those hospitalized at the Villa Rica hospital needed blood transfusions.

Among those who were treated and released were N. J. DeFore, Don Willis, Charles Dodson, John Rigsby, and Cliff Reeves. Both Charles Dodson and John Rigsby were injured in the rescue effort.

Several patients were sent from the Villa Rica Hospital to Tanner Memorial Hospital in Carrollton. Camille Adams was admitted to Tanner for treatment. Melinda Doris Hembree, the eighteen-year-old who paused in the Empire 5 & 10 Cent store to listen to the radio was admitted to the Villa Rica Hospital then moved to Tanner. Melinda had only bruises and abrasions and stayed at the hospital only a short time.

L-R Nell Baskin, Hazel Camp, Elsie Spake, Sue Ward, Hallie Dewberry, Mae Canant, Elizabeth Tackett, Joan Mayfield, Betty Loyd, Hazel Williams.
Villa Rica Nurses - 1955 Photo courtesy Ted Williamson.

At the Bremen Hospital about twenty miles west of Villa Rica, Opal Thompson, who worked in accounting heard the explosion as a small thump. Everyone in her office heard it as well. The nurses gathered around the hospital administrator, Mr. Jones, and

10. At the Hospitals

exclaimed, "What was that?" In a few minutes a call came in that there had been a serious explosion in Villa Rica. Mr. Jones told everyone to go and prepare bandages. He knew the hospital would be getting patients and they would be needing bandages and supplies. They wanted to be prepared when the call came for anything they could help with. Even though Opal worked in accounting, she was taken to central sterile where she started preparing dressings that were put into an autoclave to be sterilized.

Back in Villa Rica, Preston Lancaster, the driver of the gas tanker who had parked behind Berry's pharmacy, had been badly burned but refused to go to the Villa Rica Hospital. He flagged down someone to carry him back to Bremen where he lived.

Thirty minutes later, Preston walked into the Bremen Hospital. Someone looked up and exclaimed, "My God. What happened to you?" Preston was covered in black soot and burned badly. The skin on his hands hung down in burnt clumps. He had burns on his back and legs. He told the hospital staff who brought him into the emergency room what

L-R 1st: Estelle Conner, Yvonne Humphries, Lorene Williams, Sara Holloway, Floye Meeks
2nd row: Lois McPherson, Bitt Parker, Pearl Vaughn, Doris Pope, Myra Smith, Ina Hixon.
Red Cross Grey Ladies - 1951-52 Photo courtesy Ted Williamson

had occurred. He told them that when the explosion hit, he had been standing at the soda fountain where Ray Tyson was paying him for fuel oil he had delivered to Ray's house early that morning. He said he had been blown upward and then fell back down through the floor that collapsed.

Explosion in Villa Rica

Preston had third degree burns over most of his body and was listed in fair condition. He stayed in a sterile environment for a month. His private nurse was Eloise Manley who stayed with him around the clock seven day a week.

11

Memories, Stories, and Affidavits

*The human heart is still full of good decent things and the good in man
responded to Villa Rica in deeds of self-sacrifice
and feelings of commiseration and sympathy.
Editorial - Out of the Ashes... by Charles Williamson, Jr and Robby Robison,
The Villa Rican, Wednesday, December 11, 1957.*

The streets had been cleared; the heavy equipment had been removed; all bricks and burned timbers were hauled away. All that remained was a gaping hole where four stores had been. The people of Villa Rica had been through unbelievable tragedy, then grief. Now their memories relived the events of the day and so many have a story to tell:

As an adult Randy Wallace tells his recollections of being one of the School Safety Patrolmen: "There are events in one's life that make a lasting impression, some so ingrained in your mind that you are able to almost relive an event many years after the event. On December 5, 1957, I was a seventh grade student in Mrs. Urabell Powell's class. The classroom was located in the northwest corner of the Villa Rica Grammar School building near the intersection of Dogwood and Peachtree Streets. This would place the room about a mile from the downtown area of the City of Villa Rica.

"As one of my school duties, I got to take the lunch money and attendance record to Mr. Holloman's room every morning. I recall that the morning was routine. I had returned from delivering the morning report and was at my desk and Mrs. Powell was teaching her

Explosion in Villa Rica

class lesson for the day.

"The classroom was rather large and had a row of huge double hung windows along one side. All of a sudden there was a great boom and the windows shook violently. After a few minutes, the school was evacuated and everyone was outside the buildings. We looked toward the downtown area and saw a huge column of black smoke. We were told that there had been an explosion downtown. By that time you could hear sirens sounding.

"I was a member of the School Safety Patrol that reported to Mr. Holloman. As I

L-R 1st Randy Wallace, J. T. Wilson, Dan Davis, Tommy Tallent, Wayne Kimsey, Charles Broom
2nd row: Monroe Spake, Roy Lovell, Larry Ayers, Trooper Frank Durham, Sgt. Tom Bentley,
Photo and information courtesy Randy Wallace and Charles Broom

recall, the school patrol had about eight to ten members. Looking back on that, I guess the school patrol was sort of a quasi-playground police group. We were supposed to report to Mr. Holloman such major things as fighting, bullying, or cheating at marbles during recess.

"We wore a type of white harness that had one strap that went over one shoulder and a strap that went around the waist and fastened with a belt buckle. Fastened to the strap that went across the shoulder was a shiny metal badge. The captain of the School Patrol's harness was a bright yellow with a larger badge.

"After a short time had passed, Mr. Holloman assembled the School Patrol in the schoolyard. He informed us that since all of the law enforcement was busy working at the

11. Stories, Memories, and Affidavits

explosion site that we were going to help with traffic control. We didn't know how serious the situation was until later that day and the coming days. We were willing to do whatever Mr. Holloman asked us to do.

"We lined up in two lines with Mr. Holloman and Tyler Baswell, the School Patrol captain, at the head of the group. We marched down the road in front of the school and stopped at street corners. When we got to the corner of Dogwood and Maple Street, I was told to station myself there and not let anyone go toward town on that street, unless they lived on the street. I don't know how long we were out there but it seemed like a long time. I

L-R 1st: Ray Boyd, Tyler Baswell, George Barber, Herbie Williams, Joe Brock, James Barber.
2nd: Cap. E. B. "Red" Harbin, Lt. Ralph Crawford, Sgt. Luther Butler, Capt. Gene Thomas, Principal - E.A. Holloman, unknown student, James Terrell.
Photo and information courtesy Randy Wallace and Charles Broom.

recall that several cars came up to my street but when I told them that they were not allowed to go up the street, unless they lived on it, they would turn around or continue on toward the schoolhouse. There was one car that I still think the person driving lied to me and told me that he lived on the street. Of course, I said go on through. To this day I don't know if he lived on the street or not.

"Finally someone came around gathering us up at the street corners and we marched back to school. The buses had come to take the bus riders home. At four o'clock the Boy Scouts and the School Boy Patrolmen were released by the Highway Patrol that had arrived

Explosion in Villa Rica

to take over this duty. Later, people in the congested areas reported the Scouts and Boy Patrolmen handled their job efficiently and mannerly in rerouting the traffic through alternate streets.

"After several weeks, there was an assembly in the auditorium and some important looking state patrolman (and others) presented the Villa Rica Grammar School Safety Patrol with a plaque recognizing our effort in a time of crisis.

"I wonder what ever happened to that plaque?"

Ruth Moore, a third grade teacher at Villa Rica elementary told a newspaper reporter: "I remember the day of the explosion. I had my third grade class all lined up to go to the lunchroom when the whole building shook violently and the lights went out. I ran to the window and saw a cloud of black smoke pouring over the town.

"My first thought was that it was the filling station on the corner. It was very frightening to the children—and me, of course. By the time I got them lined up again, mothers began running into the school, coming to get their children.

"One woman kept saying 'The whole town is burning, the whole town is burning!' I assumed that was so. The woman mentioned the pharmacy, and little Ran Berry was in my class.

"We went into the lunchroom, anyway, and Ran put his head down on the table. Of course, he couldn't eat anything. He didn't know what had happened and I didn't either, so I went over and just sat with him. He lost his mother (Margaret Berry) in that explosion.

"We then went back to our classroom until word came for us to go outside as if we were having fire drill. My class lined up at the edge of the street as usual, and then someone came running to us and said to get the children away from the street because the gas mains ran along that area. So we took the children to the playground area and stayed there for the rest of the day.

"Ambulances were zooming up and down the highway. Piper cubs and small planes flew overhead all afternoon. We kept getting information from folks who would come up to tell us what was going on.

"We, the teachers, stayed until the last child was picked up to be taken home. Fortunately it was not such a cold day although it was in December. When it was safe to go, we went to town to see what had happened. The whole town was filled with cars. We had to park blocks away and walk. The National Guard was here to patrol the area and it looked like war, almost."

11. Stories, Memories, and Affidavits

Martha Fay Bailey (Beedle), remembers being a child in the colored school a half mile east of the city on the day of the explosion and tells this story "in the eyes of a young black girl" titled, "Are the Russian's Bombing Us?" :

"This was the era of the cold war between Russia and the United States. So, in saying that, we had to be prepared if Russia decided to bomb us. We had bomb drills and built fallout shelters. This was a constant concern of black and white, young and old. Our chore after school was to dig dirt out of the fallout shelter, which my granddaddy had started under the front porch.

"It was a normal day in school which was located across the tracks in 'The Crack,' now known as Cleghorn Street. This colored school was held in old World War II army barracks and had one big white board building in the center, known as the play area. The morning bell had rang and we were in our classes. In fact, we had finished our morning devotion and began our study for the day. Some of us participated by reading, or actually going in front of the class to explain a problem.

"Then all of a sudden we heard this loud BOOM. It knocked one student from the blackboard to the back of the class. RUSSIA HAD BOMBED US !!!!!

"It was total chaos. We were running and screaming. We had prepared for this. Okay, let's march out of the building single file and go to the play area in the middle of the buildings. The town was west of us. There we saw this big black cloud of smoke, and soon planes were flying over us. By then, we knew this was it.

"At the time of the explosion, my mother, Margaret Bailey, was at a dry cleaners on the west part of Montgomery Street. She was six months pregnant with my little brother. Curtis Wilson, my cousin who ran this dry cleaner shop, had a problem with the old boiler. When the explosion occurred, everybody in the shop hit the floor including my mother. They first thought the boiler had exploded. When people in the neighborhood found out there had been an explosion in town, my mother came to the school and then we all knew the Russians had not bombed us after all. We still felt bad when we learned people had been killed. I still felt scared that night.

"Faye White Williams tells her memories of being in the Empire 5 & 10 Cent Store when the disaster occurred. "My fiance Fred was stationed in the Army in Arizona. He asked me to marry him when he had a few days at home around December 25th. I went to Villa Rica to the Empire 5 & 10 Cent Store to purchase dishes and cookware for us to take back

Explosion in Villa Rica

with us to Arizona. When I arrived at the store in my Dad's car, I parked across the street.

Store layout: "As I entered the front door, there was a shelf on the left side that ran along the wall to the back of the building, and best as I can remember, it was the same way on the right side also. There were countertops with merchandise on them that ran from east to west. At the end of one of the counter tops was a cash register.

"After I had selected some dishes, I carried them to the cash register. The lady was counting my dishes, and I was waiting to pay for them. I was planning to take the dishes to the car and then come back into the store to buy cookware.

"In an instant, it was dark and the top of the building had fallen down. I could not hold my head up straight. I looked up and saw a hole, and through that hole, I could see a small blaze of fire. The lady at the cash register was screaming that her leg was pinned down and that she could not move it. I turned to see if I could help lift the debris and rubble that was on her leg, but there was no way that I could lift the material off her leg. The entire top of the building had fallen down. It was my understanding that some men had to go to the other side of the wall and dig through the wall to get to her. When they got to her she was alive, but unfortunately, she died later.

"It must have been when I saw the blaze of fire that I decided to get out or try to get out. I could not walk out on the floor. Apparently, when the explosion occurred, the counters were pushed against the shelf that was located along the wall. I climbed upon one of the countertops, although I could not stand up straight, while bent over I had just enough room to step from one countertop to the next. I remember hearing the merchandise that once was on top of the counters cracking and crumbling under my feet. When I managed to get to the front of the store, the plate glass was gone and there were broken cement blocks piled on the sidewalk. As I walked out, a man (whose name I think was Jack Thomas) took me by the hand and led me over the broken blocks. Afterwards, I stood on the hill across the road at the railroad track. It was there where I met up with my soon-to-be sister-and-law, Willette Williams. The cap shop where she worked had sustained damage, and they had to evacuate the premises. We watched the building burn.

"It was not until I got out of the building before I found out what had happened. Miraculously, I was not injured. I only had a tiny minor scratch on my leg.

"When my parents heard about the explosion, they had my sister-in-law take them to Villa Rica. While on their way, they were stopped at New Georgia store by the State Patrol. He told them that they could not go to Villa Rica due to an explosion. My mother stated to the patrolman, 'Well, I am going if I have to walk. My daughter is down there.' I imagine

11. Memories, Stories, and Affidavits

there was more conversation than that, but anyway, after the state patrol learned the reason they needed to go to Villa Rica, he let them go. I was thankful that I had parked my Dad's car across the street from the store. If I had parked on the other side next to the store, the car would have been demolished. I went home with my sister-in-law and my parents planned to drive my Dad's car home, but due to the rubble in the street and the emergency vehicles, my parents had to hire a taxi to take them home.

"I thank God for the wonderful blessing that I survived that day. This was just one of the many blessing God has given me."

Memories of Perry "Bill" Bailey: Perry Bailey, who was five-years-old at the time of the explosion and the son of Olin and Ruth Bailey who lived down Stockmar Road. His memories of that day has stayed with him for a lifetime: "It was an ordinary day as my dad came in from his job at American Thread in Tallapoosa. After we all ate a big breakfast, my brother, Andy, caught the bus to go to school to his sixth grade class. Then after my dad and my older brother, Jimmy, who worked second shift at Brown Hosiery Mill, did a few chores, we loaded up to go to town. Dad, Jimmy, and I got into our green 1954 Ford, and we headed to Villa Rica to pick up a prescription for my mom, Ruth. We left my mom and my baby brother, Douglas, at home. As a five-year-old I felt an excitement and thrill of getting to go to town and ride in the backseat anticipating what Dad might buy for me.

"I remember vaguely being in front of the drugstore, parked, as my Dad went to pick up the prescription. Jimmy and I sat there the short time and waited. I hoped that Dad would buy me a candy bar like he did sometimes.

"In a few minutes Dad came back, got into the car, and handed me a small bag. As I went through the bag, I found a small shaving mirror, my hoped-for candy bar, and Mom's prescription. Jimmy and Dad were talking about smelling gas. As we pulled out and headed toward home, I ate my candy bar and listened to them. Dad had said, 'As I was paying, I talked to Margaret Berry and asked her about the gas smell. Her reply was that they were supposed to be working on it. I had noticed when I went in that the pharmacy doors were open—I guess to let the gas smell out. I then said to Margaret. Berry that it would be dangerous if somebody came into the pharmacy smoking. Mrs. Berry replied, 'I didn't think about that but you're right.' Dad then told Jimmy that he knew people smoked in the sandwich bar area because there were ashtrays on the counter.

"As we went toward the Dallas Highway, we were almost to Walker Street when we heard a loud boom. It was like the whole ground shook. I heard my Dad say, 'What was

Explosion in Villa Rica

that?'

" My brother said, 'I don't know. Did you blow out a tire?'

"My Dad said, 'No, something has happened.' Dad pulled off on the side of the road. Both he and Jimmy got out and looked back toward town.

"I remember climbing up on the seat, looking out the back window, watching my dad and brother pointing their fingers upward toward the sky over the town we just left. They were pointing toward all the black smoke that had covered the town like a cloud. My dad and brother rushed to the car, got in, and we drove home rather than back toward town to see what had happened. Jimmy asked Dad, 'Reckon what happened?' Dad said he didn't know but that something terrible had happened. He then said, 'I'm afraid Villa Rica is gone.'

"When we got home, Dad told Mom about the big boom and the smoke, and we all decided to go back to town to see what happened. As we neared town we heard the siren that went off only every Wednesday at noon, at dinner time. If it blew at any other time, it was a signal for the Volunteer Fire Department that there was a fire. We got as close to town as the Pure Station and across the street, J & J Auto Garage. We got out of the car to walk. All I could see was a bunch of people walking and pointing toward the drugstore and lots of smoke. Some people were crying, some were scared, and we began to see ambulances coming through the crowd and across the tracks, at the depot crossing, passing us on their way to Villa Rica Hospital.

"My Mother and Daddy were asking people what happened and of course they were told that one of the stores blew up but they didn't know which one. We could see debris everywhere in downtown and bricks were thrown from the explosion as far as J & J Garage and the Pure Gas Station where we were. My brother Jimmy later told me he could remember hearing people screaming in the area where the explosion took place. I remember my dad crying and telling people that we had just left the drugstore and were driving home on Dallas Highway when it happened. He told them about smelling the gas and what he had said to Margaret Berry.

"Then we heard that school had been let out early. So we walked to the elementary school and picked up my brother, Andy. We then went back to the Pure Gas Station to see if we could find out who had been hurt or killed. The Civil Defense would not let you cross the tracks or get close to the site. They closed off this part of Villa Rica and would not let the trains through because they would block the tracks and might delay an ambulance in getting to the hospital. My dad and Jimmy offered to volunteer and were told that they had

11. Memories, Stories, and Affidavits

more rescue people coming in from other towns, but thanked my dad and brother for their offer to help.

"After a long time, we went home and had only to turn on television to watch and hear about what had taken place on that tragic day. My Dad had been trading with Berry's Pharmacy for a good while and knew the people. He kept saying, 'I can't believe it. I was just talking to Margaret Berry and now she's gone.' It was a sad day indeed for our little town. The shaving mirror that my Dad purchased from Berry's Pharmacy when Margaret Berry waited on him—we kept it, seems like forever. But no one knows where that mirror is today."

One of the unsung heros of the day was Louis Harris. Louis worked with Horace Luther, the Superintendent of the Water and Sewer Authority. Louis was on the scene immediately after the gas explosion occurred. This local man worked to pull several people out of the burning buildings. When he saw that someone had put their foot through the debris, he pulled them out by grabbing onto their leg in spite of danger to himself. He became a kind of local hero because of how long he stayed at the scene and how hard he worked. Louis is credited in stopping the gas flow from the power station to Villa Rica after the explosion. He put so much brave effort into saving others that he stayed until late to help clear the debris and haul it to the two sites where it was dumped. After working for the city in the water department, Louis served as fireman and then was the first black policeman in Villa Rica. While working at the fire department Louis lost several fingers and because of this disability he could only work part time for the city and did so until he retired.

12

The Days After the Tragedy

*In this close-knit small town of Villa Rica, there was not one church
that had not lost a member or had a member who lost a loved-one.*
Elaine Bailey, author

On Friday morning December 6, at 8:00 o'clock, work resumed at the demolished business district of Villa Rica. National Guardsmen and county prisoners began final clearing operations at the scene of the blast. Lieutenant Colonel H. T. Clary, Guard commander, said that apparently all bodies in the wreckage had been found. More help had come, but it was not until late afternoon that the debris was cleared and the crowd began to disassemble. The National Guard, Red Cross and Civil Defense pulled out about 2:00 o'clock in the afternoon. Others worked on until dark.

Emergency crews that had worked around the clock through Friday had all gone. The death toll was officially put at twelve. Different figures were published for the injured. About twenty were injured in the initial blast, but many were injured in the rescue effort. The highest estimate of both the injured at the time of the explosion and in the rescue effort came to thirty-four.

The gas service, which had been turned off approximately forty-five minutes after the blast and had left businesses and homes without heat was restored by late Friday. The work of turning on meters and lighting appliances that had begun during the evening on Thursday had continued until about 3:30 in the morning on Friday, December 6. Early Friday morning this work had resumed at 6:00 o'clock and continued until mid afternoon. By then meters and appliances had been turned on at all residences and businesses to which entry could be gained.

The loose merchandise that had been blown out in the street and had been moved into another store building in the business district had mostly been salvaged and reclaimed. A great deal of merchandise had been destroyed in the blast.

All long distance phone calls to the city continued to be tied up for a long period of time, as people who had relatives here were still trying to contact them to find out if they were safe.

"Villa Rica is far from back to normal." Mayor Griffin stated, "It will take some time for that."

The town was numbed, first in tragedy, now in grief. So many family members and acquaintances were in shock from the deaths of the twelve who died in the explosion.

On Friday, December 6, funerals were held for Rozelle Johnson; Bobby Roberts; Carolyn Davis; and a double funeral was held for O.T. Dyer and Johnny Dyer. Carl Vitner was buried in Atlanta.

On Saturday, December 7, the townspeople, acquaintances, and loved-ones of the deceased had more funerals to attend: those of Rob Broom, Oscar Hixon, and Ann Pope Smith. Dr. Jack Burnham was buried in Austell and Kenneth Hendrix was buried at Redoak, Georgia in Fulton County.

Also on Saturday, December 7, Mayor C. M. Griffin reported that the work of clearing rubble from the shattered remains of the four stores had been completed.

Three Days Later—On Sunday, December 8, 1957, funeral services were held for Margaret Berry. Just when townspeople and loved-ones thought they could stand no more grief and heartache, their beloved Margaret was buried on Sunday. She was the last to be buried of those who had perished.

On Monday, December 9, 1957, police estimated that 10,000 people had come to town Saturday and Sunday to see the scene of the disaster. The streets of the city and all highways leading into town had been jammed with non-stop traffic the entire weekend. Those attending the funerals were caught in the long lines.

After the funerals the townspeople were still filled with grief and disbelief as they quietly went to their homes to think about the events that had taken place over the last couple of days. They knew "life goes on" but it would be a struggle for many of them to try and resume a normal life when their hearts were breaking for the loss of a loved-one.

Bob Broom found out about the explosion the day after it happened. "At the time

12. The Days After the Tragedy

of the explosion, I was stationed in Baumhoulder, Germany. The explosion happened on Thursday and I read about it in Friday's *Stars and Stripes,* a military newspaper. Sue Leathers Pope, my first cousin from Villa Rica, who lived twelve miles away in Ida Obersteine, Germany with her husband also heard about the explosion and came over to see me on Friday night about 5:00 o'clock. She was very worried about her relatives who owned a service station in Villa Rica. She was afraid they might have been in town and could have been killed. I told her I had not worried at all as I knew my Dad, Rob Broom, who worked at Cannon Casket Company outside town, would be no where close to the explosion on a weekday morning."

"The next day, my company commander came to me and said I had a cablegram from the Red Cross office. It was bad news. I learned my dad, Robert L. Broom had been killed. I found out later he was a customer at the pharmacy picking up a prescription for my older sister, Mildred, who was staying at his house recovering from an operation.

"Sue Leathers Pope, my first cousin there in Germany, learned that one of her other first cousins, Ann Pope Smith, had also been killed that day. So Sue had lost an uncle, my Dad—Rob, and a first cousin, Ann, in the explosion.

One week after the explosion on Thursday, December 12, 1957, Bob Broom came home from Germany. A Greyhound bus coming from Atlanta at 3:00 o'clock in the morning stopped in the middle of the highway in Villa Rica for all the passengers to view the gaping hole where there was once thriving businesses. Bob Broom looked out the window of the bus to view the scene where his dad, Robert "Rob" Broom, had died seven days earlier. Bob had not made it home from Germany for his dad's funeral, which was held the previous Saturday.

Bob rode the bus on to Anniston, Alabama to be with his wife and two sons, but came back into town later that day to be with his mother, Eva, and his sister, Mildred.

In the Villa Rican newspaper on December 11, 1957, Robby Robison and Charles Williamson, wrote an editorial titled "Out of the Ashes."

"From all parts of the nation since Thursday morning the people of America have expressed sympathy for the people of Villa Rica. Manifested in a myriad way these heartwarming expressions have poured in by the thousands—through newspapers, television and radio, telegrams and letters; through personal contact, through gifts of money and supplies.

"Within minutes after the disaster, Villa Rica was no longer just a small town on

Explosion in Villa Rica

the map, located on the Southern Railway and Highway 78, between Atlanta and Birmingham. Villa Rica was a grief-stricken neighbor of the entire nation.

"Every heart in our town filled with gratitude for the response that came so quickly to our call for help. And deep in every grateful heart was born a new feeling—a feeling of dependency on each other and on our neighbors, as once again it was brought home to us that no person or group of persons can live alone.

"Again and again from our people of the Villa Rica community has come the same message, 'Thank God for our hospital! If only it had been large enough to take care of all the victims.'

"And so out of Thursday was born not only gratitude and a feeling of dependency, but a sense of need—need for a larger hospital with more beds, more medical and surgical facilities, more space to store medical and surgical supplies.

"Few towns the size of Villa Rica are fortunate enough to have the expert medical and nursing facilities which the people of our community have had for some time. Yet as fine as our hospital is, it was not sufficiently large to care for all those who needed it on Thursday morning.

"For months the Villa Rica Hospital Authority has been sorely aware of the necessity for an additional to the hospital. Some time ago tentative plans were drawn and approved, and application was made for enlargement. This application is still pending, due to lack of funds.

"On Thursday morning a few patients had been dismissed—sufficiently recovered

"It CAN Happen Here."

The Atlanta Journal December 1957
Courtesy Spencer Crawford.

12. The Days After the Tragedy

to return to their home. By 10:30 the six vacant beds were prepared to receive patients already on the admission waiting list—sick people of our community badly in need of hospitalization. The hospital staff alerted at all times for any emergency night or day, were prepared when the emergency came. The supply room was well stocked with both medical and surgical supplies. But the six beds were not enough; the medical and surgical supplies were not sufficient—because the hospital was not large enough.

"Out of Thursday, too, was born still another need, and another, and another. Out of Thursday came the realization that Villa Rica needs more than a Volunteer Fire Department. The men who make up our Volunteer Fire Department together with volunteer citizens, both white and negro, did a herculean job, as they have done time and time again. Risking their lives to save the lives and property of others, no firemen could have done more—with the equipment at hand.

"And out of Thursday, too, came the realization that Villa Rica needs a Civil Defense organization, prepared at all times to go into action at a moment's notice. Plans for Civil Defense were under way. The Chamber of Commerce, The Villa Rican, The City Council, The Civitan Club, had all fostered it. Such a plan needed only the backing of the citizenry. A few civic-minded citizens could not alone carry the whole load of the Civil Defense.

The Atlanta Journal December 1957

Photo Courtesy Spencer Crawford.

Explosion in Villa Rica

"Who is at fault that Villa Rica lacked so many of the things it needed on Thursday morning? The people are at fault—ALL the people.

"For years Villa Rica has been like a growing boy who, upon reaching young manhood, continues to wear the trousers of an adolescent. Blinded by selfishness, nurtured factions, steeped in petty politics, fearful of competition, with minds centered only on the present with no thought for the future, we have allowed our town to become static while progress moved to other places more willing to receive it.

"For years while we have bickered among ourselves, new industries have passed us by, our streets have gone unrepaired, our fire department remained volunteer, our Civil Defense remained unorganized, our schools and even some of our church buildings have become out-dated, all because our people lacked unity.

"Although our Mayor and Council have repeatedly warned us that our town was without sufficient funds, we as citizens have shouted to High Heaven our disapproval of higher taxes! Then as the furor subsided we returned to our complacency—until Thursday.

"Out of the ashes of every great disaster a better community has invariably risen. After every great fire, after every great flood, after every great storm, in which lives were lost—after disaster and death and destruction—only then it seems the people begin to Think!

"And so it will be with Villa Rica! Lives that have been lost can never be reclaimed. The wounds of the injured will heal—but the scars will remain, on the heart and conscience of the people.

"Villa Rica will build again. But as the bricks are laid into place, what of the people of Villa Rica? Will we simply look on while the burned stores are rebuilt, or will we unite to build a better community?

"Thursday brought to Villa Rica more than disaster and the loss of life. The siren which signaled that disaster and woke our people from their lethargy to the realization of many material needs, brought, too, the realization of a need even greater—the NEED FOR UNITY AND FOR MORAL AND SPIRITUAL GROWTH.

"In time our material needs will be fulfilled. New stores will soon replace those destroyed. With new fire fighting equipment, the savings on fire insurance alone will in time take care of the cost of a paid fire department. A Civil Defense organization will shortly be formed. An addition to the hospital is already tentatively planned.

"It has been said that 'The lowest ebb is the turn of the tide.' Villa Rica reached its

12. The Days After the Tragedy

lowest ebb on Thursday. Pray God, it brought with it a turn of the tide! A community more closely knit, pulling together for the future good of our town and our people! A community, more alert to our dependence upon each other, pulling together to acquire the material benefits for the protection of lives and property! A community, pulling together for the moral and spiritual growth of our people!"

Little by little as the days and weeks passed, the people recovered from their shock and grief. The newspaper articles each week kept them informed of those injured and still in the hospital. There were also news of stores reopening. There were plans for recovery in many phases of life in Villa Rica. But some of the newspaper articles brought unexpected and unwelcome news:

From a newspaper article on Tuesday, December 10, 1957, came an account of the status of those still in the hospital. Almost two weeks later, six of those burned in the explosion were still in the hospital with second and third degree burns. In the Villa Rica Hospital: Shirley Whitworth and Homer Vaughn were listed in "serious" condition; Ralph Fuller and Ray Tyson were in "fair" condition. Bill Berry was released on Monday, December 9th but was still recovering from injuries received and planned on going back to the job in the near future.

Preston Lancaster, a patient at the Bremen Hospital, was listed in "fair" condition with second and third degree burns. Don Bohannan was still at the Ft. Oglethorpe Hospital in Chickamauga, Georgia in "fair" condition.

Melinda Hembree and Camille Adams were released from Tanner Memorial Hospital in Carrollton. Camille Adams suffered from burns on the legs and has not been able to return to work.

On Tuesday December 10, 1957, Mayor C. M. Griffin made a statement to the local newspaper, The Villa Rican, that an official investigation would be made. "The State Fire Marshall F. E. Roberson came to Villa Rica the previous Saturday with the investigator from the National Fire Prevention organization. The officials made a thorough investigation and the city has made request for the results of the investigation." The Mayor said that there seems to be little doubt that the explosion was caused by natural gas.

Mayor Camp's article continued, "It is apparent that it was caused by an accumulation of gas, but no one knows details of where it was accumulated and what ignited it. A gas expert in Atlanta said explosions from gas as large as the one in Villa Rica are rare. 'The main factor in gas explosions,' the expert said, 'is the concentration of the gas in any given space, with the size of the space and the amount of the gas, the important things. The amount of ventilation is another factor.'"

Then in a local newspaper article came the announcement of plans by the owners of the demolished shops to reopen at temporary locations in the near future. Cliff Reeves announced that he and his wife, Eunice Reeves, planned to reopen Reeves Jewelry several stores down from the ruined location—at the west end of town until rebuilding could be done. He said he had only four thousand dollars in insurance and this would not cover even his fixtures. He did not know what the loss was, but it was tremendous. He said that he would receive help from the Retail Jewelers Association and his jewelry friends. The account books for the store were saved.

Amazing as it seemed, some of the lay-a-way packages recovered from the site were in good condition and customers would be able to pick these up at the reopening, the date of which would be announced soon. Reeves said he would be happy to accept any payments from customers on accounts at the new location during or after the reopening.

Charlotte Reeves Harrison, owner and manager of the Villa Rica Florist Shop planned to reopen at the Reeves' location with them. Charlotte stated that the florist suffered a total loss. There was no insurance, but she had been promised some help from the Florist Association and florist friends throughout the country.

The A & B Dress Shop planned to reopen as soon as possible in the building formerly occupied by the Villa Rica Trading Post. The dress shop was only half covered by insurance and they had been carrying the largest inventory of their fourteen years of business. Some of the Christmas lay-a-ways were recovered and would be available to pick up as soon as possible.

The Empire 5 & 10 Store was a total loss and no plans had been announced yet by "Red" Harris the owner of the store.

Jack Williams who owned the Tri-County Clothing Company stated in the local newspaper article that the date had not been set to reopen. The building had been badly damaged. The windows had been replaced, walls had been patched, but the top right hand corner of the facade still needed to be repaired.

James Harrison, pharmacist at Berry's Pharmacy, planned to reopen a prescription shop on Friday, December 13. James would be on duty to fill prescriptions. John Bailey and Bud Streetman would help him open and work there until a building could be built for the Berry Pharmacy at the original site.

On December 12, 1957, victims who were injured in some way or burned in the

12. The Days After the Tragedy

explosion, found out they were covered by benefits. The Social Security Office in Atlanta sent a representative to Villa Rica City Hall on Thursday, December 12 to answer questions and to aid those affected families in filling out applications for benefits. Most of the fatalities in the Villa Rica explosion were covered by federal old age and survivors insurance.

On Monday and Tuesday December 16 and 17 The Villa Rica and Sandhill Schools were closed to advert another disaster after some persons had reported "smelling gas fumes."

According to the local newspaper, J. Z. "Zeb" Morris, the principal of the high school, said, "The three gas lines serving the school buildings were checked during the weekend." Horace Luther, City Engineer, discovered the leakage in the heating system on Sunday afternoon. The detection was made by the use of the newly purchased "explosion meter" which is a device for detecting gas leakage. Fifteen pounds of pressure were put on the lines late Monday afternoon, and by 10:00 o'clock that night, the pressure had decreased to about five pounds. This indicated that there was still loss of gas from the lines or the connections in the furnace. Leaks were discovered in the boiler room in the high school and in the gas heater in one of the three sixth-grade classroom. Some leakage was found on the outside of the gymnasium. Morris reported there was not much danger since the leaks were in places that had ample ventilation.

All connections were inspected and tightened by the Daniel Boone Heating Company of Newnan, Sunday afternoon. Floor heaters in the three sixth-grades were replaced with new ceiling heaters. The city engineer again used the "explosion meter" and no gas was detected. The Atlanta Fire Marshall was asked to come out and make a final safety inspection. This inspection was made early on Tuesday morning. The heating plant and all lines and equipment has been declared safe. New heaters had been installed in the classrooms which were in the old canning building where the public came to can vegetables in the summer. These new units were ceiling heaters of the latest type. Zeb Morris, the principal, stated that the experts had approved all heating facilities at the school. "We are following the fire marshal's suggestions to the letter," Morris said.

Two and a half weeks after the explosion, on December 18, 1957, a twenty-five foot Christmas tree that had been ordered several weeks before by Oscar Hixon was put up in town across the tracks in front of the train depot. This was the largest Christmas tree the town had ever had, and it was decorated as the Christmas tree had been each year. But this year, Christmas lights were hung cheerlessly above the ruins where the explosion had taken twelve lives, and the ugly scar of ruined buildings lay spread on the streets. But the real scar

Explosion in Villa Rica

went much deeper and for much longer than this Christmas season. A cloud of sorrow lay over the rustic Georgia town. It was going to be difficult to have the usual holiday cheer.

A clerk in a nearby store told a customer, "It will be a sad Christmas in this town. Nearly everybody lost a relative or close friend."

By now the hollowed-out group of buildings had been cleared of the smouldering bricks and charred timbers. The row of shops in the surrounding blocks had been cleaned and dusted. The shelves and merchandise had been straightened. Most store fronts had new glass in the windows.

Ralph Fuller, who had been in Berry's in the snack area at the time of the explosion, was back at his job at the barbershop a few doors down from where the accident took place. He had stayed in the hospital for four days and then had gone back to work. He said to a customer as he pulled up his shirt sleeves and showed a customer the bad scars on his arms, "I was one of the lucky one."

Three blocks away at Oscar Hixon's home, a representative from the Social Security office brought Mildred Hixon a check covering death benefits for her husband. Her small children Judy, Jim, and John gathered around her. Life moves on. Families most affected by this catastrophe were picking up the broken pieces and were moving ahead.

Six doors down from the Hixon home on Westview Street, Johnny Dyer's young widow, Winnie, visited her parents, Fate and Nellie Leathers. Winnie and Johnny had already bought toys for their daughter, Marion Ann, age two-and-a-half, before the accident. Winnie told her parents, "I've picked out a small tree. It's not as big as the one we usually have."

Porter DeFoor and Mrs. Boots Griffis and her friends brought all the presents the little girl needed for Christmas. Everyone made sure Marion Ann had a happy holiday."

Across town at the Villa Rica Hospital, three patients were still in the hospital but were doing well. Ray Tyson's condition was reported "much improved." Homer Vaughn had been in serious condition but was improving. Shirley Whitworth, the eighteen-year-old girl from the Empire 5 & 10 Cent Store who had been burned badly in Berry's, had been told she could go home for a few hours on Christmas day. She was hoping it would not be long until she could go home for good. Her long blond hair that was cropped to the scalp had started to grow a little. Her legs were still badly burned but the burns on her face and arms had cleared up in the last three weeks without leaving scars and the doctors said she was getting along fine.

Ray Tyson had spent the last three weeks recovering from his back surgery, and from the burns and injuries sustained in the explosion. "This was the worst thing that ever

12. The Days After the Tragedy

happened to me," he told a newspaper reporter. "I lost my money that day; my car was demolished, and I was seriously burned and injured."

On December 21, a special election was held at City Hall, for the mayor and for a councilmen seat in Wards 1 and 2. The election had been originally slated for December 5 when the explosion occurred. At the time of the blast, about 11:00 o'clock, only seventy-six votes had been cast. These ballots were then locked up at the Villa Rica City Hall to be destroyed. The ballot in the special election read as follows: For Mayor—C. M. "Charlie" Griffin; For Ward 1—Herman Newell and Frank Black; For Ward 2—H. Grady Brown.

By Saturday, December 21, there were building plans—the talk around town was that the four stores destroyed in the blast would soon be rebuilt. As the months went by, the citizens of Villa Rica demonstrated resilience and lost no time in rebuilding what had been lost.

By June of 1958, Bill Berry opened one of the most modern drug stores in west Georgia in the same location as the pharmacy that had been destroyed. This new Rexall Drug Store was thirty-by-one-hundred feet, had an all glass front, all new fixtures, was air conditioned, and had a complete new stock of drugs and sundries. A new soda fountain was planned to open two months later at the Grand Opening.

Things would never quite be the same around Villa Rica, but its citizens realized that progress had to go on and that time makes some things a little easier. This small town was gradually making a come-back.

13

New Organizations

News of this catastrophic disaster spread around the world.
The Villa Rican, December 18, 1957

Letters and articles ran in the The Villa Rican, the local paper, for the next several weeks after the explosion explaining the needs of the victims' families. Within days after the explosion The Villa Rica Relief Fund was set up for these families.

The Villa Rican kept residents informed as to the needs and to the donations that came: "This week several donations have been received by Villa Rica Hospital through church groups and individuals, who stated that they wished to help defray expenses of some of the victims who were injured in the disaster of December 5th. The total received to date is $348.67.

"The Hospital Authority would like for the people of our community, and in particular those who so generously sent their donations, to know that your dollars will be carefully and wisely used.

"The hospital has made no charge for the treatment of out-patients who were injured in the explosion and fire or injured in rescue work. Some of these brave citizens are still being treated for burns and other injuries received that day. Hence a portion of this fund will be used to cover the actual cost of tetanus shots, drugs, and dressings for those who were cared for among the injured but who did not require hospitalization.

"The remainder of the fund will be pro-rated as needed among the injured who were hospitalized. If you would like to contribute to this fund as a part of your Christmas

Explosion in Villa Rica

giving, please mail or bring your donation to the Villa Rica Hospital, or to any member of the City of Villa Rica Hospital Authority: Herman Holloway, Sr, Chairman; Robert Jeffers, Vice-Chairman; John B. Bailey, Sr, Treasurer; Jack Lassetter, Secretary; W. D. Tyson, Cliff Reeves, Ray Matthews, Jack Candler, Paul Meek."

Funds began to pour in from all over the nation and abroad as the Associated Press picked up the story of this disaster. Contributions came pouring in even before this letter of appeal appeared in the local newspaper.

Letter of appeal from the Fourth District Post Commanders Adjutants, Child Welfare Chairmen and Service Officers:

"I feel sure all of you are aware of the tragedy that struck Villa Rica this past week. We have been advised by the post at Villa Rica that there is a great and emergent need for financial assistance.

"There is one family in particular—he is a veteran, his wife is unable to work, and they have two small children. He will be hospitalized for at least twelve months from injuries received in this disaster. The local Post has given all they have, and I feel sure all the Posts in the surrounding area would want to help out in this emergency.

"Checks or money orders should be made payable to The Villa Rica Relief Fund and mailed to Felton Hall, Villa Rica, Georgia. Please advise your District Commander, Bill Pitts, McDonough, Georgia, the amount your Post contributes.

"Let's do everything possible to assist these people during this emergency.
Best Wishes,
Sincerely Roy Cousins,
Department Commander."

13. New Organizations

This article printed page after page of letters that poured into Villa Rica from all over the world. Letters of concern, sympathy, support, and regret were received by Mayor Charles Griffin:

"*Mayor Griffin:*

"*Ten years ago my husband and I were marooned in Villa Rica by an ice storm in which several persons were killed. At the time there were no motel, no hotels. The manager of the bus station tried to find a place for us to stay but couldn't.*

"*A citizen of your town (whose name I do not recall) was kind enough to let us spend the night in his house. We have never forgotten that kind act.*

"*Please accept this check for your present disaster.*

Yours,

Mrs. C. M. Griffith,

Yazoo City, Mississippi"

"*James H. Vaughn, Villa Rica Hosiery Mills*

Dear Jim:

"*Joan and I would like to extend our sympathy to the many people in Villa Rica who were bereaved or seriously affected by the disastrous explosion last Thursday. It was a very sad experience for the community of Villa Rica and a great shock to the rest of the nation.*

"*We feel that we are a part of Villa Rica as much as if we lived there, and yet, helpless to help as a good neighbor would. Following a disaster of this type, there is always suffering afterward, and those who need help. We are enclosing a check for $50.00, and we would greatly appreciate your directing it to where it will do some good.*

Sincerely yours,

Joseph C. Smith, Joan Maggio"

Explosion in Villa Rica

"Mrs. J. H. Pope:

Each Christmas I give something to someone I don't know, who is in need. This year my thoughts return to my birthplace. When I read the papers yesterday of the terrible explosion of Villa Rica landmarks it made me very sad, and I am sure it is worse than I can imagine. Will you give Frank my enclosed check and ask him to use it as he sees fit for the 'Needy Blast Victims.'"

Aline Cobb Owens,
St Petersburg, Florida
The check for $100.00 was turned over to the Disaster Relief Fund of the city."

On January 8, 1958 in the local newspaper, Mayor Charlie Griffin reported that the disaster relief fund had reached $656.

In the Villa Rican on March 12, 1958, Mayor Griffin reported that the victims of December 5, 1957 received $6,000 (total) from the Red Cross as relief funds were presented on the basis of need, not loss.

An organization that became much more active after the explosion was the Villa Rica Civil Defense Unit. Three months before the tragedy at the August 28, 1957 City Council meeting, the thought of organizing a Civil Defense unit came up. There was discussion, and a City Council-sponsored Civil Defense organization was formed. Discussion was focused on purchasing equipment and on how to fund this equipment.

The Mayor was Charles M. Griffin; the City Council was made up of Sam Black, Chester Ergle, Hoyte Easterwood, John Bailey, Sr, Jack Candler, Dr. Ernest Powell and Horace O. Luther who was the Superintendent of the Water Department.

There was discussion on the type of equipment to buy, but then the purchase was postponed as the City Council did not see that the funds were available at that time. The city's only firetruck was a 1942 Chevrolet firetruck.

After the explosion, Dr. Ernest Powell, Jr a member of City Council, termed the city's Civil Defense organization "semiactive." We had done a lot of organizational work on Civil Defense," he added. "It's one of those things a lot of smaller towns are working on. We were a little slow realizing what it could mean. I hope this makes a lot of small towns

13. New Organizations

realize what it could do."

Dr. Powell, Jr, who was on the scene minutes after the disaster struck said lives might have been saved with equipment the city's Civil Defense had planned to buy some day. "We could have done a tremendous job those first thirty minutes," said Dr. Powell, Jr, "if there had been more fire and emergency equipment." He mentioned specifically an air compressor and a bulldozer. "Both items," he said, "were on a list of equipment the City Council-sponsored Civil Defense organization knew were desirable and had considered obtaining eventually.

"The air compressor to make holes in walls of adjoining buildings and the bulldozer to push aside the burning debris to get at trapped victims were desperately needed in the

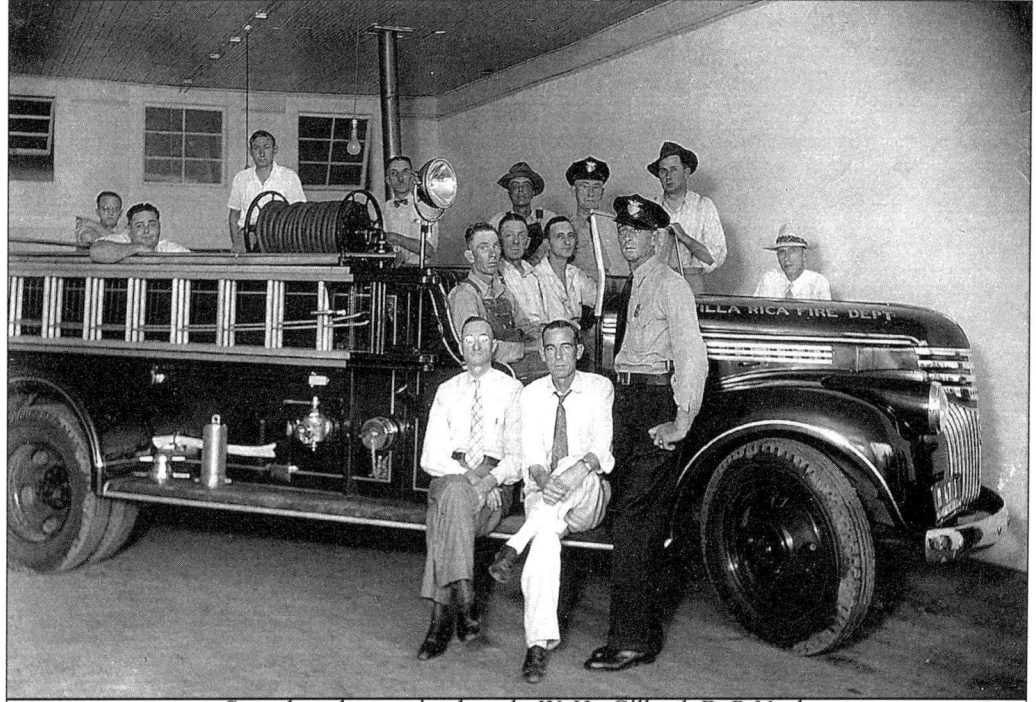

Seated on the running board - W. H. Gilland, B. P. Neal; Standing in front: Horace Luther; seated behind the windshield - Calvin Freeman, Sam Black, Mr. Boyd; Back row - Ralph Smith, A. V. Bilbo, Lewis Talley, H. G. Roberds, Oscar Griffis, R. R. Knight, Loyd Smith and F. S. Pope. Photo courtesy Ted Williamson

first few minutes," he said.

"Could lives have been saved?" he was asked by a newspaper reporter right after the explosion.

"That's hard to answer," Dr. Powell said. Then he added: "But I know one or two could have." He said he talked to either two or three persons who tried to help a woman

Explosion in Villa Rica

trapped in the ten-cent store. He told of holes being knocked in the adjoining Tri-County Clothing Store wall so that water could be sprayed on the trapped person. By the time holes were knocked with hammers, it was too late.

"Another firetruck and much more hose also were badly needed," Dr. Powell said. "Applications have already been made to get a firetruck through the Federal Civil Defense Administration. The City Council decided after discussion to find out where its priority stood and to try to get one another way, if necessary."

About local preparedness, Dr. Powell said, "The thing I kept realizing is that as big as this was, it was small compared with a bomb. If this could cause that much havoc, you can see the need for so much more."

On January 16, 1958, in the first City Council meeting of the new year, fifty new members were present and an active Civil Defense Unit was formed. J. L. "Jack" Grantham, Sr, the state Civil Defense Communications Coordinator, was present at the meeting as an advisor.

W. C. Cole was elected co-chairman of communications of the newly restructured Civil Defense. In later years, W. Cole issued the following statement to the newspaper as a summary of the progress of the Civil Defense.

"The 1957 gas explosion in Villa Rica impacted the city in such a way that a very strong and active Civil Defense Unit was formed that had long-lasting effect on other Civil Defense Units across the state. On the day of the explosion, we realized how handicapped the city was, so we got busy and began to acquire the necessary equipment that could be used in rescue operations. In January 1958, the month following the explosion, Mayor Charles Griffin directed the formation of a robust and well equipped Civil Defense Unit in Villa Rica. In response to the mayor's direction the unit was formed, more than thirty members were recruited, including the auxiliary police. They purchased a lot of surplus equipment such as a jeep, an ambulance, a two-and-a half-ton truck, a weapons carrier, and all kinds of small tools necessary for rescue purposes.

"The Civil Defense unit was organized with Jack Candler as director; Robert Jeffers and W. C. Cole, co-chairmen of communications; J. C. Williamson as radiological chief; J. C. Green and Gordon Byram as rescue co-chiefs.

"The Villa Rica unit became very active and from time to time went all over the state on missions....search and rescue missions, drownings and rescues…in many sections throughout the state.

"The explosion was a major event in the city and led the Civil Defense Unit to

13. New Organizations

become very active, not only in our area, but in many sections throughout the state.

"The actions taken by Villa Rica following the explosion on December 5, 1957 generated increased awareness of the need for ready and capable Civil Defense organizations throughout west Georgia and across the state. The impact of these actions persists today. The CD unit created in 1958 has transitioned over the past half century into what is now the Emergency Management Agency of Carroll County.

"The far reaching impact of the Villa Rica disaster affected Civil Defense Units around the entire country, well into the future."

14

Lawsuits Against Southern Natural Gas Company

"This was a terrible time and although the terrible disaster was years behind us, every court date brought it back to the dinner table of the people of Villa Rica."
Mrs. Sarah Camp, wife of Mayor Paul Camp, 1961

After the town had buried its dead and after the injured began to heal, the investigation into what had caused the blast began to take center stage. The local newspapers and even the *New York Times* reported that the suspected cause had been a faulty gas line. Since many people had reported smelling gas in the days prior to the explosion, it was assumed that there was indeed a leak in the line.

Now the big question was: What really happened and who was at fault? In the following months after the disaster, the City Council heard accusations attempting to place the blame.

The City Council voted unanimously to inspect all the gas lines. With the help of the Department of Public Safety they then began a city-wide inspection of all gas installation and gas appliances. They started with the public buildings, manufacturing plants, and churches. When these were completed, the inspectors went to the homes, checking each installation for faulty venting, safety valves and gas leaks.

If any default was found in the gas installation or appliance, the customer had ten days to correct the problem from the time of inspection. After a second inspection was made,

Explosion in Villa Rica

if the service was still found to be unsafe and dangerous, gas service was discontinued.

A five dollar inspection fee was charged to each gas customer, but the City Council had to reconsider the charge after receiving hundreds of complaints. Later they continued the inspections at no charge to the citizens. The City Council members were unanimous in their attempts to do everything in their power to insure the safety of the community.

When the community seemed to be getting back to normal then the hint of litigations began. A few weeks after the explosion, insurance companies urged those injured and those who lost loved-ones to start law suit proceedings. A lawyer came to Donald Willis' house and asked if he wanted to sue. Donald Willis who worked in the cabinet shop across at an angle from Reeves' had been hurt when he rescued Camille Adams. The lawyer said that he had a good case. Donald Willis told him "no." He was there to help and so many others got hurt worse than he did that he wasn't going to sue anyone.

When eight property damage suits were filed in Superior Court against Dr. William L. "Bill" Berry, of Berry's Pharmacy, the City of Villa Rica which distributed the natural gas, and Southern Natural Gas which supplied the natural gas, many of the property owners publicly stated they were unwilling parties to the damage suits and that insurance claims were involved.

When Camille Adams, of A & B Dress Shop filed suit, she released a statement a few days later to the local paper hoping to make it clear that she was not personally interested in suing anybody. She said she had been forced by the insurance company to be named in the suit because of the injuries she received and the total loss of her business. A reporter for the local paper contacted the insurance authority who said that the suits were a "normal action and procedure" following an incident such as the December 1957 disaster.

Bill Berry stated that an insurance company had filed suit against the city of Villa Rica and Southern Natural Gas company without his approval. He moved to have the case dismissed.

One authority on insurance stated the action was a normal procedure when something happens like the December 1957 tragedy. "They call it the use of subrogation rights," the authority stated in the newspaper.

Superior Court Judge Sam. J. Boykin dismissed these charges in a brief hearing Friday, February 27, 1958. It was indicated that at least eleven other suits were pending and that cases resulting from the tragic blast and fire could be in the courts for years. Four cases were on the court calendar for hearing March 13, 1958. Four other suits were on file in Fulton County while three more were filed in Coweta County. Attorneys reported that

14. Lawsuits Against Southern Natural Gas Company

these remaining suits were filed by relatives of persons killed in the explosion.

Citizens of Villa Rica followed the law suits as the latest was printed in the local newspaper, The Villa Rican: "A Federal court in Newnan, Georgia, Saturday awarded a total of $127,940 damages in three of the cases growing out of deaths in the Villa Rica explosion. The three suits were a portion of the eleven such cases to be heard during this year (1958) in Newnan, Atlanta, and Carrollton.

"Two of the three Federal Court (Newnan) suits were filed against the City of Villa Rica, Southern Natural Gas Company, and Bill Berry. Each of these suits asked $250,000 in damages.

"The third suit, seeking $250,000 in damages, was filed against the gas company and Bill Berry. In the three decisions, Bill Berry was not held liable in any of the cases."

O. W. Roberts, Jr from Carrollton was the attorney for the plaintiffs and Boykin and Boykin of Carrollton served the defendants.

The U.S. District Court awarded $27,000 to one plaintiff. She had filed suit in the death of her loved-one. Another plaintiff was awarded $37,000 by the court with the City of Villa Rica and the gas company ordered to pay that amount in the death of her loved-one.

On November 18, 1959, five Villa Rica residents filed suites in Fulton Superior Court asking damages totaling $650,000 because of deaths of their loved-ones in Villa Rica on December 5, 1957.

Southern Natural Gas Co., a Delaware corporation which had an agent in Atlanta, was named as the defendant in five suites. Bill Berry, operating the drugstore destroyed by the explosion, was named defendant in four of the suits, and the City of Villa Rica in one.

The suits were filed by attorneys Joseph L. Llop and Bobby Lee Cook on behalf of two plaintiffs who asked $250,000 each. Three of those injured, each asked for $50,000.

One plaintiff filed the only suit against all three defendants.

All of the plaintiffs except one were in the drugstore when the explosion occurred or had loved-ones killed there. All except one pointed out they were seeking damages for personal injuries incurred in the explosion.

The suits alleged the gas company had knowledge that gas was leaking for several days before the explosion but did not take precautions to stop the leakage. It was also alleged the company knew that Villa Rica was maintaining untrained and unskilled employees in the operation of the gas system.

As reported in the local newspaper, "The town was shocked and citizens were outraged by the lawsuits and accusations. The local government moved quickly to assure citizens that the explosion had been an unforeseeable accident. Still blame was debated all over town in the barber shops and grocery stores. Emotions were stirred again as that terrible day in Villa Rica was discussed and relived by those whose lives had been affected that December morning almost two years before."

In the Federal Courts, 5th Circuit—July 22, 1960, the trial began against the Southern Natural Gas Company. The Honorable William Boyd Sloan was the presiding judge. Attorneys for the plaintiffs, the victims or family of the victims in the Villa Rica explosion, were attorneys Bobby Lee Cook; Joseph L. Llop; Hamilton Lokey; Oscar Roberts; and W. Frank Lawson. Representing the Southern Natural Gas Company were the attorneys Emerson Garner and Hugh Wright.

To begin: the following facts of the contract between Southern Natural Gas Company and the City of Villa Rica was made known. Under the December 29, 1953 and July 16, 1954, Natural Gas Act (15 U.S.C.A.717 et seq.) the Federal Power Commission legally authorized Southern Natural Gas Co., 'a natural gas company within the meaning', to began selling gas to Villa Rica in 1954. The Southern Natural Gas Company was ordered to serve the City of Villa Rica, Georgia, which was a 'municipal corporation' which was engaging in the local distribution of natural gas. Southern Natural Gas Company was to deliver natural gas to a point about six and one-half miles south of Villa Rica (at Sandhill), and it has since continued to do so pursuant to the contract which, providing for quantities and cost of gas and fixing the place of delivery as above.

'Purchaser' (City of Villa Rica) shall also construct, maintain and operate pressure regulating equipment of standard type for the purpose of reducing the pressure of gas as delivered by 'Company' (Southern Natural Gas Company) to a pressure suitable for introduction into Purchaser's system and an odorizing plant to introduce a warning odor into the gas after delivery by the 'Company.'

The summation of the trial is as follows: "Appellant, Southern Natural Gas, is here urging upon us that, under the undisputed facts, it was under no duty to odorize the gas and, therefore, was not responsible for the negligence, if any, of the City of Villa Rica, or any other person, in respect thereto and a verdict should be directed for it.

"It is equally settled law that Southern having sold, and Villa Rica having purchased, the gas with knowledge on the part of both that Villa Rica should and would odorize the gas, and, under the undisputed evidence it has made provision to do so, Southern was under no duty to odorize it and was not responsible for the explosion and the damages caused by it.

"Meeting all of appellees' contentions head on, including the contention that there

14. Lawsuits Against Southern Natural Gas Company

is adequate proof that the gas was not odorized. Southern argues that, since there was positive evidence that the gas was odorized and none that it was not, and the only reliance of appellees to support their position that it was not is on the opinion testimony of some of the witnesses that they did not smell gas. The case is one of an attempt by negative evidence to overcome positive evidence, and in Georgia this cannot be done. In support it cites: Georgia Code, 38-11, which provides:

"The existence of a fact testified to by one positive witness is to be believed, rather than that such fact did not exist because many witnesses who had the same opportunity of observation swear that they did not see or know of its having existed.

"Arguing in further support of this contention, that when the evidence taken as a whole is considered in the light of the undisputed evidence (presented by experts) that if the leaking gas was not in the atmosphere of the drugstore but was underneath its floor or under the floor of the shop next door and was properly odorized it could not have been smelled until it came into the store and into contact with the nostrils of the witnesses, it insists that the finding of the jury, if it did so find that the gas was not odorized, was without evidence to support it and was based only on surmise and suspicion.

"… Southern could presume that Villa Rica's gas system and its personnel were such that it could and would properly deal with the gas, and further, that, absent such knowledge, Southern had no duty to inspect Villa Rica's system or personnel . . .

"… Appellant takes its stand firmly on the proposition that a wholesaler supplier of gas to a local retailer has no duty to the ultimate consumer to odorize it where the supplier has no reason to believe that the gas will reach the consumer unodorized. . . .

"… The subsequent negligence of the City of Villa Rica was the independent, intervening and proximate cause which, superseding Southern's negligence, was in law the responsible cause."

Frank Bennett, witness for defendant Southern Natural Gas Company, testified in part and in substance as follows: "I live in Atlanta, Georgia, and am an engineer for the Atlanta Gas Light Company. I am in charge of engineering design for odorization plants, orifice meters for such plants, and telemetering equipment. The Atlanta Gas Light Company is a privately owned distribution company, distributing natural gas in some 30 to 35 communities in Georgia. I have been employed by this company for 19 years. I was educated at Georgia Tech, with a B.S. degree in mechanical engineering, and I have been to two schools for gas measurement, which included odorization as part of the curriculum. I am familiar with odorizing substance put in natural gas. Natural gas has no appreciable odor and, in order to give an indication that gas is present in the atmosphere, a malodorant is put into it to give it an odor that can be detected... The Villa Rica odorizing station at Sandhill has a Peerless odorizer... It is considered to be far superior to any other odorizer that is manufactured.

"It is impossible to tell the concentration of gas merely by the smell. When one smells gas, he cannot judge that the gas he is smelling is either lower or higher than the explosive limit. All you know is that you smell gas... I would say that odorized natural gas smells like most raw petroleum products such as diesel fuel oil, kerosene, and similar products. Generally speaking, one gets a lot of different opinions as to what odorized gas smells like. The higher the concentration of odorized gas in the air, the stronger the odor will be noticed...

"The question concerning a drugstore of about thirty by one hundred feet with a front door or two front doors which swing in and out and a back door and back window, ... several people had smelled natural gas in and about the store, and they had smelled it intermittently and not continuously by those in the store, and before the explosion occurred customers going in and out of the store opened and closed the front door and the back door and windows were opened for 45 minutes to one hour a short time before the explosion. My opinion would be that the gas they did smell would not necessarily be improperly odorized. This is true because there are many factors other than the amount of odorant in the gas that have a bearing on the smell.

"One point is the amount of gas that is in the air in the store which would be changing when the ventilation occurred. Another point is that the sense of smell of individuals differ in regard to detecting the odor of gas. Another point is that remaining in the presence of the odor will develop an immunity or numbness or desensitivity of the nerves which are in the nose. If one stays in an odor for any length of time, the strength of the odor decreases. Of course, to smell odorized gas, it has to go into the nostrils. If a breath of fresh air comes along and blows the odorant in it, a greater concentration of that gas will give a stronger smell than a lower concentration. If gas is escaping in a building and building up in concentration starting on Wednesday and increasing to Thursday, and if you have a confined space with no ventilation, the strength of the odor should increase. But if there are doors and windows and other means of ventilation and the place is ventilated, during the period of ventilation the concentration will go down."

Charges were dropped against the defendant: The Southern Natural Gas Company.

15

Lawsuits Against Dr. William L. "Bill" Berry

"Did you at any time undertake to ventilate your premises that morning?"
"We opened the back doors, back windows and the…
double front doors of the pharmacy."
From Bill Berry's testimony, 1960

In the Federal Court hearings, 5th Circuit, at Newnan, Georgia that began on July 22, 1960, charges were brought against Dr. William L. "Bill" Berry by plaintiffs, those involved in the explosion or on behalf of those killed in the explosion. The Honorable William Boyd Sloan was the presiding judge. Attorneys for the plaintiffs were Bobby Lee Cook; Joseph L. Llop; Hamilton Lokey; Oscar Roberts; and W. Frank Lawson. Attorney for the defendant were N. Cook Barwick, T. I. Bentley, and Shirley C. Boykin.

Extensive testimony was given in a step-by-step retracing the events of Monday, December 2; Tuesday, December 3; Wednesday, December 4; and the morning of Thursday, December 5, 1957. The hope was to find the cause of the explosion and why it occurred. Testimony was given in defense of Bill Berry and plaintiff's lawyers cross examined each witness.

It was established by expert witnesses in the field of gas who gave evidence that the floor of the pharmacy splintered upward indicating the gas was in the crawl space underneath the pharmacy. This was confirmed when those victims who survived testified to being blown upward. The several expert witnesses who testified came to a strongly indicated conclusion based on the collective testimony of Don Bohannan, Bill Berry, M.D. Henslee, and especially Ray Tyson. The eye witnesses' testimonies and other evidence strongly pointed to the source of one of the leaks. This leak was in the heater line that went from underneath the floor up into the ceiling heater then on up to the two heaters in Dr. Burnham's office on the second floor of the pharmacy building.

At the instance of the initial explosion there was the appearance of a sudden puff or a tall cloud of black smoke in the area of the overhead heater, indicating that the adjacent chimney was probably stopped up. Both the hot water heater and the overhead hanging heater vented into this chimney. This probably explained the smell of backdraft and masked the smell of the odorized natural gas. This black puff of smoke came an instant before a yellow-orange or red flash of flame came from the rear of the pharmacy.

Then Ralph Fuller, who had been taking a coffee break in the snack bar before the explosion occurred, was called to testify. Ralph testified to being thrown against the left or east wall of the snack bar area which was located down a few steps and in the back right side of the pharmacy. This would indicate to the experts at the trial that gas also exploded from under the A & B Dress Shop west (to the right) of the pharmacy. A secondary explosion happened when the gas pipes in question ruptured. No one will ever know if this same leak was the one detected earlier in the A & B Dress Shop or if the escaping gas from underneath the crawl space (of the dress shop) came from this same, or another source.

It was also brought out that M.D. Henslee went upstairs to check Dr. Burnham's heaters with a lighted straw. When he checked the heater in the reception area and the heater in Dr. Burnham's dental office, he found the one in Dr. Burnham's office to have a small leak. He testified that he cut that heater off about 10:30 that morning. Were the leaks there significant to also be part of the explosion? If so, there was gas from three sources: underneath the pipe of the overhead heater in the crawl space under Berrys; under the A & B Dress Shop; and also some amount—small or large—upstairs in Dr. Burnham's office.

It was also emphasized that for an explosion to happen, there had to be just the right mixture of gas and air and then an ignition. There would have to be five percent natural gas and ninety-five percent air. If there was even as much as twenty-five percent gas there would <u>not</u> be enough air to cause an explosion.

The ignition might have been a light switch flipped on as many remembered being the source of later rumors. Many said that the plumbers, O.T. Dyer and Johnny Dyer or the Gas Superintendent, Oscar Hixon, may have switched on the light where the hot water was located. It is not probable that any one of them switched on a light as every other light switch in the pharmacy had already been turned on when the store opened that morning

15. Lawsuits Against William L. "Bill" Berry

when Don Bohannan and Ray Tyson came in together.

Ray Tyson testified as to what he saw from his limited line of vision from the soda fountain to the backs of O.T. Dyer, Johnny Dyer, and Oscar Hixon standing in line at the end of the soda fountain. Where the Dyers stood—to the middle right of the store, at the hanging overhead heater, Oscar Hixon almost blocked his view, standing behind them. But Ray Tyson *did* see one of the plumber's arm moving up and down a few times as if he were tightening a pipe with a wrench. Tightening the pipe could have created a spark that triggered the explosion just when the gas and air mixture was capable of exploding. No one will ever know the answer for sure, but after weeks and weeks of testimony from all who were at the scene these explanations are as close as possible to what happened.

Ray Tyson, witness for defendant Berry, testified in part and in substance as follows for M. Cook Barwick attorney for William L. Berry. Statement from actual court records:

"I live four and one-half miles west of Villa Rica and work for Dr. Berry in his pharmacy and did so on December 5, 1957. I have worked for him since 1949. My duties were fountain manager, but I helped all over the store and made deliveries. During the week of the explosion, I detected a kind of unusual odor first on Wednesday before the explosion happened on Thursday. No one reported to me that he smelled anything unusual on Monday or Tuesday. I have smelled odorized natural gas; it is hard to describe but I know it when I smell it. The odor I smelled on that Wednesday was not the odor of odorized natural gas…

"As to whether O.T. Dyer was working on the space heater at the time of the explosion—if he had been working on the space heater, which was in [sic] the overhead, he would have had to stand on something… The space or overhead heater was piped with gas from underneath the store. I lit that overhead heater once a year, when it got cold, and it stayed on all winter.

"As to what else he could have been working on, there was one more pipe that leads from below the store through the floor that went to the water heater. It had a pilot light that stayed on all the time. The water heater was about half way in the store and to the left of the overhead heater. I would guess the store was about one hundred feet in length. There was a radiant heater in the back of the pharmacy which was not automatic and had to be lighted with a match every morning. I had smelled natural gas out of that heater before the explosion.

"There were electric wires in the crawl space, but there was no light or socket down there. Oscar Hixon reached the Dyers before the explosion occurred. As to how many minutes, I answer that from the time that the Dyers and all went in, I will say it was between five and six minutes.

"I saw the black smoke about [sic] in the area where the hole was blown in the A & B Dress Shop. The wall there had a vent in it; the chimney down [sic] there. In my opinion, the smoke came from the water heater. It could have come from the chimney, but I can hardly answer that."

> The following is the cross examination of Ray Tyson by Mr. Barwick and Mr. Boykin for the plaintiffs:
> MR. BARWICK:
> Q. Now you testified about a black cloud of smoke, does that indicate on here (a diagram) directly the area next to your soda fountain from the A & B Dress Shop where the hole was blown?
> A. Yes, sir, right about where the hole was blown sir.
> Q. Was it in that area that you saw the black smoke?
> A. Yes, sir. It was.
> Q. Was it in that area, was the [sic] wall, the wall had a vent in it there?
> A. Did the wall have a vent in it there?
> Q. Yes, sir. That chimney came down through there?
> A. Yes, sir. They [sic] was a chimney there.
> Q. All right. Now could that black cloud have come out of the hole where the water heater, where those heaters were vented into it?
> Mr. LOKEY: May it please Your Honor, I would object to that question as being leading and suggestive of the answer.
> THE COURT: Objection sustained.
> MR. BOYKIN:
> Q. Well, state, please sir, whether in your opinion, whether it would have been possible for that cloud of smoke that you have described to come out of the heater. State in your opinion if you know where it came from.
> A. Out of the water heater.
> Q. From the vent up there, the chimney?
> A. Well, it could have, but I couldn't [sic] hardly answer that.

15. Lawsuits Against William L. "Bill" Berry

Q. Well, I understand you don't know.

MR. BOYKIN: That is all.

MR. BARWICK:

Q. Now, did you or did you not on Wednesday or Thursday consider the possibility of sewer age gas?

A. Well, I don't believe I did before but after that, after the explosion I have thought about it and wondered if it could have been sewage gas or what it could have been.

Q. Yes. Now where were you standing with reference to this hole that was blown in the side of the A & B Dress Shop?

A. I was near the front from that.

Q. Well, were you -

A. I was about, I guess twenty feet from -

Q. About as far as from you to me?

A. Something like that, yes, sir.

Q. Yes, sir. And the puff of black smoke you saw was back toward where that hole was, is that right?

A. Yes. Sir.

Q. Now, did you have occasion to see that floor of the A & B Dress Shop after this thing?

A. Yes, sir.

Q. Now I will ask you whether the splinters came up toward the sky, or whether they went down in toward the ground?

A. Sir, I didn't even examine them, I just saw the hole.

Q. Didn't check that?

A. Now I was kind of hurt, and I didn't walk around.

MR. BARWICK: That is all.

A great part of the court time was spent with individuals who reported what they had smelled in the days prior to the catastrophe. More than twenty witnesses testified they were in or around the four stores involved for some amount of time from Monday, December 2, to the time of the explosion on Thursday December 5, about 11:00 a.m. All of the witnesses interviewed were very familiar with odorized natural gas. Many of the witnesses had heaters which used natural gas and testified that they had lit these heaters that very morning. Each noticed that their heater(s) gave off the familiar odor they usually smelled each morning as they lit them.

At least ten or so witnesses who were in the pharmacy or the adjacent buildings testified to noticing a backdraft smell—a peculiar odor—unlike anything they had smelled anywhere before. Several witnesses said their eyes and nose burned from this strong backdraft type smell. Many of these witness who testified smelled odorized natural gas in the atmosphere but said nothing to anyone about it.

At least half of the witness who were in the pharmacy or the adjacent stores several times during this same time frame, testified to smelling nothing out of the ordinary whatsoever. One person was in the pharmacy the day before for five hour doing inventory and testified to not noticing any unusual smell. Many were in and out of the pharmacy that morning and did not notice any odor.

Horace Nunley, a witness for the defendant Bill Berry, testified in part and in substance as follows: "I have lived in Villa Rica for fifteen years. I am director-secretary of Villa Rica Housing Authority and raise thoroughbred horses and farm a little. I was in Dr. Berry's Pharmacy in Villa Rica on Monday of the week when the explosion occurred. I did not smell any odor when I went into it [sic] on that day. I did not have a cold nor was there anything wrong with my smelling apparatus. I also went into the drugstore on Tuesday. I did not smell anything on that day. I also was in the drugstore on Wednesday. I did not smell anything there on Wednesday. I also was in the drugstore on the morning of Thursday, December 5, 1957, before the explosion. I also did not smell anything in the drugstore at that time. Thursday morning I was in there about an hour and a half. On Thursday morning I did not hear anyone say anything about smelling an unpleasant odor. I heard no conversation about it at all.

"I saw the Dyers come in. They came in single file and strode toward the back of the store. Two of them were carrying pipe wrenches. Oscar Hixon was with them. I did not hear him make any statement. I know that the Dyers had worked on gas installations for people. I left the store about six minutes before the explosion occurred. During the time I was there I talked with Dr. Berry. At no time did he say anything about an odor of gas in the place. I did not notice my eyes stinging or anything that morning. Dr. Berry said nothing about his eyes stinging or watering. The Dyers and Oscar Hixon went on toward the back of the building out of my sight."

Dr. Ernest Powell, Jr, was called to be a witness for defendant Berry, and testified in part and in substance as follows: "I am a physician and have lived in Villa Rica all of

15. Lawsuits Against William L. "Bill" Berry

my life. I stopped by Berry's Pharmacy Thursday morning shortly before the explosion to leave some prescriptions. I did not have a bad cold nor was there anything impairing my sense of smell that morning. I detected nothing unusual in respect to odor while in the store. There were normal odors there, but no odor of gas or anything of that kind. I did not smell anything that smelled like rotten eggs or dead cats or polecats or onions or anything of that kind. I was in the store ten to fifteen minutes. I have smelled mercaptan (the odorant put in natural gas). It has an odor between onions and garlic; I did not smell anything in the store that morning that smelled like mercaptan. Full strength mercaptan would smell stronger than natural gas odorized by it. To some individuals odorized gas might smell like a polecat (skunk). Odors may smell differently to different individuals. One person's sensitivity to odor varies from another person considerably. One person may smell something and another person around the same odor might not smell it.

"The olfactory nerve of an individual varies with that of another individual. It does not vary perceptibly among normal individuals unless they have a cold. There is a very definite range of odor perception in individuals but their interpretation of it varies. I have heard of olfactory fatigue. If one stays around odor any length of time he either becomes unaware of the odor or the nerves becomes fatigued. I am familiar with the smell of odorized natural gas. I did not smell any at any time that morning in the drugstore."

As the court trial of Villa Rica plaintiffs verses Bill Berry continued, several witnesses were questioned. It was established that Tom Pope, the Assistant Gas Superintendent was in Douglasville getting a load of gravel the morning of the explosion. Then Ralph Smith, the assistant to the Clerk at City Hall was questioned about Bill Berry calling about 8:30 that morning to get the Gas Superintendent to come to his pharmacy.

Next was the testimony of Ray Dodson, City Clerk at City Hall, for the defendant Bill Berry:

Q. Mr. Dodson, do you recall that Dr. Bill Berry called early
(on December 5th) to City Hall to complain about the peculiar odor in his
store?

A. I don't know of that.

Q. You don't know of that?

A. No, sir.

Q. You mean that Ralph Smith, your assistant, didn't relay information like
that to you?

A. No, sir.

Q. But if Ralph Smith got the information, he did nothing about it—you just didn't know about it—is that right?

A. I didn't know it.

Q. You had no system about recording complaints that came in, did you, making a written record of them?

A. No, sir. We make a note of it and then we take it out to the parties concerned, the department head that is concerned of all complaints.

Q. And there was no arrangement whereby your assistant notifies you in the event he got a call?

A. No, sir.

MR. LOKEY: That is all.

Then Ray Dodson was cross examined by Mr. Barwick, attorney for the plaintiffs:

Q. Mr. Dodson, if Bill Berry had told you that he had thought he had a gas leak in his drugstore you would have probably gotten in your car and beat it out [sic] looking for Oscar Hixon?

A. Yes, sir.

Q. Well what would you have done?

A. We would have gone and found Oscar Hixon. The City Council pays Ralph Smith for each trip looking for department heads when we need them.

Q. Yes.

A. We pay them twenty-five cents a trip.

But every time there is an odor whether it is from sewer gas or rotten food or something, you don't go get Hixon off the job to go check that right on the spot but—

A. No, sir.

Whereupon the witness was excused from the stand.

Dr. William L. Berry was called to the stand to be cross examined by Mr. Lokey for the plaintiffs:

Q. Dr. Berry you did go to City Hall the morning of the explosion, did

15. Lawsuits Against William L. "Bill" Berry

you not?

A. Yes, sir.

Q. And said, you were looking for Oscar Hixon, is that right?

A. Yes, sir.

Q. When you returned to your premises, did you at any time cut off the gas leading into you premises?

A. No, sir.

Q. Did you direct anyone to cut it off?

A. No, sir.

Q. Did you at any time undertake to ventilate your premises that morning?

A. We opened the back doors, back windows, and the double front doors, and of the pharmacy.

Q. And what was the purpose of opening the back doors and the back windows?

A. To get this odor, and what we were smelling out.

Q. You were concerned at that time that it was gas?

A. No, sir.

Q. Well now, how long did you leave the back doors and the back windows open?

A. I would hate to say, but I would say forty-five, minutes to an hour, something along there.

Q. Then you closed them?

A. That's right.

Q. They were closed at the time of the explosion?

A. As far as I know.

Q. Did you at any time give any warning to your customers in the store about odors that you smelled?

A. No, sir.

Q. You at no time directed any of your customers and specifically Rob Broom to vacate the premises that morning, did you?

A. No, sir.

Q. Now when Oscar Hixon came into the store did he make any statement about odor that you had been concerned about?

A. I heard him make a statement, I mean, I didn't see him come in or didn't ever see him but I heard him say, "This odor is not gas."

Q. You heard him make the statement, "This odor is not gas?"

A. Yes, sir.

MR. BARWICK:

Your Honor please, I would like at this time to make a motion or a directed verdict in behalf of Dr. Berry on the grounds that the testimony that has been adduced by the plaintiff has failed to carry the burden of proof against Dr. Berry. There is no evidence that the realization came to him because of the fact that it was so pungent and so overpowering that it was a dangerous odor of natural gas. In other words, there is no evidence as to where it came from, whether it was coming from the outside or where, and there is no evidence to demonstrate that he was on notice that there was any duty which he had to perform. But still, going, assuming that he did not realize there was natural gas escaping. I believe the jury will say that he did all he could to find out the source and not hold him alone accountable for what happened.

The jury ruled in favor of Dr. William L. Berry.

16

Lawsuits Against the City of Villa Rica

5% natural gas plus 95% air equals an explosion when ignition comes.
So based on this area involved, I estimate there was 944 cubic feet of natural gas.
Chester A. Roush, engineer, witness.

In 1960 the U.S. Fifth Circuit Court of Appeals trial and testimony began with the plaintiffs against the City of Villa Rica. The Honorable William Boyd Sloan was the presiding judge. Attorneys for the plaintiffs, the victims or family of the victims in the Villa Rica explosion, were attorneys Bobby Lee Cook; Joseph L. Llop; Hamilton Lokey; Oscar Roberts; and W. Frank Lawson. Attorney for the defendant, City of Villa Rica, was Shirley C. Boykin. The trial was held in Newnan, Georgia.

Three exhibits were prepared ahead of time and presented as witnesses were questioned. Exhibit # 7 was the Valve Book which described the entire gas system of Villa Rica showing the location of each cut-off valve. Exhibit # 8 was the blueprints of the Villa Rica gas system on the block of the stores bordered on the west by Candler Street; on the south by Wilson Street; on the east by Carroll Road; and on the north by Montgomery Street. Exhibit # 11 was the customer set-up of gas piping that led to each separate customer location.

The first witness called to testify for the plaintiff(s) against the City of Villa Rica was Dr. Thomas H. Goodgain.

Dr. Thomas H. Goodgain, witness for plaintiff, testified in part and in substance as follows: "I live in Atlanta and am associate professor of chemical engineering at Georgia

Explosion in Villa Rica

Institute of Technology. I have been in that capacity since 1957. I have a bachelors degree in chemical engineering, a master of science, and a doctor of science in chemical engineering. I attended the Atomic Energy Commission Institute in Nuclear Engineering and presently work with and consult with the Atomic Energy Commission in a professional and engineering capacity. I have had experience working with natural gas but not actually in natural gas explosions. I am familiar with the engineering details of a natural gas system."

"The properties of natural gas are that it is odorless, colorless and tasteless and that it is lighter than air. The reason for odorization is to give a warning to humans that gas is in the atmosphere. Natural gas is dangerous if not odorized. Natural gas in amount of five (5%) percent by volume in air is explosive. It should be odorized such that it can be smelled when there is one (1%) percent of natural gas in the atmosphere…

"As to what should be done in a building thirty feet by one hundred feet if natural gas had been smelled for one or two days, the people should first be gotten out of the building, the sources of fire shut off, and the building ventilated thoroughly. Then the supply of gas should be shut off. After that, leaks should be checked."

Then Tom Pope, witness for plaintiff, testified in part and in substance as follows: "I live in Villa Rica, am twenty-eight-years-old, and on December 5, 1957 was employed by the Gas Department of the City of Villa Rica… The City received natural gas from the Southern Natural Gas Company at Sandhill, which is about six and a half miles south of Villa Rica and between Villa Rica and Carrollton. We received it at one hundred pounds per square inch pressure. It passed through a meter of Southern Natural and then Villa Rica odorized it and the gas then went on into town. The last time I put odorization in the system was in June or July when three drums of mercaptan were delivered from the Barnes Freight Lines. We put it right into the station, that is, Oscar Hixon and I. There were fifty (50) gallons in each drum. That amount of mercaptan will last six to eight months. I do not know how much mercaptan was automatically dropped into the gas that flowed into the system.

"The gas was sufficiently odorized that it could be smelled. I was familiar with the odorizing machine. It contained a storage tank and then (the gas) left the storage tank and went into the line. The odorizing station is from ten to fifteen feet from the Southern Natural Gas Meter Station. The gas goes immediately through the odorizing station and then flows into town through Villa Rica's regulator station. At the regulator station, the pressure is cut from one hundred (100) pounds to fifteen (15) pounds per square inch. There is no way for the gas from Southern Natural Gas Company not to pass through Villa Rica's odorizing station.

16. Lawsuits Against the City of Villa Rica

"On December 5, 1957, there was mercaptan to odorize the gas in the odorizing station. The gas then flows through a steel pipe to the regulator station, and after being reduced to fifteen (15) pounds is distributed to the City of Villa Rica. Before the gas is used by customers it is reduced again to about four (4) ounces per square inch. The system is a Rockwell system. If the pressure gets too high, there is a pop-off valve. If it gets too low, there is an alarm system which would turn on a light and alarm.

"Mercaptan, the odorizing agent, has a very unpleasant odor. Raw gas and gas fumes have different odors. The fume does not smell like the natural gas which is odorized. No one made any complaints to me about leaking gas and I found none in the lines.

"The purpose of the odorizing station was to put odorant into the gas because the gas did not have any odor when Villa Rica receives it; that is, Southern Natural supplied Villa Rica with unodorized gas, and the Gas Department of the City of Villa Rica knew that and that is why they operated the odorizing station and put odorizing substance into it.

"The more gas that was used the more odorant would go into it and the faster the odorant would be used up. I believe the capacity of the odorizing tank was from two to three hundred gallons. You can see the odorant going into the gas through a glass tube which shows the odorant dropping down. I put into the tank three fifty five gallon drums around July of 1957.

"Oscar Hixon's practice was to check the odorizing station about every day; I would go with him perhaps once a week. After the explosion I did not put any additional odorant into the system until the time Gus Cobb came. When Gus Cobb came about three (3) months after the explosion, the tank was about half full.

"I identify defendant's exhibit No. 11 as a typical customer set-up of piping that leads to each separate customer in Villa Rica. Both Reeves Jewelry Store, the A & B Dress Shop, and the Berry's Pharmacy had such a set-up in regard to gas piping. If the valve shown in this exhibit had been cut off for each of the customers in that block, all the gas going into the stores in that block would have been cut off.

"I identify defendant's exhibit No. 8 as the blueprints of the Villa Rica gas system as constructed. My attention is called to page 6 of this exhibit and to the block bounded on the east by Carrollton Road, on the south by Wilson Street, on the west by Candler Street, and on the north by U.S. Highway No. 78, which is Montgomery Street. The rectangles show the different stores. The one near Candler Street is Reeves Jewelry Store and the A & B Dress Shop; and the next is Berry's Pharmacy.

Explosion in Villa Rica

"The dotted line with the little circle at the eastern end could represent the two and one-fourth inch gas main running back of these stores. The circle is the valve at the head of the main which I was unable to find immediately after the explosion. If this valve had been shut off, all the gas passing in a westerly direction in this main behind the stores would have been shut off."

Next Gus Cobb, who took over Oscar Hixon's job, was called to testify for the plaintiff: "I am presently employed by the City of Villa Rica as Manager of its Gas Department. Prior to that time I had worked for the City of Tallapoosa (Georgia) in their gas system. I worked for the Gas Department of Tallapoosa from 1949 until March of 1958, when I began work for the City of Villa Rica. I have examined the odorizing equipment in the City of Villa Rica's gas system. As far as I know it is the same equipment that was there at the date of the explosion. We use mercaptan as the odorant. It is a liquid and is kept in the reservoir tank. A Hancock valve allows the liquid to go into the gas. It can be adjusted to increase or decrease the flow of mercaptan going in. This is done by turning the valve. It can be turned so that the odorant is cut off altogether, or it can be turned the other way so that a steady stream may go in, or it can be adjusted so that it will go into the gas drop by drop. The valve controls the flow such that the more gas passes through, the more mercaptan enters the system. You can see the flow of odorant into the gas by looking into a peep valve.

"When I became manager of this system, I did not find any written records concerning the amount of mercaptan that was put into the gas before the date of the explosion. I am familiar with the odor of odorized natural gas after mercaptan has been added to it. The odor smells like sulphur, asafedita and wild onions. It smells like a dead rat. It causes me to have a headache. It does not cause my eyes to burn or smart.

"After arrival at Villa Rica, I checked the odorizing tank. There was odorant in it. I would guess about 150 pounds or approximately one-half full or something like that. I checked the odorizing tank once a day."

Next J. E. O'Toole, witness for defendant City of Villa Rica, testified in part and in substance as follows: "I am a consulting engineer who attended the University of Alabama and studied engineering there. I have an office in Birmingham, Alabama and have been in the practice approximately fourteen years. My firm designed and drew the plans for the natural gas system of Villa Rica...The Buchanan Pipe Line Company constructed this system. It was supervised in construction out of my office with an engineer in the field. This engineer was C. W. Kelpe. He was the project engineer. This system was designed and engineered in accordance with the accepted practice and standards of installing such systems for small

16. Lawsuits Against the City of Villa Rica

communities. The gas main from the point of connection with Southern Natural Gas Company at Sandhill to the City of Villa Rica's regulator station was six and five-eights inch OD standard weight steel pipe. The rest of the system in regard to mains was of mechanical joints and cast iron pipe in sizes from six inches in diameter to two-and-one-quarter inches. Cast iron pipe is standard equipment for such a distribution system. It was built in 1954. The odorizer was a Peerless machine. It is approximately twenty to twenty-five feet from the Southern Natural Gas meter station.

"The gas comes from Southern Natural Gas Company's station and goes through the odorizing station. The Peerless station is an automatic machine, and goes into the transmission main and is delivered to the regulating station into the distribution system of the city. The city's regulator station reduces the pressure and controls it from the main supply in the system. From the mains the gas goes to each customer through a service line which is one-inch galvanized line connected to the main and it goes through a meter at the end of it. There is also a small regulator ahead of the meter which further reduces the pressure before it goes into the customer's appliances. To me, odorized natural gas smells like a polecat (skunk). To someone else, it might smell a little different. I have heard it described as smelling like sulphur, rotten eggs, and a polecat. I would say that approximately a gallon of odorant should go into a million cubic feet of gas. The amount of odorant going into the gas would depend upon the flow of gas. The City's odorizing station is easily observable by employees of Southern Natural Gas Company at their meter station."

J. E. O'Toole is Cross Examination by Mr. Boykin, attorney for the defense of the City of Villa Rica.

Q. Tell the court and jury about exhibit #7.

A. That is what we call a Valve Book. It has sheets in it with the locations of valves at each intersection on the natural gas system as built.

Q. That describes the entire system and the valves?

A. The system, the location of the valves on the system.

Q. Yes. This Valve Book prepared in your office?

A. Yes, sir.

Q. I will get you to state to the court and jury was the system in Villa Rica designed and engineered in accordance with the accepted practice and standards of installing systems of this type.

A. Yes, sir.

Explosion in Villa Rica

Q. For small communities?

A. Yes, sir.

Q. Was there any brittle or plastic pipe used in the laying of that system anywhere?

A. No. Sir.

Q. Did you have [sic] any, Oscar Hixon employed by you in connection with the building of this system?

A. No sir. He wasn't employed by us.

Q. Well, I mean, did he work with you during the—

A. Well he was employed by the City of Villa Rica but was on the job along with our engineer.

Q. He was there during the entire construction of it?

A. Yes, sir.

Q. Did you have occasion to see him and talk with him?

A. Yes, sir.

Q. Look him over so to speak?

A. Yes, sir. I did, on occasion.

Q. Tell the court and jury whether you thought he was an intelligent man, how he impressed you.

A. Well, my impression of Oscar Hixon was that he was a very capable young man in that he was, I would say very intelligent. He could grasp situations pretty quick, he was ready and willing to learn, and he was willing at all times to do whatever he could to further the work on the job.

Q. Was he present when the system was finally completed, the installation finally completed?

A. Yes, sir.

Q. Now from your knowledge of Oscar Hixon, seeing him there in Villa Rica, let me ask you first—how long did he work with you, I mean during the installation of the system?

A. From about June or July, I forget the exact month, until sometime about January 1955.

Q. I will get you to state to the court and jury if in your opinion he was a capable man of managing and running the system, gas system from your observation of him and what you had seen him do and what he had learned

16. Lawsuits Against the City of Villa Rica

in connection with the system.

A. Well, from my observation of Oscar Hixon and from the way he conducted himself during the construction, trying to learn and become acquainted with the system and materials, it was our opinion that he would make a qualified superintendent, and he had the resources of trying to learn all the time new things and why things were done, and for that reason we felt that he was, would make a very capable operator.

Q. And you felt after your experience with him that he would make a capable superintendent?

A. Yes, sir.

Q. When was it that you parted company with him in '54, or '55?

A. Somewhere around about the end of '54 or part of '55.

Q. Now, assuming that he had continued to work on as the manager of the gas system there, he would have become pretty familiar with the odor of natural gas, that had these foreign odorizing substances, wouldn't he?

A. We had had the experience of the system being out—in sections prior to that which had odor in it and he was acquainted with that, yes, sir.

Q. So he would be more familiar with it than would say the mayor of the town or say some layman who might be running a barbershop or filling station or grocery store, isn't that right?

A. Very definitely.

Q. Now, if, I will ask you this hypothetical question, if he, if Oscar Hixon walked into a pharmacy or any other building which was demolished within some three or four minutes after he entered and if he made the statement "that odor you smell in here is not the odor of natural gas," would you think that he was mistaken or that he knew what he was talking about?

MR. GARDNER: Now, Your Honor, that is speculating on what another man says, thinks, feels or does. I think that is beyond the realm of this witness to speculate on it.

THE COURT: Yes. I think that is —

MR. BARWICK: All right. I withdraw the question.

BY MR. BARWICK:

Q. I will ask you this. If Oscar Hixon walked in, I will ask you if Oscar Hixon had been advised by someone that there was an odor in a building and if he went into the building, a building within just a few minutes was demolished, and smelled something, in your opinion would he be able to tell whether or not that smell was the smell or odorized natural gas?

A. Yes, I think he would.

Mr. BARWICK: All right. That is all.

Next Charles W. Kelpe, was called to the stand to testify for the defendant, the City of Villa Rica:

"I am in the J. E. O'Toole Engineering Company and have been in the engineering field for over 25 years. I attended the University of Michigan where I studied engineering for three years. I worked under Mr. O'Toole in directing the course of construction as a supervising engineer on the job. The system was installed in accordance with the plans and specifications. I instructed Oscar Hixon in all the details of the system, including the odorizer. I went through the odorizer with him and took the bonnet off and showed him the functions of the machinery in it and showed him the meter and showed him the possibilities of trouble. I explained to him all the workings of the odorizing equipment during the period that the system was being installed."

Charles W. Kelp was cross examination by Mr. Boykin for the defense of the City of Villa Rica: I was in Villa Rica a little over a year of which time I was devoted to gas from sometime in June, I think the early part of June on through January the following year, which was '55.

Q. Did the City of Villa Rica have Oscar Hixon working with you continuously?

A. Yes, sir. He did continuously.

Q. Well, just tell what kind of man you found Oscar Hixon to be.

A. From the first days after meeting Oscar Hixon, I found through conversation that he did have the ability to develop into a Gas Superintendent. Oscar has followed me through that construction. I have taken Oscar and showed him every phase of it. When the delivery of the regulators arrived, sometime shortly after they were delivered, I have taken the regulators apart and explained part by part the function of the various regulators, the high pressure farm tap, normally called farm tap and explained to him where they do have some difficulty by getting some parcels that get up under them and cause them to leak, how that is corrected. I have also explained to him of

16. Lawsuits Against the City of Villa Rica

the regulator valve, the pressure regulator valve that the customer service could be cut off because of a rupture, excessive high pressure, how that is corrected. I have taken the service regulator which is the regulator that reduces the pressure from fifteen pounds down to four ounces, or thereabout. I have taken that regulator apart and showed him how it is. I have taken him into every phase of it.

When the odorizer was installed I went through the odorizer the same way. I have taken the bonnet off or had the bonnet taken off by the contractor's men, raised the bonnet off to show him just exactly the functions of it and showed him the motor and told him how it is repaired. Explained to him also that the needle valve on there, how the gas functioned through the orifice face by creating the differential, showed him the needle valve how he assessed the quantity into the regulator and explained to him that regardless of how much gas flows through the main that proportionately he gets the same odor as he would whether it was one million cubic feet, two million, five million or whatever it was, it would depend on the setting, and the quantity of gas that goes into it proportionately to the amount of gas that flows.

Q. Well, did he do any, did he watch the installation or do any work during the installation period? Did he do any of the actual labor or watch it when you were constructing.

A. Yes, he was there watching, yes, sir.

Q. Up until that time did Oscar Hixon still stay with you through every phase?

A. Yes, sir. He did. Oscar Hixon was with myself making the required tests on the individual service lines. That is the home plumbing.

Q. As I understand you to say that you turned the gas on in sections?

A. We began to distribute gas before the entire system was completed.

Q. Now, Mr. Kelpe, you said Oscar Hixon worked continually with you during the time over there. What kind of a man did you find Oscar Hixon to be, tell the Court and jury.

A. I have a very high impression of Mr. Hixon.

Q. Well, did he receive the instructions and operations and understand how to operate this system?

A. Yes, he did. He absolutely had a thorough, thorough knowledge when that system was completed. He had a thorough knowledge as to the functions and its operation.

Q. Well and to his intelligence, can you tell the court and jury whether he was a man of just common intelligence, a man of high intelligence, the average competent man or the extraordinary?

A. Well I don't think I could flatter him regardless of what all I could say about the man. That is how my opinion of how fine a gentleman he was. There was no question but what I think. I believe that would be borne out with anyone in Villa Rica as to the quality, the principle, the character of that individual. I have been in a position to learn a great deal with that man for I have been with him for all that time, from morning 'til night, and know his every thought. He was definitely a very capable man in any endeavor that he would undertake, in anything and do it well.

Q. Now, Mr. Kelpe, when you completed the system and you made the final test did you turn the system over to the City of Villa Rica?

A. Yes, we turned it over to the City of Villa Rica with the complete documents which were made up of the Valve Book, the plan drawings, and other literature that may have been with the equipment, and we turned it over to the City of Villa Rica.

Q. Did you recommend to the City of Villa Rica that the system had been built according to those plans and specifications and they accepted it?

A. Yes.

Q. Did you recommend or did you feel in your, well it was your opinion as to Oscar Hixon being a capable man to operate the system.

A. I did make the commitment, to the board or to the Council, that he was very capable and they could all place all confidence necessary in him in operating that system successfully as the Superintendent of the Gas System of Villa Rica.

Then Chester A. Roush, witness for defendant City of Villa Rica, testified in part and in substance as follows: "I am an engineer, with an engineering firm, and in the natural gas business. We engineer and build and operate utility systems. I have more to do with natural gas systems than with other types of utilities. Until recently, I have been assistant to

16. Lawsuits Against the City of Villa Rica

the President of the Jacksonville Gas Corporation. I am Vice President of Coastal Natural Gas Company, which is a new pipe line in South Georgia. I am a graduate of Georgia Tech in 1946 in Chemical Engineering. I have a masters degree from Harvard University. I then went to Texas and started several businesses which distributed propane hydrous ammonia, which is a gas used for fertilizers.

"The City of Villa Rica hired me early this year, about January, 1959, to make a complete inspection of their entire system.

"I saw the odorizer that was used by the City of Villa Rica. It is a Peerless type MO Odorizer. The description of it given by witness Bennett in detail was correct and I subscribe to it.

"In Berry's pharmacy, the water heater and the overhead space heater were both vented into an old chimney. I think the smoke previously referred to could have been from that chimney or vents. There was not an explosive mixture of gas in the drugstore when the lighted taper was used to check the line. Also, there was a source of ignition from the lighted pilot in the space heater and the pilot in the water heater.

"The tank in the odorizing system of the City of Villa Rica has a rated capacity of two hundred fifty gallons. It probably holds closer to three hundred. The Peerless Odorizer is probably the commonest odorizer used.

"The system of Villa Rica is what is known as an open grid system. Once the gas passes the regulator which reduces it to fifteen pounds pressure, it then goes through a grid of pipes throughout the town. All the valves are left open at the corners and intersections of the street so that the pressure at any time in that system will be approximately the same at one point as at any other point. *It is impossible to have a higher pressure in one portion of the system than there is in another portion.* There were recording gauges in the system at the regulating station, at the City Hall, at the hospital, and on the meters at Villa Rica Mills, Golden City Mills, and Browns Mill. I have checked the plans of the system as constructed and the specifications. They are entirely according to industry standard.

"In regard to odorization of gas, the odorization diffuses entirely throughout the system. *Once it is dissolved in the gas stream, it would be impossible to have odorant in one part of the system and not have odorant in another part of this grid of mains that I described.* Once the odorant is placed in the gas stream, it would be diffused evenly throughout all portions of the system. The odorant stays in the gas until it is burned out. If Southern Natural Gas Company had odorized the gas before they delivered it to Villa Rica, it would have been odorized all the way through and after delivery. The minimum concentration of natural gas in air for there to be an explosion is five percent natural gas with ninety-five percent air. After the concentration reaches five percent, there must be some ignition to set off the gas. The explosion then results from a rapid burning of the gas.

"From the testimony, (of those in the explosion) it would indicate that a combustible gas ignited in the pharmacy, which was visible to the persons who stated they saw the flash. I cannot say that inside the pharmacy was the only place that gas ignited. It is difficult to tell exactly how gas explosions propagate. After an initial explosion, it may be that a fraction of a second later there will be another explosion, or a secondary effect from the original explosion. The fact that there were men who were blown up(ward) but who saw flame coming from the rear is not consistent because the flame coming from the rear would indicate an explosion from the rear, which would not have knocked the men upward. If there was an explosion from underneath the floor and there was gas in the atmosphere in the drugstore above the floor, the ignition from the basement would not set off the gas inside the store unless they were connected. If people were standing on a floor and they were blown upward and they came back down and there was no floor there, that would indicate that there had been an explosion underneath the floor. If there was an explosion underneath the floor which ruptured the floor and if there was gas above the floor, the gas above the floor would explode also.

"Conversely, if there was an explosive concentration of gas above the floor and also below the floor and if the gas above the floor exploded, and if there was a connection between the two, the gas underneath the floor would explode. In an explosion the forces move outward and have their greatest affect on objects which have the least resistance. If there is a masonry wall and a wooden floor, and the explosive force is exerted against both of them, the floor would be more apt to go than the masonry wall, with one exception. The exception is if the concentration of gas were trapped against the masonry wall, and concentrated against it, the wall might be blown at the same time as the rest of the area.

"The rear frame construction of Berry's Pharmacy was blown out and the brick and masonry wall about twelve to sixteen inches thick between Berry's Pharmacy and the A & B Dress Shop was completely destroyed. If there had been an explosion under the A & B Dress Shop, it would have blown a hole in the floor as shown in the diagram and it might well have blown through the masonry wall if the explosion had been concentrated against it. It would be very possible to have a concentration of gas in this crawl space.

"There is another reason that this could have happened. When gas exceeds a concentration of about twenty five (25%) percent in air, it becomes nonexplosive because there

16. Lawsuits Against the City of Villa Rica

is not enough oxygen left to continue the explosion. Therefore, in a confined space where there is an explosion, you may have a large area of gas left which does not explode at the first instant because there is not enough oxygen left to explode all the gas. If the crawl space had gas above this percentage concentration, it may not have exploded at the first instant. But at the next instant where all of the gas surges through the hole there may be an additional amount of oxygen to become mixed with the gas and there would be another explosion in a mere fraction of a second.

"Assuming that there was an explosion under the A & B Dress Shop which blew through the brick wall, it could well have carried enough gas under the first floor of Berry's Pharmacy so that the second explosion could have been there. This is particularly true because of the old-time brick chimney that was in the brick wall which would give a passageway through which the first surge could have gone up and out and accounted for the flash of flame coming forward.

"This could have accounted for the fact that the boy (Ralph Fuller) in the back was blown eastward and could have accounted for the subsequent explosion under the floor blowing the other witnesses upward. This would be a series of circumstances which would explain the evidence. The flue or chimney was in the solid masonry wall. The chimney on either side would have been perhaps one brick thick. If the explosion had hit the wall and gone up the flue, it would have knocked the vent out in Berry's pharmacy. It would then have entered the back part of the drugstore and could have accounted for the black smoke."

Lawyer for the plaintiffs gave a summary: "The evidence of several eyewitnesses to the explosion supported the contention that escaping gas had permeated the air throughout the pharmacy so that when it reached the explosive concentration of five per cent and was ignited, a wall of flame swept through the pharmacy and a violent explosion destroyed the building and killed twelve people in the process. Numerous witnesses testified to the fact that they detected no odor in the pharmacy shortly before the explosion, or that they detected only a slight odor. The evidence was undisputed that natural gas when properly odorized should give an impact odor when it reaches a concentration of only one percent (1/5th) of the concentration necessary for an explosion.

"There was likewise evidence that at concentrations above 1 per cent, properly odorized natural gas should become so offensive to the sense of smell as to make it difficult to remain in the presence of the escaping gas. No witness testified as to any such strong odor in the pharmacy. The testimony of these witnesses was sufficient to support the conclusion

Explosion in Villa Rica

of the jury that the natural gas supplied to Berry's Pharmacy was not sufficiently odorized. The evidence provided by the defendant City of Villa Rica fully supports the contention that the gas was not sufficiently odorized.

"Tom Pope, the Assistant Superintendent of the Gas System, testified that one hundred sixty five gallons of mercaptan were placed in the odorizing machine in June of 1957, and that this amount represented a six months' supply of odorant. Gus Cobb testified that sometime after March 1, 1958, when he became Superintendent of the Gas System, he inspected the odorizing machine and found it contained one hundred fifty gallons. The expert witness for the City of Villa Rica testified that the capacity of the machine was two hundred fifty gallons. While there was no evidence as to how much the machine contained after the one hundred sixty five gallons were added in June of 1957, it is perfectly obvious that the machine could not have contained more than two hundred fifty gallons. *If 150 gallons remained some 10 months later, it necessarily follows that not more than 100 gallons of odorant were used over a 10 month period, when 165 gallons was the proper amount to use during a 6 month period.*

"The testimony of the witnesses as to the lack of odor or the faintness of the odor in Berry's Pharmacy on the morning of the explosion is not necessarily inconsistent with the testimony of the three workmen who smelled the odor of gas when working on a pipe on the other side of town that morning. These witnesses testified that they cut into a pipe containing a pressure of fifteen pounds to the square inch and that the gas under this pressure blew out directly upon them. With such a volume and concentration of gas, even a weak malodorant would be noticed by them.

"We submit that the evidence in this case clearly establishes negligence on the part of the defendant City of Villa Rica not only for failure to properly odorize the gas, but also for failure to properly deal with a condition of leaking gas after actual notice to it that gas was leaking in and around Berry's Pharmacy."

On July 22, 1960 judgement was passed against the City of Villa Rica for negligence. It was established that the gas had not been odorized, a safety proceedure that is normally done by the distribution company. "Gus Cobb, the present (1959) superintendent of the Villa Rica Gas system, and several other expert witnesses, testified that the safe procedure in checking for a gas leak is to first cut off the gas where it enters the premises, then ventilate the premises, then test for leaks in the pipes and fixtures by the use of air pressure or other similar safe procedures. The testimony of at least three witnesses established that Hixon

16. Lawsuits Against the City of Villa Rica

and the Dyers entered the premises at approximately the same time and that they were in Berry's Pharmacy for six minutes before the explosion took place.

"Although the store building was only one hundred feet long, Hixon did not during the six minutes he was in the store go to the back of the store to cut of the flow of gas into the store; nor did he ventilate the premises; nor did he warn anyone of the danger incident to escaping gas prior to the explosion which destroyed the pharmacy.

"On the contrary, according to Dr. Berry, Hixon stated that the odor was not that of escaping natural gas. From this statement of Hixon alone, the jury was authorized to conclude either that the gas was not properly odorized or that Hixon was not sufficiently familiar with the smell of odorized natural gas to recognize it. The latter would support the conclusion that the defendant City of Villa Rica was undertaking to operate its gas system without sufficiently qualified personnel. The failure to cut off the flow of gas, the failure to ventilate the premises, and the failure to warn persons of the danger incident to escaping gas would clearly authorize a jury to conclude the defendant City of Villa Rica was guilty of negligence in the premises."

The Federal Court Circuits, 5th Circuit July 22, 1960—Summary by attorneys for the City of Villa Rica: "While, as we have said above in connection with Southern's appeal, we are of the clear opinion that the finding of the jury, if it did so find, that the gas was not odorized, was without evidence to support it and was based only on surmise and suspicion, we think it equally clear that the jury could, and did, find that the City was negligent in not taking proper precautions after complaints of escaping gas had reached it, and that such negligence was the proximate cause of the damages sustained and recovered by plaintiffs…

"The record furnishes ample proof to support the finding implied in the verdict, that Villa Rica had ample notice of leaking gas, not only in Berry's Pharmacy but also in adjacent premises, and that its negligent failure to take prompt corrective action commensurate with the dangers involved proximately caused the explosion.

"The evidence established: that the odorizing station designed and constructed for Villa Rica through which the gas was purchased from Southern moved on its way to customers was of approved design and capacity; that that type of odorizing equipment used, 'Peerless Odorizer,' the most commonly used odorizer, was a superior type of equipment manufactured by a reputable company, and was the best in its field.

"The undisputed testimony shows that the gas was odorized with mercaptan, an odorant which has a sulphur base and produces distinct and separate olfactory reactions on different people.

"It was testified, and no one disputed, that a sufficient quantity of mercaptan odorant was kept in the automatic odorizing plant, or station, at all times, and that before and after the explosion, there was sufficient mercaptan odorizer in the automatic odorizing station, and the odorizing plant was working at all times.

"Natural gas is its natural state is odorless and sightless. When odorized at a point before it goes into any distribution system, it becomes odorized at any and every point in said system. There is no way to get the odor out, save burn it out. This is particularly true with reference to a system of the type installed by the City of Villa Rica. In the City of Villa Rica system, the one main gas line coming from the Southern Natural Gas line supplies the entire system. Any gas reaching any customer of the Villa Rica gas system necessarily passed through the automatic odorizing station.

"On the morning of the explosion, many people in the City of Villa Rica smelled and detected the odor of odorized natural gas. Some of these detected and noticed the odor of odorized natural gas when lighting the heater, etc.

"Oscar Hixon, the manager of the Villa Rica Gas Department with three laborers was making a new tap on the gas line within the system within the City of Villa Rica, at the time he received notice from the defendant Berry, by and through his clerk and employee, Ray Tyson, that a peculiar odor was prevalent in the drugstore. These workers testified that within a few minutes of the time of the explosion on the morning of December 5, 1957, they noticed and detected the odor of odorized gas.

"There was no direct or positive evidence whatever disputing the facts above stated, and there was also direct and positive evidence from many of the twenty witnesses, who testified to their sensations, that they had smelled odorized gas in and about the block where the explosion occurred during the week of the explosion; and negative testimony of many of them that they had not smelled it.

"Reeves Jewelry Store, two doors from Berry's Pharmacy, reported a gas leak on Monday before the explosion on Thursday, but no leak was found.

"Bernie Bell, the operator of the dress shop next to the drugstore testified that Tyson told her Thursday that they had been smelling gas for three days in the drugstore and it had been burning their eyes.

"Defendant Berry testified that on the morning of the explosion he ventilated his drugstore to remove the odor which was a 'peculiar odor' different from normal odors in the prescription department. His eyes burned. He went to the City Hall to find the Gas Su-

16. Lawsuits Against the City of Villa Rica

perintendent and later called the City Hall in a further attempt to find him.

"Witnesses Preston Lancaster, Homer Vaughn, Don Bohannon, and Ray Tyson, all of whom were in the drugstore at the time of the explosion, testified that they were blown up(ward) and fell back into the wreckage.

"Both expert witnesses, Dr. Thomas Goodgain and Chester Roush, testified that, for a person to be blown up, the explosion would have to be underneath the floor. Dr. Thomas Goodgain testified that if the gas were under the floor and not in the building, it could not be smelled by those in the building, even though properly odorized, and in a building with front and back doors and windows open, gas in the building would be dispelled and the odor dissipated.

"On the issue of notice to Villa Rica of gas leakage and its negligence in respect thereto in not taking proper action against danger, the following facts were established without contradictions:

"Tom Pope, who testified that one of his duties was to look for leaks, checked Reeves Jewelry Store for leaking gas on December 2 at Gas Superintendent Hixon's request, upon complaint of Eunice Reeves. Hixon checked it at Reeves' request at 6:00 o'clock that night on December 4. He then explained to Mr. Hixon that the odor seemed to be coming from the back of Berry's Pharmacy. Hixon knew that the Berry's Pharmacy had been converted from a butane service system. Hixon examined the Reeves' building only. No pressure test was made to check the Reeves' complaints. At no time did Pope cut off the gas to Reeves' store or undertake to ventilate the premises. Nor did he make an air test for leaks. On Tuesday Hixon checked Reeves' store. On Wednesday Hixon checked Reeves' store and was told the odor seemed stronger 'up toward the back of the pharmacy.' After checking around the jewelry store Hixon advised Reeves that he did not have a leak. Apparently no effort was made to see if the leak was somewhere else in the row of stores.

"Bill Berry called the City desk December 5, complaining of gas odor and later came over personally about 9:30 (that morning) complaining of an odor which had existed for two days, stating that he had become dubious about it. No records are kept of prior complaints. The City Clerk did not attempt to get in touch with the Gas Service Department, although the City has a method for locating department heads. The City also has a radio-police setup for this contingency.

"Dr. Bill Berry resorted to sending one of his employees for Oscar Hixon and Hixon arrived at Berry's Pharmacy minutes before 11:00 o'clock. When Hixon arrived, he did not go to the back of the pharmacy, did not order the premises ventilated, did not take charge of the situation, did not order the occupants out, but walked in and said: 'This is not gas I smell.' Hixon came in as the Dyers did; walked over to where the Dyers were standing and watched them 'tightening up something.' They had been there only a short time when the explosion occurred.

"When a warning odor is detected, flames should be extinguished, electric motors shut off, premises ventilated, and a check made for leaks. There was a cut-off back of Berry's Pharmacy.

"Dr. Goodgain testified as an expert on handling of natural gas that the safe procedure to follow in searching for a gas leak is: (1) get the people out of the building; (2) shut off sources of fire, such as pilot lights, electric motors and things that may spark; (3) ventilate the building thoroughly to get the gas out; (4) shut off the gas supply to the building; and (5) test for leaks with a device that is safe in the presence of explosive mixtures.

"Gus Cobb, who succeeded Oscar Hixon as superintendent of the Villa Rica gas system, testified that the safe method in inspecting for gas leaks is: (1) cut off the gas going into the premises; (2) ventilate the premises; and (3) test for leaks with a gas detector pump. He testified that it was unsafe to search for a leak inside the premises without first cutting the gas off. Mr. Frank Bennett, an expert witness for appellant Southern, testified that not to ventilate premises when the odor of gas is present 'is the worst thing you can do.'"

On July 27, 1960 the U.S. Fifth Circuit Court of Appeals affirmed a judgment against the city of Villa Rica. The U.S. Court of Appeals found the city solely responsible for the December 5, 1957 explosion. After exhaustive testimony, the jury felt there was ample proof that the City of Villa Rica had been negligent by not responding to complaints of escaping gas and that negligence was the proximate cause of damages to the plaintiffs.

After judgment was passed on the City of Villa Rica they could not pay the plaintiffs. In July of 1961 when the city of Villa Rica had failed to pay the judgment plus interest to those plaintiffs that had been awarded judgement, they cited insufficient funds available for the payments. The City of Villa Rica officials were served a summons in the form of a Mandamas, a written command that an order be fulfilled. The summons stated, "That if the city does not have the funds to discharge the judgements, it should levy a tax on all property within the corporate city limits to pay said judgments."

In October 1961, Mayor Paul Camp took a stand and told Judge L. R. Morgan that the City of Villa Rica simply could not pay the amount of money it had been ordered to pay. Tax assessors took the stand and testified that the city was under assessing the property of the town in an attempt to keep from paying. Testimony from both sides was fierce. The

16. Lawsuits Against the City of Villa Rica

judge adjourned at noon that day to take the question under advisement and asked both attorneys to file briefs.

Mrs. Sarah Camp, whose husband, Paul Camp, was the mayor in 1961 said that the city simply did not have the money. She said that the lawyers were feverishly negotiating to work out a settlement with the plaintiffs.

On November 12, 1962, a surprise announcement came that both shocked and pleased the citizens of Villa Rica. At the November Villa Rica City Council meeting the council reached a settlement with representatives of the plaintiffs and reached a final agreement. Then the city issued checks for a total of $125,000. This amount was agreeable to all parties whereas the original demands had been for a total of nearly one million dollars. The funds needed to satisfy the demands of the plaintiffs were borrowed from private citizens at a five percent interest for a period of five years. A sinking-fund was set up to repay the debt. As to how the extra one thousand two hundred and fifty dollars per month would be obtained the council admitted they were still unsure, but provisions were in the works. The five years of staggering uncertainty that had hung over the city were finally over. This payment each month for five years placed a considerable financial burden on the city.

By 1967, the monetary debt was finally paid off when Villa Rica finished paying the private financiers. Villa Rica had tried to sell the gas company quickly, but due to pending litigation it was not sold until February 1, 1979. The City of Villa shouldered the blame but all along they proclaimed the fault did not lie with the city.

The far reaching implications of the Villa Rica disaster caused changes in the requirements to incorporate odorizers into the natural gas supply to facilitate identification of leaks and adherence to pressurization standards.

The Villa Rica tragedy generated increased attention to natural gas safety throughout the state. Attention to gas safety influenced the consciousness of everyone during that tragic time and ultimately that consciousness of the dangers of gas has continued even today.

The far reaching impacts of the Villa Rica disaster caused the Villa Rica Civil Defense Unit to become one of the best in the state and in turn set a precedent for better Civil Defense Units in each county throughout the state.

This story was put together from written records, but no one really knows every detail of what took place. There are conflicting stories and fading memories. Only those who died in the catastrophe know for sure and they are not here, but live in our hearts. Of those that survived the blast many since that day, have passed. There is no one left to tell, for sure, all that happened.

17

40th Anniversary and 50th Anniversary Remembrance Ceremony

"The town is growing and it's important for people to know the history of the city they live in, and this was the biggest, most devastating thing to ever happen to this town."
Valerie Berry Wilhelm, daughter of Bill and Margaret Berry, 2007

On December 5, 1997, a brief Fortieth Anniversary Memorial Service was held on the side of Montgomery Street in front of the original site of the Berry's Pharmacy building (then the Rexall Drug Store). A low, white marble marker had been placed on the edge of the right side of the street between the scene of the explosion and the railroad tracks. The marker was engraved with the names of the twelve who lost their lives that same day forty years before. A group of about twenty five gathered at the road's edge to gaze reverently at the engraved names. There was a moment of silence as Mayor Monroe Spake read the names of each of those who died on the tragic day. The service opened with a prayer, followed by a brief commemorative speech then Ethyleen Tyson read her touching and appropriate poem dedicated to the residents of Villa Rica. All of those who attended were solemn in their memories as she read:

Great is Thy Faithfulness
In everyday and every hour
Secure in our Father's love
And His Majestic Power

Explosion in Villa Rica

His unseen presence surrounds us
Through trials of every kind
For the love of our God is broader
Than the measure of man's mind.

When we have not a smile to give
And not a song to sing
Then we will feel His sweet peace
Beneath His sheltering wing.

When dark steep paths appear
Just trust His love and care
He is there to direct our steps
And wipe away our tears.

On December 5, 2007, fifty years later, exactly, from the day of the explosion, Mayor J. Collins and the councilmen of Villa Rica along with the Berry family held a Fiftieth Anniversary Remembrance Ceremony. The Villa Rican newspaper had published special articles of commemoration every Thursday for six weeks prior to the December 5th service.

Valerie Berry Wilhelm, daughter of Bill and Margaret Berry, had related in an article that preceded the day events, "We went to the high school to hear the band that would preform in the remembrance ceremony. The director asked the students who had heard of the explosion and only five raised their hands. The town is growing and it's important for people to know the history of the city they live in, and this was the biggest, most devastating thing to ever happen to this town."

Two special events were planned in commemoration of this special day. A new building was to be dedicated and an historical marker was to be unveiled.

After the explosion, a one story Rexall Drug Store building had been built at the site of the demolished two story red brick building that Berry's Pharmacy had occupied. The Rexall building was owned and occupied by Robert Woodall, who had purchased it from the Berry family. The old Rexall building had stood empty since 2004. Then the Berry family bought the property back from Robert Woodall. In the last few years, massive renovations had turned the building back to the 1895 glory of the original two-story building, known as

17. 40th and 50th Anniversary Ceremonies

the Powell Marchman building. Restoration had been perfected down to the oak flooring and walls of cinder blocks and brick. The glass trimmed double front doors, windows, and stonework were copied from early photographs of the Powell Marchman—1895 building. Many parts of the building give the feel of the late 1800's structure. While most sections resemble the original, the design was updated for use in today's environment. The soda fountain was put in the same place as it was in 1957. Villa Ricans brought out photos from attics and dusty boxes and displayed the memorabilia on the walls. An inlaid fireplace and electric logs gave off warmth to visitors that gathered in clusters to reminisce. This new structure would be opening as the 'Berry and Bean' restaurant serving light breakfast, lunch, and desserts. A ribbon cutting was planned on the day of the anniversary ceremony.

A committee worked toward having the historical marker ready to unveil on the day of the anniversary ceremony. The Villa Rica Historic Preservation Committee had worked diligently for the past nine months to insure the historical marker would be placed for this occasion. Members of the Historical Preservation Committee were Barbara Daniel, Patricia Proctor, and Valerie Berry Wilhelm.

Then on December 5, 2007, Candler Street, a side street adjacent to the Powell Marchman building was blocked off, a large tent was set up in the street, and chairs were arranged in wide rows. The day was cold and the wind was sharp as it whipped around Wilson Street and whirled from Montgomery Street, now usually referred to as Highway 78 or Bankhead Highway.

A podium and microphone were set up. Dignitaries came from local, state, and federal governments. Many of those who had grown up in Villa Rica made the trip back to attend the ceremony including about forty surviving relatives of those that had perished.

Programs were distributed to the many guest that poured into the downtown area as the Villa Rica High School Symphonic Band led by Derek Able played appropriate music for the occasion. At 10:30 that morning, J. Collins, Mayor of Villa Rica, gave a welcome to everyone. Bernice Brooks gave an opening prayer. Franklin Richardson, Villa Rica resident and local musician, sang a beautiful and moving song, *To Where You Are*.

Several people stood when their names were called in recognition as those being in the buildings but surviving the blasts. Then those who had helped in the rescue effort were recognized for their brave and heroic efforts. About forty more people stood and were recognized as family members of those who had been killed. Their memories must have been heavy that day as the crowd sat adjacent to the very buildings that had collapsed.

Mayor J. Collins spoke: "Fifty years ago our city had its darkest day, that day when

Explosion in Villa Rica

in an instant lives would be changed forever. Families would be changed; families would lose loved-ones. It was a day that over the past fifty years has stood out for many people as they drive down Montgomery Street and remember maybe helping rescue someone from the debris; remembering their loved-one that may have been killed that day; and I can only think how it must feel for many family members who have gathered here to remember their loved-ones and to have to relive that day today."

"As you can see, this effort in the City of Villa Rica was aided by many, many entities," Mayor Collins continued. "When we called upon those entities to help, they answered the call, and we're forever grateful to our friends and neighbors from down the street or across the state. Today we want to say 'thank you' to those friends and neighbors who helped us."

Mayor Collins then read from a history research paper his mother, Brenda Busbin Collins, had written in 1993 about the explosion when she attended West Georgia College. As *Explosion in Villa Rica* was read, the audience was somber as their thoughts went back to the sad time half a century before. Many remembered where they were when the explosion occurred, or how they first heard about it. They thought about the ones who were killed. Most everyone knew someone who had perished or who had been directly affected by this life-changing day.

Carroll County Fire Chief Gary Thomas and Randy Wallace

Photo courtesy Randy Wallace.

Randy Wallace, who had been the eleven-year-old boy on the school safety patrol

17. 40th and 50th Anniversary Ceremonies

directing traffic that day long ago, now stood and read the names of those who lost their lives. "With love and respect we remember…" he began. A moment of silence followed each name, then Carroll County Fire Chief, Gary Thomas, tolled a medium-size bell. The vibrating sound chimed through the cold air creating a deep somber moment. After a moment of silence, the next name was read and the bell struck again. All sat quietly listening to each chime fill the air with a melodic note that lasted for a while, lingered for a moment, then quietly died out. As the tone sounded then subsided, each person had a special story locked in the memories of his or her heart.

Jessica Tyson, a Villa Rica High School senior, honor student, and the granddaughter of Ethyleen Tyson, went to the podium and read her grandmother's poem, *Great is Thy Faithfulness*. As Jessica read, some seated in the audience looked toward the Fortieth Anniversary marker visible to them across the street at street level.

Jessica Tyson reads a poem to those gathered on Candler Street.

Photo courtesy Ethyleen Tyson

Franklin Richardson and Patrick Henrickson sang a special musical rendition of *Unending Love, Amazing Grace*. Patrick Henrickson, another local resident and musician, played the accompaniment on the guitar.

Kippard "Kip" Berry, son of Bill and Margaret Berry, dedicated the new Powell-

Explosion in Villa Rica

Marchman building: "We're not trying to bring back the past; we're just trying to honor those people, Kip Berry said. "We acquired the building from Robert Woodall, who had purchased it from my dad. The building had been shut down since 2004. We had it rebuilt to the way it looked before the explosion as a tribute to our parents and to the victims and their families, and the city itself."

All in the audience moved toward the adjacent building where Mayor Collins cut a broad yellow ribbon draped across the double glass front doors.

After the ribbon was cut, all of the onlookers turned toward the veiled historical

W. C. Cole and Mayor J. Collins

Photo courtesy W. C. Cole.

marker. Christy Crisp, Program Manager for the Georgia Historical Society, made these statements, "These markers tell the story of Georgia's past. Sometimes that story is not always happy; it's not always pretty, but it's all part of the picture. That's why we think the marker program is so important and that's what people are going to see when they walk by Berry's building now."

"There are people who have walked by this storefront, no doubt, for the past fifty years with no idea what happened there," she said. " Now, residents and visitors alike will have that opportunity. Now when people come through Villa Rica, they'll know a little bit more about the events that transpired here fifty years ago. This marker is dedicated on the

17. 40th and 50th Anniversary Ceremonies

50th anniversary of the explosion in remembrance of those who died, and to commemorate the courage of neighbors who ignored their own safety to rescue victims trapped in the debris created by the blast."

The newspaper photographer snapped pictures as the crowd anxiously gathered around the veiled marker and when the cloth was pulled off, Christy Crisp read to the crowd that had gathered more closely around. Then as the crowd shifted, small groups moved and paused a couple of minutes to read the marker that stood a few inches from the sidewalk exactly in line where the double doors had been opened fifty years to the day, to let out the gas fumes. Somber faces were upturned as serious eyes followed the bronze, raised lettering.

Villa Rica Explosion
Erected by Georgia Historical Society
Dedicated December 05, 2007
Region: Piedmont
County: Carroll
GPS: M33 43.8951/W084 55.17768
Location: 130 Montgomery Street/GA Hwy. 78

Around 11:00 a m on December 5, 1957, a natural gas leak under Berry's Pharmacy caused an explosion that destroyed four buildings and damaged several others in Villa Rica's downtown. The explosion killed twelve and injured twenty. The tragedy highlighted the need for both an organized local emergency response unit and the use of odor in the natural gas supply. The civil defense unit that resulted became a model for west Georgia. Ensuing litigation placed a considerable financial burden on the city, suppressing economic development for years. In terms of injury and loss of life, the explosion remains the most catastrophic event in Carroll County history.

Erected by the Georgia Historical Society, City of Villa Rica, the Villa Rica Historic Preservation Committee, and Villa Rica Downtown Development Authority.

In Memoriam

To every thing there is a season: A time to be born,
and a time to die;... A time to weep;...
a time to morn;... and a time to embrace.
Ecclesiastes 3:1-5

On Thursday December 5, 1957 the community of Villa Rica saw more devastation than anyone could have imagined. The town was stricken again, this time with sorrow, when it had to bury nine of its citizens. On Friday, five funerals were held in that one day. On Saturday the cloud of sorrow and heartbreak continued when three more funerals were held. Then on Sunday their beloved Margaret Berry was buried. Two of those killed were from Atlanta and one from Austell. Their funerals were held also on Friday and Saturday in their community.

Margaret McCree Berry:
March 18, 1918—December 5, 1957

Funeral services for Margaret Berry were held on Sunday, December 8, at the Villa Rica Methodist Church with Reverend Floyd Walden officiating.

Margaret Berry taught Sunday School at the Villa Rica Methodist Church in the children's department. Margaret, a native of Texas, lived in Florida a number of years before coming to Villa Rica some ten years before. She was one of Villa Rica's outstanding civic leaders and was active in every phase of community life. She was a former president of the PTA, director of the Camp Fire Girls and active in the Cub

In Memoriam

Scouts.

She was survived by her husband, Dr. William L. "Bill" Berry; one daughter, Valerie Ann; two sons, Kip and Ran Berry; mother, Mrs. W. A. McCree of Orlando, Florida; sisters Mary Stiler, Melba Yatsuk, and Zelma Durrenberger all of Orlando Florida, Norma Lee Loyd of Chanute Kansas; brothers, Dr. A. G. McCree, and W. A. McCree of Orlando, Florida; and Dr. D. G. McCree of Bremerton Washington.

Jones Funeral Home was in charge of arrangements.

Reverend Allen Phillips, pastor or Wesley Memorial Church and former pastor of the Villa Rica Methodist Church, said, "Regardless of how busy she was, Mrs. Berry always had time to help out any person or organization." He described Mrs. Berry as an 'ideal mother.' "Her husband, Bill, was an alumnus of the University of Georgia and she went with him and their two boys Kip 10, and Ran, 8, on Sunday to see the Tech-Georgia game. This was typical of her spending time with her family."

A picture or Mr. and Mrs. Berry and their two boys attending that Tech-Georgia game had been in the Sunday, Atlanta Journal Constitution five days before the explosion that took her life.

Robert Lee Broom, Sr:
April 20, 1903 December 5, 1957

Robert Lee Broom, Sr, age fifty four, was born in Floyd County Georgia, the son of Marcus Joel Broom and Sarah Norris Broom. His wife, Eva Gibbs Broom was born in Blount County, Alabama. He was a member of Wesley Chapel Methodist Church and had been employed at the Cannon Casket Company in Villa Rica for seven years.

He was survived by his wife Eva Jeanette Gibbs Broom; his mother, Mrs. Sarah Norris Broom of Villa Rica; a daughter Mrs. Mildred Holloway and a grandson Gary Holloway of Alexander, Alabama; one son, Private Robert Lee "Bob" Broom of the U.S. Navy stationed in Germany, daughter-in-law Sara Louise Winkler Broom; grandsons Stanley Broom and Ronald Broom all of Anniston, Alabama; five brothers—Lyndon Broom, Cliff Broom,

Herman Broom, Willie Broom and Joe Broom; three sisters—Essie Broom Leathers, Mattie Broom Perkins, and Ethel Broom Lloyd.

Funeral services for Robert Broom were conducted on Saturday, December 7, 1957 at Fullerville Baptist Church with Reverend Ralph Tapley and Reverend Jimmy Summerall officiating. Robert Lee Broom was buried at the Villa Rica Hillcrest Cemetery with Robert Miller Funeral Home in charge.

On the day of the explosion, someone went to get Eva Broom, Rob's wife, who worked at the Hosiery Mill in Fullerville. His demolished car had been found parked out front of Berry's Pharmacy and he was thought to have been inside. Eva Broom thought he was home with their daughter, who was recuperating from an operation, but found out later he had gone to pick up a prescription for her.

When Rob's brother, Lyndon, came from work down Bankhead Highway toward Villa Rica, he was stopped at the road block where cars were banned from going on into Villa Rica. He told the patrolmen his name, and they checked the list of those killed and found the name "Rob Broom." That is when he knew his brother had been killed. The patrolmen let him go on through to Villa Rica.

Dr. Hugh J. "Jack" Burnham, Jr:
1924—December 5, 1957

Funeral services were held on Saturday, December 7, 1957 at Spring Hill in Atlanta. Entombment was in Westview Abbey, in Atlanta, Georgia. In addition to his wife, Mrs. Burnham, survivors included his father, Dr. H. J. Burnham Sr, Jackson, Mississippi; two sisters, Mrs. Kenneth Cox, New Orleans; and Mrs. Syd Speer, Meridian, Mississippi and a brother Bill B. Burnham, Dallas, Texas.

Prior to the accident, Dr. Burnham was a thirty-six-year-old dentist who had his regular office days in Villa Rica on Wednesdays and Thursdays. He had practiced in Villa Rica and in Douglasville for about a year. Dr. Burnham resided at 16 Perkerson Drive in Austell where he and his wife moved from 128 E. Andrews Drive., N. W. Atlanta about a month before.

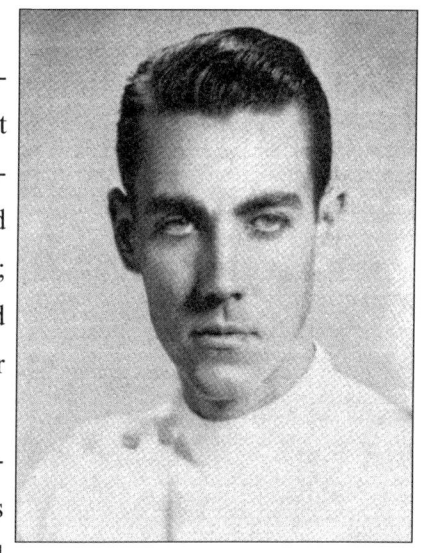

Dr. Burnham, a native of Jackson Mississippi, came to Georgia after serving as a

In Memoriam

navy officer in World War II. He finished part of his medical education at the University of Mississippi in 1943 prior to entering the service. Later he completed his medical and dental training at Emory University Medical School and graduated from Emory University School of Dentistry and practiced in Marietta.

Dr. Burnham was active in professional and social fraternity work at Emory and was a member of St. Luke's Episcopal Church in Atlanta.

Carolyn Davis: April 27, 1935 December 5, 1957

Carolyn Davis was born in Haralson county, the daughter of Evie Barber Davis and Carl B. Davis. She was a beautician employed at Marie's Beauty Salon in Villa Rica at the time of her death. She was a member of District Line Methodist Church.

Besides her parents, Mr. and Mrs. Carl B. Davis, she was survived by her maternal grandparents, Mr. and Mrs. Virgie D. Barber, Temple, Georgia; and paternal grandmother, Mrs. J. M. Davis, Winston, Georgia. Funeral services were conducted Saturday afternoon, December 7, at the District Line Methodist Church in Haralson County. Carolyn Davis was buried at the District Line Methodist Church Cemetery. Hightower Funeral Home of Bremen had charge of the arrangements.

Johnny Marion Dyer: June 24, 1927—December 5, 1957

A double funeral was held for Johnny Dyer and his father O.T. Dyer on Friday December 6, 1957, at the First Baptist Church in Villa Rica at 4:00 o'clock in the afternoon with Reverend E. Bunyan Collins, Reverend John L. Smith, and Reverend Archie McNair officiating.

Johnny Dyer, age 30, was a member of the Villa Rica Presbyterian Church, Woodmen of the World, and the American Legion. He and his father operated the Dyer Heating and Plumbing and Company.

He was survived by his wife, Winnie Leathers Dyer; one daughter, Marion Ann Dyer; mother, Mrs. Vera Goggins Dyer; two sisters, Marie Harrrison and Elizabeth Dyer Tackett; two brothers, Judson Dyer and Harold Dyer, all of Villa Rica.

In Memoriam

Johnny Dyer was buried at Hillcrest Cemetery in Villa Rica. Almon Funeral Home of Carrollton was in charge of arrangements.

Later Winnie, Johnny wife, relates how so many orders for flowers came in from all over the world to be sent to the Dyer family and for others who died in the explosion. The small town of Villa Rica just could not fill all the orders as there were not that many plants and flowers in town since the Villa Rica Florist located in Reeves Jewelry Store was demolished. What was needed could not be furnished by the few other florists in town nor could what was ordered be brought in from neighboring towns in time for the ten funerals that were held within the span of three days. The florist kept track of the orders and filled the Dyer orders over the next two years, two at a time. Winnie and Mrs. O.T. Dyer were given the cards showing who ordered floral arrangements, so when they wanted fresh flowers on the two graves, they let the florist in town know when to deliver to the two grave sites.

Olin Thomas Dyer:
November 28, 1897—December 5, 1957

A double funeral was held for Olin Thomas Dyer and his son Johnny Marion Dyer, on Friday December 6, 1957, at the First Baptist Church in Villa Rica at 4:00 o'clock with Reverend E. Bunyan Collins, Reverend John L. Smith, and Reverend Archie McNair officiating.

Olin Thomas Dyer was born in Carroll County, the son of the late Zodie Fields Dyer and John Dyer. O.T. was a member of the First Baptist Church.

Mr. Dyer was survived by his wife Vera Goggins Dyer; two daughters, Mrs. Winton Tackett and Marie Harrison of Villa Rica; two sons, Judson Dyer and Harold Dyer of Villa Rica; four sisters, Shirley Harper, Mrs.

In Memoriam

Monroe Jacobs, Mrs. Claude Morris and Grace Martin; and four brothers, Youles Dyer, Roy Dyer, Herman Dyer, and Henry Dyer.

O.T. Dyer was buried in the Wesley Chapel United Methodist Church Cemetery. The Robert Miller Funeral Home of Villa Rica was in charge of the arrangements.

Kenneth Clifton Hendrix: April 20, 1935—December 5, 1957

The funeral for Kenneth Clifton Hendrix was held on Saturday, December 7, at Red Oak First Baptist Church in Red Oak, Georgia, an unincorporated town close to Fairburn, in Fulton County. Kenneth was survived by his parents, Clara and Lewis Hendrix, four sisters, Myra, Janice, Karen, and Pansy; and one brother, Billy. He was buried at the Forest Lawn Cemetery, in Red Oak, Georgia,

Kenneth and his wife Kitty Crutshaw Hendrix, of Florida, had been married for three years and lived in Mountain View in Clayton County, Georgia. Kitty worked for IBM. On May 1, of that year, Kitty, age twenty-two, died in childbirth, from complications of heart trouble. Their infant also died. Kenneth then moved back to his parents' home in Red Oak and got a job with the Atlanta Linen Service.

James Oscar Hixon: January 22, 1925 December 5, 1957

Oscar Hixon, age thirty two, was buried at Pleasant Grove Baptist Church Cemetery in Villa Rica where the funeral service was held on Saturday December 7, 1957. Jones Funeral Home was in charge of the arrangements.

Survivors were his wife, Mildred Parrish Hixon; and their three small children, Judy, John, and Jim; parents, Guy Hixon and Addie Brooks Hixon formerly of Temple, Georgia; grandmother, Mrs. W. J. Brooks; and aunts, uncles, nieces and nephews.

Oscar was an active member of his church and community. He was the Sunday School Superintendent, a deacon, and chairman of the church building committee. Oscar was also chorister at Pleasant Grove Baptist Church as well as president of the Villa Rica PTA, a Mason, and a member of the Villa Rica Chapter of the American Legion.

In Memoriam

Many have said, "He was one of the kindest and best persons who ever walked the face of this earth." The entire town and surrounding community mourned the passing of Oscar Hixon.

Rozelle Johnson:
September 17, 1914 - December 5, 1957.

Miss Rozelle Johnson, age forty three, of Hays Mill Road, Carrollton, Georgia was a member of the Shiloh Methodist Church in Carrollton. Rozelle was survived by her father Thomas Watson Johnson; stepmother, Marie Dobbins Johnson; a sister, Lucille Johnson Wilson, Atlanta; a brother, Bob E. Johnson, of Carrollton and a step-brother, Jewell Sutton of Atlanta.

Funeral services were conducted with Reverend John Lanthey officiating. Rozelle was buried in the church cemetery. Almon Funeral Home was in charge of arrangements.

Rozelle Johnson had been employed as a manager at the Empire 5 & 10 Cent Store in Carrollton for a number of years before she was transferred to the Villa Rica store. She had been the manager there for a few years. She lived on a two hundred acre farm with her parents and brother, Bob Johnson, who took her to Alabama Street in Carrollton each morning to catch the bus to Villa Rica to work at the dimestore.

Robert "Bobby" Charles Morris Roberts: June 11, 1945—December 5, 1957

Bobby Roberts, age thirteen, was survived by his mother, Marie Roberts Couch; stepfather, Sergeant Boyd C. Couch; dad, Nobel Earl Roberts; one brother, Ronald "Ron" Roberts; grandparents, Mr. and Mrs. C. W. Hamrick; and great grandmother, Mrs. J. H. Williams.

After a small service at Bobby's home, the main funeral service at the First Methodist Church, on Friday, December 6, 1957, drew a huge crowd. One of his heroes, an Atlanta Cracker baseball team player, Chuck Tanner, attended the funeral when he heard

In Memoriam

of the explosion and was told that Bobby had been a big fan. A popular Atlanta lawyer and friend of the family, Bobby Lee Cook, also came to console the family. The midget football team from his school were an honorary escort. Entombment was at Hillcrest Mausoleum in Villa Rica.

Bobby, a seventh grader and a straight-A honor roll student, was a bright young man admired by his teacher and friends. He was awarded six pins for perfect attendance in Sunday School and for Bible study where he attended church at the First Methodist Church in Villa Rica. He wore these six pins on his baseball cap. He played guard on the midget football team at school. Remembered as such a friendly, happy kid, Bobby earned two nicknames, "Smiley" and "Facey." "He always wore a blond crew cut and a big smile," was later quoted in a newspaper. His football team had been scheduled to play in the Allstar game at the Georgia Tech Field in Atlanta. When that game was played on December 14 between Carrollton and Avondale there was a moment of silence and prayer before the kick-off in Bobby's memory.

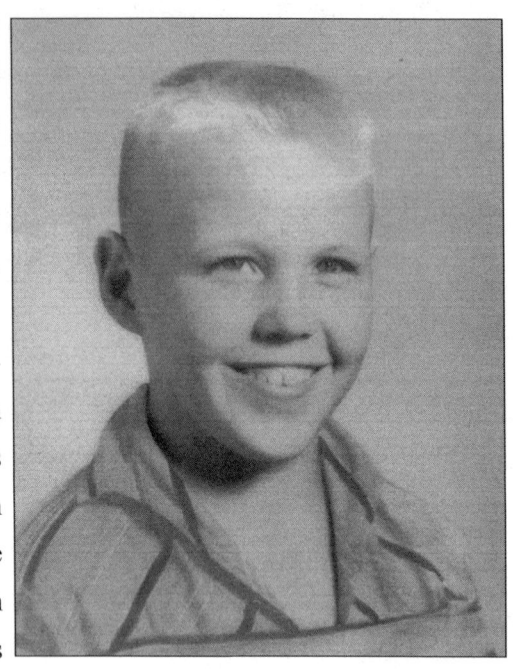

Bobby was a youth leader in the church he attended and occasionally took over junior services handling himself like a veteran. Friends reflected fondly that they had "never heard a prayer come from anybody's lips like Bobby prayed last Sunday." That's the way they liked to remember him: praying eloquently, playing guard, or putting up a scrap. Or smiling.

Upon hearing of his death, the family went into shock. Later his younger brother said, "I just could not believe it for a long, long, time."

Robby Roberts was loved by all who knew him and was missed by his peers in school and at church.

In Memoriam

Annette Pope Smith:
October 7, 1934—December 5, 1957

Ann Smith, age twenty-three, the daughter of Gladis Leathers Pope and William Roy Pope, was an employee of Berry's Pharmacy. She was survived by her husband, James "Billy" Smith, age twenty four; parents, Mr. and Mrs. William Roy Pope; three sisters, Mildred Pope Johnson, Nell Pope Holloway, and Catherine Pope; two brothers, William C. Pope, Bobby Pope; in-law parents, Mr. and Mrs. Ray Smith; sister-in-law, Mrs. Curtis Golden; and nieces and nephews.

The funeral service was held on Saturday December 7, at the Villa Rica Methodist Church in Villa Rica with Reverend Floyd Walden and Reverend R. C. Owens officiating. Ann Smith was buried at Hillcrest Cemetery in Villa Rica.

Ann Pope Smith had lived in Villa Rica all of her life. She was popular and well liked by all who knew her. She was voted "the most athletic" in her graduating class of 1952. Everyone said, "She will be missed by many who knew and loved her."

Carl Vitner: 1931—December 5, 1957

Carl, age 26, attended Henry Grady High School and graduated from Southern School of Pharmacy (now Emory) in 1953. He worked at Jacob's Drug Store in Atlanta before taking a sales job with Young Pharmaceuticals where he worked for two years. Carl wanted to increase his income in order to open his own pharmacy, so he went into sales. He and his wife Jackie Frankel Vitner had been married for eighteen months and had a six-month-old daughter, Lynn Ellen. They lived in the Woodland Avenue area of the Northeast section of Atlanta.

In Memoriam

Carl was survived by his wife, Jackie Frankel Vitner; their daughter Lynn Ellen; his parents; Mr. & Mrs. Sigmund Vitner; two sisters, Mrs. Morris Robbins and Mrs. Saul D. Stein, both of Atlanta; and a brother, Dr. Saul Vitner, St. Louis. Services for Carl Vitner were held on Friday, December 6, 1957, at Blanchard's Funeral Home Chapel with Rabbi Dr. Harry H. Epstein officiating. Burial was at the Greenwood Cemetery in Atlanta.

Carl's parents, Sigmund Vitner and Fannie Exelbirt were immigrants from Romania who met in 1908 in New York at a social event sponsored by the local Jewish synagogue in the Lower East Side of Manhattan. Sigmund, handsome in his streetcar conductor's uniform, met Fannie, a seamstress, who loved to dance. Sigmund who came from Harlow, a tiny village twenty miles from the Russian border where Russian teamsters brought fine work horses to do all manner of work, liked to talk of the old country. Fannie, who came from a tiny poor community, had a father who was a spiritual leader in their community and believed in hard work and in helping the poor.

Sigmund and Fannie later married and had four children. Beatrice, Sylvia, Saul, and Carl, the youngest. Saul became Dr. Saul Vitner, a prominent physician in Atlanta for many years.

At the time of the explosion, Carl's body went to one of the funeral homes. After determining his identity from papers in his wallet, the police called his parents who then lived on Spring Valley Lane in the Highland Avenue area in Atlanta.

Out of the blue the family got a call about 4:00 o'clock that evening from a policeman who told them that their son, Carl, had been killed in an explosion. They were overcome with shock and grief. Fanny was flushed and weak from mourning. When Carl's wife, Jackie, came into their house and learned of Carl's death, she fainted."

The victim's brother, Dr. Saul Vitner later said, "The family had listened to radio reports of the Villa Rica tragedy during the day. We had no reason to suspect Carl was involved.

Credits

Preface

1. *History of Villa Rica: City of Gold,* Mary Talley Anderson, 1935, pages 1-6.
2. *Villa Rica Jumps Dahlonega's Claim,* Dan Chapman, The Atlanta Journal and Constitution, July 9, 2009.
3. Interview with Carl Lewis, historian at Pine Mountain Gold Museum.
4. *'City of Riches,' Now Highly Industrialized,* The Atlanta Constitution, Friday, December 6, 1957.
5. *Rocket Flop Cancels Talk by Scientist,* The Miami Herald, Saturday, December 7, 1957.
6. *7 Big Fires In 5 Years At Villa Rica,* The Atlanta Constitution, Friday, December 6, 1957.

Chapter 1—The Days Before the Tragedy

1. Federal court records, testimony of Tom Pope, pages 1-5, 25-35, 60-69, 914-917.
2. Federal court records, testimony of Will Pope, page 15, 198-202.
3. Federal court records, testimony of Mrs. L. W. Leathers, page 15-16.
4. Federal court records, testimony, and cross examination of Ray Tyson pp. 46-50, 541-546, 758-763.
5. Federal court records, testimony of M.D. Henslee, page 28-31, 546-549.
6. Federal court records, testimony of Bill Berry pp. 16-19; 211-219, 919-938.
7. Federal court records, testimony of Joe F. Cutcliff, pages 28, 541-543.
8. Federal court records, testimony of Cliff Reeves 22-24.
9. Interview with John Bailey.
10. The Villa Rican, April 17, 1957, *W. L. Berry Elected President of Georgia Pharmaceutical Association.*

Chapter 2—Early Morning, December 5, 1957

1. Interview with Donald Willis.
2. Interview with Don Bohannan, Federal court records, testimony of Don Bohannan, pages 26-26, 435-445.
3. Interview with John Bailey.
4. *Happy Lad Keeps Date With Death,* The Atlanta Journal, 12/5/1957.
5. *Villa Rica Debris Sifted,* The Atlanta Constitution Friday, December 6, 1957.
6. Federal court records, testimony of Bill Berry pp. 212-219, 377.
7. Federal court records, testimony of Ray Tyson pp. 46-50 and pp. 758-779.
8. Interview with Winnie Dyer Baxter.
9. Federal court records, testimony of M.D. Henslee, pages 28-31, 546-549.
10. Interview with Ricky Hammond.
11. Interview with Shirley Whitworth Garner.
12. Interview with Martha Wynn Swann.
13. Interview with Larry Bishop.

Credits

14. Federal court records, testimony of James Bailey pages 40-41, 704-707, Horace Chism, page 40, and Harold E. Evans pages 40, 696-701.

15. *James Harrison Does Believe in God,* Frank X. Ellis, The Villa Rican, Thursday, December 4, 1997.

16. *Death Calls,* The Atlanta Journal, Friday, December 6, 1957.

17. Tom Pope, Court Testimony and cross examination, pages 1-5, 33-40, 60-69, 914-917

18. Cliff Reeves, Court Testimony, pages 22-24

19. Interview with Earnest Lee "Buck" Jackson.

Chapter 3—The Moments That Decided Life of Death

1. *Brave Villa Rica Struggling Back*, The Atlanta Journal and Constitution, Sunday, December 22, 1957.

2. Interview with Don Bohannan, Federal court records, testimony of Don Bohannan, pages 26-27, 445-455.

3. Interview with Earnest Lee "Buck" Jackson.

4. *James Harrison,* Frank X. Ellis, The Villa Rican, Thursday, December 4, 1997.

5. *Death Call,* The Atlanta Journal, Friday, December 6, 1957.

6. Federal court records, testimony of Ray Tyson pages 46-50, 806-813.

7. Federal court records, testimony of Bill Berry pages 16-19, 217, 919-939.

8. *I Ran to the Window, Saw Black Clouds of Smoke*, Ruth Moore, Progress-Villa Rican, February 22, 1989.

9. Interview with Herman Holloway.

10. Interview with Ralph Fuller, Federal Court Testimony and Cross Examination pages 24-25.

11. M.D. Henslee, Court Testimony, pages 28-31, 546-549.

Chapter 4—The First Minutes After the Explosion

1. Interview with Donald Willis.

2. *Many Spontaneous Heroic Acts Performed in Holocaust's Agony,* Atlanta Constitution, Friday Morning, December 6, 1957.

3. Interview with Martha Wynn Swann.

4. Interview with Don Bohannan, Federal Court Testimony and Cross Examination pages 26-27, 435-445.

5. Interview with John Bailey.

6. *Radio Tune Held Girl In Building,* The Atlanta Journal, Friday, December 6, 1957 Newspaper quote of Ray Tyson.

7. Interview with Karen Gustafsol.

8. Interview with Mary Bailey.

9. *Death Calls,* The Atlanta Journal, Friday December 6, 1957.

10. Federal court records, testimony and cross examination of Ralph Fuller, pages 24-25, 357-371.

11. *Brave Villa Rica*, The Atlanta Journal

Credits

and Constitution, December 22, 1957

12. Carroll County Georgian, Tuesday, December 10, 1957.

13. Drew Brown and Frank X. Ellis, *Gas Explosion Survivors,* The Times Georgian, December 4, 1997.

14. Brenda Busbin Collins, *Explosion in Villa Rica,* a history research paper, August 5, 1993.

15. Interview - Shirley Whitworth Garner.

16. Interview with Ricky Hammond.

17. *Eye-Witness Recalls Explosion's Horror,* The Atlanta Journal, Friday, December 6, 1957.

18. Interview with Mark Berry.

18. Federal court records, testimony and cross examination of Preston Lancaster, pages 13-14, 170-179.

19. Federal court records, testimony and cross examination of Homer Vaughn, pages 14-15, 189-197, 1044-1046.

20. Interview with Joe Doyle, viewing of 8 mm video.

21. Interview with Ed Elsberry.

22. *Blast Victims Rites Tomorrow,* The Miami Herald, Saturday, December 7, 1957.

23. *Cooperation of Friends, Towns Helped in Villa Rica Tragedy*, The Villa Rican, Wednesday, December 11, 1957.

24. Interview with Herman Holloway, Jr

25. Interview with Jeff Robison.

26. Interview with Ann Bell.

27. Interview with John and Nancy McPherson

Chapter 5—The Community Reacts to the Sudden, Violent Blast

1. Interview with Ann Bell.

2. Interview with Charlotte Doyle.

3. *Cooperation of Friends*, The Villa Rican, Wednesday, December 11, 1957.

4. Memories of Martha Fay Bailey Beedle.

5. Interview with Frances Hughie.

6. Interview with Bud Streetman.

7. Gas Explosion in Georgia, New York Times 12/6/1957.

8. *…Bodies Removed in Villa Rica Blast,* The Atlanta Journal, Friday December 6, 1957.

9. Drew Brown & Frank X. Ellis, *Gas Explosion Survivors,* Times-Georgian, December 4, 1997.

10. Frank X. Ellis, *Ethyleen Tyson Recalls,* Times Georgian, Thursday, December 4, 1997.

11. Anderson, Mary Talley, *History,* page 72.

12. Interview with W. C. Cole.

13. Interview with Herman Holloway, Jr;

14. Interview with Ann Morris Broom;

15. Interview with Charles Broom.

16. Interview with Alfred B. Smith.

17. Interview with Mark Berry

18. Interview with James Conner.

19. Interview with Louise Watts, Demetric Watts, and Tony Watts.

Credits

Chapter 6—The Search for Loved-Ones
1. Interview with Winnie Dyer Baxter;
2. *Villa Rica Debris Shifted,* The Atlanta Constitution, Friday December 6, 1957.
3. *A Town Is Suddenly Shattered and a Family Begins Grim Hunt,* The Atlanta Constitution, Friday, December 6, 1957.
4. *People Were Calm, Says Salesman Who Reached Villa Rica Early,* The Atlanta Constitution Friday, December 6, 1957.
5. *Death Calls,* The Atlanta Journal, Friday, December 6, 1957.
7. Interview with Herman Holloway, Jr
8. Times Georgian, Thursday, December 4, 1997.
9. Interview with Mary Knights Bailey.
10. *Villa Rica Debris Sifted,* The Atlanta Constitution, December 6, 1957.
11. Interview with Herman J. "Billy" Keaton, Jr.
12. Interview with Martha Wynn Swann.
13. *Eyewitnesses Called it a Loud 'Whoomp' that Day,* Frank X. Ellis, The Villa Rican, Thursday, December 4, 1997.
14. St. Petersburg Times, December 6, 1957.
15. *Explosion,* The Carroll County Georgian, Thursday, December 5, 1957.

Chapter 7—Rescue Efforts: Civil Defense/Red Cross/National Guard
1. *Gas Explosion in Georgia,* The New York Times, 12/6/1957.
2. *...Bodies Removed,* The Atlanta Journal, Friday December 6, 1957.
3. Interview with Herbert Willis.
4. Interview with Hughlene Cook Folds.
5. Interview with John Bailey.
6. *Number of Injured Expected to Exceed 30,* Atlanta Journal, December 6, 1957.
7. Documents of Valerie Berry Wilhelm.
8. Interview with Bob Broom.
9. Rome News-Tribune, December 6, 1957.
10. Patricia Proctor. *Ordinary People Perform Heroic Acts in Face of Tragedy,* The Villa Rican, November 15, 2007.
11. *Eyewitnesses Called,* Frank X. Ellis, The Villa Rican, Thursday, December 4, 1997.
12. *Volunteers Prisoners Rush Rescue,* The Atlanta Constitution, Friday, December 6, 1957.
13. *Gas Explosion Survivors,* . Ellis, Times Georgian, Thursday, December 4, 1997.
14. *Points Up Red Cross Role, Says Gen. Clay,* The Atlanta Constitution, Friday, December 6, 1957.
15. *People Were Calm,* The Atlanta Constitution, Friday December 6, 1957.
16. *State Civil Defense Heads Agencies Channeling Aid Into Stricken City,* The Atlanta Constitution, Friday, December 6, 1957.
17. *Mercy Crews Nurse Town In Aftermath,* The Atlanta Journal, Friday, December 6, 1957.
18. Interview with June Albertson;

Credits

19. New York Times, December 6, 1957.
20. Interview with Mark Berry.
21. Interview with W. C. Cole.
22. Interview with Herman Holloway, Jr
23. *Villa Rica Boy Scouts Do Day's 'Good Deed,'* The Carrollton Times Free Press, Tuesday, December 10, 1957.
24. Interview with Alfred B. Smith.
25. Interview with Charlie Dodson.
26. Interview with W. C. Cole.
27. Interview with Ran Berry.
28. Interview with Kip Berry.
29. Interview with Buford G. Kittle.

Chapter 8—Families Learn of the Disaster

1. Interview with Mark Berry.
2. Affidavit by Annie Powell Berry courtesy of Mark Berry.
3. Memories by Leslie Powell Carter.
4. *Villa Rica Gas Explosion,* The Atlanta Journal & Constitution, Sunday, December 8, 1957.
5. *Villa Rica Explosion Excites Atlantans,* The Atlanta Constitution, Friday, December 6,1957.
6. *Melvin Ayers Heard it on the Radio in Atlanta,* Frank X. Ellis, The Villa Rican, Thursday, December 4, 1997.
7. Interview with John and Nancy McPherson.
8. Interview with Ruth Waller.
9. *Gas Explosion in Georgia Kills Ten,* Chicago Sun Times, December 5, 1957.
10. Interview with Ethyleen Tyson.

Chapter 9—A Town, Crippled

1. *Gas, Phone Service Stalled in Villa Rica,* The Atlanta Constitution, December 6, 1957.
2. *Keeper of the Flame: The Story of Atlanta Gas Light Company*, by James H. Tate, page 211-212.
3. Interview with Bobby Fendley.
4. Court Documents, Carroll County Courthouse Book FF pp 387-392, 469-479.
5. Interview with Emily Roberson and Diane Roberson Shadix.
6. Interview with Gene Roberson.
7. *Disaster Call Stopped Ham's Casual Gabbing,* December 6, 1957, The Atlanta Journal.
8. *Gas, Phone Service Stalled in Villa Rica,* The Atlanta Constitution, Friday, December 6, 1957.
9. *Volunteers,* The Atlanta Constitution, Friday, December 6, 1957.

Chapter 10—At the Hospitals

1. *Fire Officials Investigate Explosion,* The Carrollton Times Free Press, Tuesday, December 10, 1957.
2. Valerie Berry Wilhelm - Documents.
3. *Nurse Toils, Brother and Father Dead,* The Atlanta Constitution, December 6, 1957.
4. Rome News Tribune, December 6, 1957.

Credits

5. Interview with Don Bohannan.
6. Interview with John Bailey.
7. Rome News-Tribune, December 6, 1957.
8. Interview with Opal Thompson.
9. *Explosion Remembered,* Ellis Brown, Times-Georgian, December 4, 1997.
10. Brenda Busbin Collins, *Explosion in Villa Rica,* a history research paper, August 5, 1993.
11. *Villa Rica, Struck Without Warning,* The Atlanta Journal December 6, 1957.
12. Interview with Richard Smallwood.
13. Interview with Shirley Smallwood.
14. *Villa Rica Veteran Barber Well Remembers,* The Villa Rican, Thursday, December 4, 1997.
15. *Christmas Dies For Villa Rica,* The Atlanta Journal, Friday, December 6, 1957.
16 Collins, *Explosion,* a history research paper, August 5, 1993.
17. *Villa Rica Hospital Opens,* The Villa Rican, January 1, 1957, .
18. *Flu Causes Record Absenteeism,* The Villa Rican, November 20, 1957.

Chapter 11—Memories, Stories, and Affidavits

1. Memories of Faye White Williams with Kalina Grimm.
2. *School Safety Patrol Helped Ease Explosion Confusion,* by Randy Wallace, The Villa Rican, Thursday, November 8, 2007.
3. *Villa Rica Boy Scouts Do Day's 'Good Deed,'* The Carrollton Times Free Press, Tuesday, December 10, 1957.
4. *I Ran to the Window, Saw Black Clouds of Smoke,* Ruth Moore, Progress-Villa Rican, February 22, 1989.
5. Memories of Perry "Bill" Bailey.
6. Interview with W.C. Cole.
7. Interview with Mark Berry.
8. Interview with Ran Berry.
9. Interview with Kip Berry.
10. Interview with Louise Watts, Demetric Watts, and Tony Watts.

Chapter 12—The Days After the Tragedy

1. *Sister of Orlandoans Is Victim,* The Miami Herald, December 6, 1957.
2. *Many People See Tragedy Scene,* The Villa Rican Wednesday, December 11. 1057.
3. *The Curious Jam Villa Rica Streets,* The Carrollton Times Free Press, December 10, 1957.
4. Interview with Bob Broom.
5. *Businesses Destroyed in Fire Plan Early Re-opening Here,* The Villa Rican, Wednesday December 11, 1957.
6. *Fire Officials Investigating Explosion, Scene Cleared,* The Carrollton Times Free Press, Tuesday, December 10, 1957.
7. Interview with Bob Broom.
8. Interview with Paul Free.
9. *Schools Close Monday, Tuesday for Heating Plant Inspection,* The Villa Rican

Credits

December 18, 1957.

10. *School Holidays to End January 2,* The Villa Rican, Wednesday, December 18, 1957.

11. *17 Days After Catastrophe,* The Atlanta Journal and Constitution, Sunday, December 22, 1957.

12. Documents—Valerie Berry Wilhelm.

13. *Modern Berry Pharmacy Now Open in New Location,* The Villa Rican, Wednesday, May 28, 1959.

14. Interview with John Bailey.

15. *Villa Rica Explosion,* Carroll County Georgian, Thursday, December 19, 1957.

16. The Carroll County Georgian, Thursday, December 12, 1957.

17. *Fire Officials Investigate Explosion, Scene Clears,* The Villa Rican, Tuesday, December 10, 1957.

18. *Official Probe Of Blast Cause Still in Doubt,* The Atlanta Journal, December -1957;

19. Interview with Reba Nell Tapley and Gail Norred.

Chapter 13—New Organizations

1. *To: Fourth District*, The Villa Rican Wednesday, December 18, 1957.

2. *Villa Rica Doctor Cites CD Equipment Need,* The Atlanta Journal, December 1957.

3. *Relief Fund for Disaster Victims,* The Villa Rican, December 18, 1957.

4. *Letters of Sympathy, Regret Received by Mayor Griffin,* The Villa Rican, Wednesday, December 11, 1957.

5. *In Sympathy,* The Villa Rican, Wednesday, December 18, 1957.

6. *Former Resident Sends Help to Disaster Victims,* The Villa Rican, Wednesday, December 18, 1957.

7. *Disaster Relief,* The Villa Rican, January 8, 1958.

8. *The Red Cross Gives Aide,* The Villa Rican, March 12, 1958.

9. *Civil Defense Unit Grew from Explosion's Aftermath,* by W. C. Cole, The Villa Rican, Thursday, November 29, 2007.

10. *Out of the Ashes...* by Charles Williamson, Jr and Robby Robison, The Villa Rican, Wednesday, December 11, 1957.

11. Carroll County Court Records Book FF pages 469-479.

12. Valerie Berry Wilhelm - Documents.

13. *The Elected for 1957,* The Villa Rican, January 1, 1957.

14. *Civil Defense Unit,* The Villa Rican, January 23, 1958.

Chapter 14—Lawsuits Against Southern Natural Gas Company

1. *Federal Courts Award $237,940 in Explosion Suites*, The Villa Rican, June 3, 1959

2. *The Explosion in Villa Rica,* Brenda Busbin Collins, a history research paper, August 5, 1993

3. *Villa Rica City Gas Dept. Starts Inspec-*

Credits

tion of Gas Installations, The Villa Rican, February 28, 1958.

4. *Gas Inspections to Continue but the City Won't Foot the $5.00 Charges*, The Villa Rican, March 12, 1958.

5. *Local Merchants Give Views on Law Suites from Explosion,* The Villa Rican, January 14, 1959.

6. *Villa Rica Explosion Suits are Dismissed in Friday Hearings,* The Villa Rican Wednesday, March 11, 1959.

7. *Five Villa Ricans Ask $650,000 For Damages From Explosion,* November 18, 1959, The Villa Rican.

Chapter 15—Lawsuits Against Dr. William L. "Bill" Berry

1. Federal Circuits Records, 5th Circuit July 22, 1960.

2. Federal court records, testimony of Dr. Ernest Powell, Jr pages. 27-28, 859-864.

3. Federal court records, testimony and cross examination of Dr. William L. Berry, pages 16-19, 378-384.

4. Federal court records, testimony of Horace Nunally pp. 41-42, 715-727

Chapter 16—Lawsuits Against the City of Villa Rica

1. Federal court records, testimony and cross examination of Tom Pope, pages 25-35, 60-69, 914-917.

2. Federal court records, testimony and cross examination of Dr. Thomas H. Good-gain pages 7-12, 505-514, 519-524.

3. Federal court records, testimony of Gus Cobb pages 19-20,

4. Federal court records, testimony and cross examination of J. E. O'Toole pages 37-38, 639-657.

6. Federal court records, testimony and cross examination of Charles W. Kelp pages 39, 661-685.

7. Federal court records, testimony of Frank Bennett, pages 31, 34-36.

8. Federal court records, testimony, and cross examination of Ray Tyson pp. 46-50, 806-813 ;

9. Federal court records, testimony and cross examination of Chester A. Roush pages 56-61, 942-981;

10. *Explosion in Villa Rica*, Brenda Busbin Collins, a history research paper, August 5, 1993;

11. *An Ordinance Between The City of Villa Rica and the Atlanta Gas Light Company*, January 29, 1979.

12. Summary: Federal 5th Circuits Records, July 22, 1960.

Chapter 17—40th Anniversary and 50th Anniversary Remembrance Ceremony

1. Interview with Kip Berry.

2. Ethyleen Tyson, *Great is Thy Faithfulness,* The Villa Rican, Thursday, December 4, 1997.

3. *Historic Berry's Pharmacy Renovation Nears Completion,* Spencer Crawford, The

Credits

Villa Rican, Thursday August 9, 2007.

4. *State Will Forever Mark Site of Historic Berry's Pharmacy Explosion*, Spencer Crawford, The Villa Rican, Thursday, November 22, 2007;

5. *Remembrance Ceremony to Mark Berry's Explosion 50th Anniversary*, Spencer Crawford, The Villa Rican, Thursday, November 29, 2007.

5. *Community Remembers Victims of Villa Rica's 'Day of Infamy,'* Spencer Crawford, The Villa Rican, Thursday, December 6, 2007;

In Memoriam

Margaret Berry:

1. *Funeral Services Held for Margaret Berry,* The Villa Rican December 11, 1957.
2. Interview with Valerie Berry Wilhelm.
3. *It Was a Routine Day When Death Called for Her Citizens,* The Atlanta Constitution, Friday, December 6, 1957.
4. *Fatality List*, The Carrollton Times Free Press, Tuesday, December 10, 1957.
5. *Sister of Orlandoans Is Victim,* The Miami Herald, December 6, 1957.

Robert Lee Broom, Sr:

1. *Robert Lee Broom Rites Saturday Morning,* The Villa Rican, December 11, 1957.
2. Interview with Bob Broom.
3. *Fatality List,* The Carrollton Times Free Press, Tuesday, December 10, 1957.

Dr. Charles Burnham:

1. *It Was a Routine Day,* The Atlanta Constitution, December 6, 1957.
2. *Fatality List,* The Carrollton Times Free Press Tuesday, December 10, 1957.
3. *Doomed Dentist Said He Smelled Fumes,* The Atlanta Journal, Friday, December 6, 1957.

Carolyn Davis:

1. *Last Rites Held for Miss Carolyn Davis,* The Villa Rican December 11, 1957.
2. *Fatality List,* The Carrollton Times Free Press, Tuesday, December 10, 1957.

Johnny Marion Dyer:

1. *Fatality List*, The Carrollton Times Free Press, Tuesday, December 10, 1957.
2. Interview with Winnie Leathers Dyer Baxter.
3. *Funeral Services Held for Mr. Johnny Dyer,* The Villa Rican December 11, 1957.

Olin Thomas Dyer:

1. *Fatality, List* The Carrollton Times Free Press, Tuesday, December 10, 1957.
2. *Funeral Services Held for Mr. Thomas Dyer, 60,* The Villa Rican December 11, 1957.
3. Interview with Winnie Dyer Baxter.

Kenneth Hendrix:

1. *It was a Routine Day,* The Atlanta Constitution, Friday December 6, 1957.

Credits

2. Collins, *Explosion - A history research paper, August 5, 1993*.
3. Interview with Karen Gustafsol, sister of Kenneth Hendrix.

Rozelle Johnson:
1. *Fatality List*, The Carrollton Times Free Press, Tuesday, December 10, 1957.
2. *Funeral Services Held for Rozelle Johnson,* The Villa Rican December 11, 1957.
3. Interview with Bob Johnson.

James Oscar Hixon :
1. *Funeral Services Held for Oscar Hixon,* The Villa Rican December 11, 1957.
2. *Fatality List*, The Carrollton Times Free Press, Tuesday, December 10, 1957.
3. Interview with Jane Walker.
4. *Happy Lad,* The Atlanta Journal, Friday, December 6, 1957.

Robert "Bobby" Roberts:
1. *Master Charles Roberts Funeral Held Friday,* The Villa Rican December 11, 1957.
2. Interview with Ron Roberts.
3. *Christmas Dies*, The Atlanta Journal, Friday, December 6, 1957.
4. *Happy Lad*, The Atlanta Journal, Friday, December 6, 1957.

Ann Pope Smith:
1. *Rites Held Saturday for Mrs. James Smith,* The Villa Rican December 11, 1957.

2. Interview with Bobby Pope.

Carl Vitner:
1. *It Was A Routine Day,* The Atlanta Constitution, December 6, 1957.
2. Interview with Bennett Stein.
3. *Fatality List*, The Carrollton Times Free Press, Tuesday December 10, 1957

Bibliography

Newspapers

Chicago Sun Times
Progress-Villa Rican
St Petersburg Times
The Atlanta Journal
The Atlanta Constitution
The Carroll County Georgian
The Carrollton Times Free Press
The Miami Herald
The New York Times
The Rome News Tribune
The Times Georgian
The Villa Rican

Manuscripts

Atlanta Gas Light Company, *Keeper of the Light*, Magazine article, December 1957
Bailey, Perry "Bill" *Memories of Perry "Bill" Bailey*
Berry, Annie Powell - *Affidavit of Annie Berry*, courtesy of Mark Berry
Beedle, Martha Faye Bailey - *In the Eyes of a Young Black Girl*, a memoir.
Collins, Brenda - *Explosion in Villa Rica*, a college history research paper, August 5, 1993.
Carter, Leslie Powell - *Memories of a Young Girl*, story.
Tyson, Ethyleen - *Great Is Thy Faithfulness*, a poem.
Wallace, Randy - *Recollections of a School-boy Patrolman*, article.
Williams, Faye White - *Memories* story.

Newsreels/Videos/Microfilm

Bailey, Perry "Bill"—*Explosion in Villa Rica*, documentary.
Doyle, Joe—8 mm film taken at the scene of the disaster.
The Gold Rush in Georgia—The Pine Mountain Gold Museum, Villa Rica.
Nichols, Richard—50th Anniversary Remembrance Ceremony Video http://www.douglaspix.com.
Universal Newsreel #100—Explosion in Georgia. Now shown on Youtube.
Microfilm, The Villa Rica Library, The Villa Rican, June 1956—June 1958.

Court Documents

Carroll County Civil Records, Issue Docket Bench 5, July 24, 1960, September 8, 1960, Case numbers 2214, 2215, 2222, 2223, 2224, 2226, 2227, 2228, 2229, Book 31, Carroll County Courthouse, Carrollton Georgia.
Federal Circuits 5th Circuit, July 22, 1960, Case numbers 466, 467, 486 - AS123204; Case numbers 526, 527—AS 123205; The Federal Archives, Morrow, Georgia.

Photographs Courtesy Of:

Baxter, Winnie Leathers Dyer—original collection.
Bailey, Perry "Bill"—collection of original pictures.

Bibliography

Broom, Bob—individual photograph.

Carnes, Irma Ree—individual photograph.

Cole, W.C.—individual photograph.

Crawford, Spencer—photo journal prints and photographs.

Holloway, George—collection of original photographs—courtesy of Ann Bell and Frances Hughie.

Johnson, Bob—individual photograph.

Kave, Mildred Hixon and Jane Walker—individual photograph.

Lee, Charlotte Reeves—individual photograph.

McPherson, John—collection of original photographs.

Roberts, Ron—individual photograph.

Robison, Robby—collection of original photographs—courtesy of Jeff Robison.

Stein, Bennett J—individual photograph.

Tyson, Ethyleen—individual photograph.

Watkins, Nancy, Emory University School of Dentistry, Library Archives—individual photograph.

Wallace, Randy—collection of original photographs.

Wilhelm, Valerie Berry—collection of photographs.

Williamson, Ted—photographs from his collection.

Newspapers Courtesy of:

Barber, Charlotte

Baxter, Winnie Leathers Dyer

Bollen, Patsy

Crawford, Spencer

Doyle, Charlotte

The Villa Rica Library

Wilhelm, Valerie Berry

Books

Anderson, Mary Talley, *History of Villa Rica City of Gold,* Villa Rica: 1935, Georgia Bicentennial Committee, 1976, 2000

INDEX

Adams, Camille - 8, 21, 38, 96, 100, 102, 106
Albertson, Bill - 77
Albertson, June - 77, 79
Allen, Pat - 72
Ariail, J. A. - 55, 73
Ayres, Larry - 106
Ayres, Melvin - 86, 87

Bacon, Hudson - 77
Bailey, James - 25
Bailey, Jimmy - 111, 112
Bailey, John, - VI, 7, 14, 16, 19, 43, 48, 100, 122
Bailey, John, Sr - 46, 47, 48, 66, 71, 130
Bailey, Margaret - 108
Bailey, Mary Knights 1, 66, 67
Bailey, Olin - 111
Bailey, Perry "Bill"- 2.110, 111, 198, 199
Bailey, Ruth -111
Barber, Charlotte - 2, 199
Barber, George - 107
Barwick, M. Cook - 143, 144, 145, 148, 150, 157, 158
Baskin, Nell - 102
Baswell, Tyler - 106, 107
Baxter, Winnie Leathers Dyer- 2, 59, 125, 182, 183, 189, 191, 197, 199, 201
Beedle, Martha Fay Bailey - 3, 107, 198
Bell, Ann - 2, 191,199
Bell, Bernice "Bernie"- 8, 21, 38
Bennett, Frank - 139, 168, 196
Bentley, I. T. - 141
Bentley, Sgt. Tom - 54, 55, 75, 106
Berry, Annie Powell - 2, 10, 82, 192, 198
Berry, Dr. R. L. - 84
Berry, Dr. William L. "Bill"- 8, 10, 12. 13, 14, 15, 16, 18, 20, 29, 38, 39,82, 84,85,86,96, 98,101,121,125,136,137,141,146,147,147,167,189,190
Berry, Kippard William "Kip"- 2, 82, 174, 176, 193, 194, 196
Berry, Margaret - 8, 13, 24, 30, 39, 43, 53, 63, 74, 81, 82, 83, 84, 85, 108, 109, 110, 111, 112, 113, 117, 172, 179, 197
Berry, Mark - 2, 81, 191, 192, 193, 198-
Berry, Randall Lewis "Ran"- 2, 82, 108, 180, 193, 194
Berry, Sara - 81
Bilbo, A. V. - 131
Bishop, Gladys - 24
Bishop, Larry - 189
Black, Frank - 125
Black, Homer Grady "Bill" 31, 69
Black, Sam - 131
Bohannan, Don C. - 10, 15, 16, 17, 19, 24, 29, 30, 43, 101,121. 141,143, 189, 190, 192,
Bollen, Patsy - 2
Boyd, Ray - 107
Boykin, Judge Sam J. - 136
Boykin, Mr.- 137, 144, 155, 158,
Boykin, Shirley C. 141, 151
Boyd, Mr. - 131
Brock, Joe 8, 43
Brock, Joe Jr - 107
Brooks, Bernice - 173
Broom, Charles - 106
Broom, Jr, Robert Lee "Bob" - 117, 192, 194, 197
Broom, Sr Robert "Rob" Lee 30, 52, 53, 74, 116, 117, 149, 180
Brown, Clarence - 82
Brown, Grady- 25
Burnham, Dr. Hugh J. "Jack"- 8, 19, 21, 22, 24, 63, 64, 74, 83, 116, 142, 181, 182, 197
Butler, B. H. - 91
Butler, Sgt. Luther - 107
Byram, Gordon - 132

Camp, Hazel - 102
Camp, Paul - 134, 168, 169
Camp, Sarah - 64, 134, 169
Canant, Mae - 102

Index

Carnes, Frank - 35
Carnes, Irma Ree - 2
Carter, Leslie Powell - 2, 81, 83, 193, 198.
Candler, Jack - 120, 131, 133
Candler, Kathleen - 56
Chism, Horace - 25, 190
Clary, H. T. - 115
Clower, Evelyn - 64
Cobb, Gus - 153, 154, 164, 168, 196,
Cole, Jeff - 20
Cole, W. C - 54, 132, 133, 176, 191, 192, 193, 195.
Collins, Brenda Busbin - 2, 190, 194, 194, 195, 196, 197, 198
Collins, J.- 2, 172, 173, 174, 176
Conner, Estelle - 103
Conner, James - 52, 53, 191
Cook, Bobby Lee - 137, 138, 141, 151, 186
Cousins, Roy - 128
Crawford, Lt. Ralph - 107
Crawford, Spencer - 2, 118, 119, 197
Crisp, Christy - 176, 177
Cutcliff, Joe F. - 15, 189

Daniell, Barbara - 173
Davis, Carolyn - 19, 24, 64, 74, 117,183
Davis, Carl - 64

Davis, Evie Barber - 64
Davis, Dan - 106
DeFoor, Porter - 124
DeFore, N.J. - 102
DeGarrett, Dr. Irving - 63
Dewberry, Hallie - 102
Dodson, Charles - 102
Dodson, Charlie - 193
Dodson, Ray - 69, 147, 148
Doyle, Charlotte - 2, 191, 199
Doyle, Gene - 43
Doyle, Joe - 191, 198
Doyal, Robyn - 89
Durham, Trooper Frank - 54, 106
Dyer, Elizabeth - 97
Dyer, Johnny Marion - 26, 27, 29, 74, 116, 124, 142, 143, 182, 183, 197,
Dyer, Marion Ann - 20, 59, 124, 182
Dyer, Olin Thomas "O.T." - 10, 16, 26, 27, 29, 60, 116, 142, 143, 183, 184

Easterwood, Hoyte - 9, 44, 130
Easterwood, Dora Mae - 44
Elsberry, Ed - 47, 48
Ergle, Chester - 130
Evans, Harold E. - 25, 190

Fain, Captain - 54, 73
Farr, Juanita - 90

Fendley, Bobby - 93, 193
Folds, Hughlene Cook - 192
Free, Paul - 2, 194
Freeman, Calvin - 131
Fuller, Ralph - 23, 30, 40, 101, 121, 124, 142, 163, 190

Gilland, W. H. - 131
Golden, Martha - 65
Goodgain, Dr. Thomas Harper 151, 167, 168, 196
Grantham, Sr, J. L."Jack" - 69, 70, 90, 132
Green, J. C. - 132
Griffin, Charlie M. - 67, 116, 117, 121, 125, 129, 130, 132, 194
Griffis, Mrs. Boots - 124
Griffis, Oscar - 131
Griffith, Mrs. C. M. - 129
Grimm, Kalina - 194
Gustafsol, Karen - 190, 197

Hall, Felton - 128
Hambrick, C. W. - 56
Hambrick, Mae - 19
Hammond, Ricky - 22,23,49,189,191
Harbin, Capt. E. B. "Red"- 106
Harris, Louis - 57, 58, 113
Harrison, James - 10, 15, 16, 25, 32, 122, 190
Harrison, Lewis - 97, 98

Index

Harrison, Marie - 96, 97, 98, 182
Helton, Gerald - 87
Hembree, Melinda Doris - 33, 42, 102, 121
Hendrix, Kenneth - 35, 47, 73, 117, 184, 197
Henslee, M.D. - 8, 13, 14, 18, 20, 21, 22, 24, 26, 32, 44, 53, 141, 142, 188, 190
Henrickson, Patrick - 175
Hixon, Ina - 103
Hixon, Oscar -10, 11, 14, 15, 20, 22, 24, 25, 26, 27, 28, 54, 74, 117, 123, 124, 142, 143, 146, 148, 149, 152, 153, 154, 156, 157, 158, 159, 160, 164, 165, 166, 167, 168, 184, 185, 198, 199
Holloman, E. A.- 73, 107
Holloway, George -2, 39, 41, 46, 47, 48, 65, 72, 99
Holloway, Jr, Herman - 31, 32, 55, 61, 140, 191, 192, 193
Holloway, Sr, Herman - 31, 129
Holloway, Nell Pope - 62
Holloway, Sara - 103
Hughie, C. T. "Cula"- 51, 52
Hughie, Frances - 51, 52, 191, 199
Humphries, Yvonne - 103

Jackson, Ernest Lee "Buck"- 26, 31, 191
Jeffers, Robert - 128, 133
Johnson, Bob - 185
Johnson, Rozelle - 33,42,46,47,48,67,73,96,116,185
Jones, Clyde - 64,65,83

Kelpe, Charles - 154, 158, 159
Kennedy, William - 90
Kimsey, Wayne - 106
Knight, R.R. - 131
Knowles, Thelma - 45

Lancaster, Preston - 26,27,30, 40,41,45,103,121,167,191
Lassetter, Jack - 128
Lawson, W. Frank - 138, 141, 151
Leathers, Fate - 124
Leathers, Mrs. L. W. - 10, 189
Leathers, Nellie - 124
Lee Harrison, Charlotte (Reeves) - 9, 35, 37, 122, 199
Lokey, Hamilton - 138, 141, 148, 151
Logan, James - 91
Lovell, Roy - 106
Loyd, Betty 102
Luther, Horace - 57, 58, 59, 113, 123, 131

Maggio, Joan - 129
Manley, Eloise - 103
Maret, Lamar - 91

Martin, Henry - 69
Matthews, Ray - 128
Mayfield, Joan - 102
McClung, Jerry "Moe" - 55
McPherson, John - 1, 49, 82, 88, 193, 200
McPherson, Marjorie Eloise 89, 103,
McPherson, Nancy - 49, 82, 88, 191, 193
Meeks, Floye -103
Meek, Paul - 128
Mees, Col. Donald - 70
Miller, Robert - 95, 96, 181, 184
Moore, Ruth - 108, 190, 194
Morris, Alton - 56
Morris, Ann - 56
Morris, Stella - 56
Morris, Zeb - 123
Moseley, Elbert - 48
Mullinax, Gene - 8, 45

Neal, B. P. - 131
Newman, Otis - 69
Nunley, Horace - 146

O'Toole, J. E. -
Owens, Aline Cobb - 130

Parker, Bitt -103
Pitts, Bill - 128
Pope, Bobby - 198
Pope, Catherine - 61, 63

Index

Pope, Doris - 103
Pope, F. S. - 131
Pope, Gladis Leathers - 63
Pope, Mrs. J. H. - 130
Pope, Sue Leathers - 116
Pope, Tom - 10, 17, 57, 58, 90,147, 164, 167
Powell, Annie Berry - 2, 10, 82. 83. 192, 198
Powell, Jr, Dr. John Earnest - 38, 39, 65, 81, 96, 98, 130, 131, 133, 146, 196
Powell, Sr. Dr. John Earnest- 84, 96, 98
Powell, Urabell - 105

Ramsey, Jennie - 77
Redding, "Monk" - 55
Reeves, Cliff A. - 8, 14, 15, 20, 37, 38, 101, 102, 122, 128, 189, 190
Reeves, Eunice - 8, 10, 11, 14, 23, 122, 167
Richards, Roy - 74
Richardson, Franklin - 173, 175
Robison, Jeff - 1, 60, 191, 200
Robison, Robby - 25, 39, 42, 48, 57, 76, 77, 78, 79, 105, 117, 199
Rigsby, John - 102
Roberds, H. G. - 131.
Roberson, Emily - 91, 93, 193
Roberson, F. E. - 121

Roberson, Gene - 93, 193
Roberson, Guy - 92
Roberson, Roy - 93
Roberts, Bobby - 19, 24, 56, 63, 64, 74, 83, 85, 90, 116, 185, 186, 198
Roberts, Oscar - 138, 141, 151
Roberts, Ron - 19, 57, 185, 198, 199
Robertson, Ruth - 97
Robison, Robby - 25
Robinson, Gid - 60
Roush, Chester A. - 151, 161, 167, 196

Shadix, Diane Roberson - 92, 193
Smallwood, Richard - 94, 96, 97, 98, 194
Smallwood, Shirley - 97, 98, 194
Smith, Alfred B. - 71, 191, 192
Smith, Ann Pope - 8, 23, 27, 30, 61, 67, 82, 187
Smith, James "Billy" - 8, 198
Smith, Joseph C - 129
Smith, Loyd - 131
Smith, Myra -102
Smith, Ralph - 20, 23, 25, 131, 147, 148
Spake, Elsie - 102
Spake, Monroe - 106, 171
Spinks, J. P.- 43

Stein, Bennett - 198, 200
Streetman, Bud - 55, 122, 191
Stewart, Horace - 72
Stewart, Robert - 72
Sutton, Jewell - 185
Swann, Martha Wynn - 24, 43, 68, 189, 190, 192

Tackett, Elizabeth 96, 102
Tackett, Willie Mae - 43
Tallent, Tommy - 106
Talley, Lewis -131
Tant, Ellen - 51
Tate, James H. 193
Terrell, James - 109
Thomas, Gary- 174, 175
Thomas, Capt. Gene 109
Thomas, Jack - 110
Tyson, Ethyleen - 3, 59, 171, 175, 191, 193, 196, 198, 199,
Tyson, Jessica - 175
Tyson, Leonard - 88
Tyson, Ray - 8, 13, 18, 20, 21, 22, 23, 24, 25, 26, 27, 30, 41, 42, 101, 103, 121, 124, 142, 143, 144, 166, 167, 188, 190,196
Tyson, W. D. - 128

Vaughn, Homer - 25, 26, 27, 30, 41, 121, 124, 167, 191
Vaughn, James H. 129
Vansant, Dr. J. I. - 85
Vaughn, Pearl 103

Index

Vitner, Carl - 30, 74, 116, 187, 188, 189

Walker, Jane - 198, 199
Wallace, Randy - 2. 105, 106, 171, 175, 195, 198, 199
Ward, James - 92
Ward, Sue - 102
Watts, Demetric - 192, 194
Watts, Louise - 192, 194
Watts, Tony - 192, 194
Wayne, Lewis - 67
Wheeler, Harry L. - 73
Whitworth, Cora - 101
Whitworth, Janie - 101
Whitworth, Shirley - 23, 31, 39, 40, 51, 101, 121, 124, 189, 191
Wilder, E. B. - 91
Wilhelm, Valerie Berry - 2, 12, 13, 82, 172, 173, 180, 192, 193, 195, 197, 199.
William, Fay White - 2, 110, 195, 199
Williams, Hazel - 102
Williams, Herbie - 109
Williams, Imogene - 64
Williams, Jack - 46, 47, 48, 49, 81, 122
Williams, Mrs. R. L. - 25
Williams, Lorene - 103
Williams, Rosa Lee - 25
Williams, Willette - 110
Williamson, J. C. - 132

Williamson, Ted - 1, 12, 30, 102, 103, 131, 199
Willis, Donald - 17, 36, 37, 38, 39, 72, 96, 101, 136, 189, 191
Wilson, Curtis - 109
Wilson, J. T. -106
Wynn, Metta - 43

Yearty, Roy - 69, 71, 75